EAT TO
BEAT
YOUR AGE

Also by Janette Marshall

Fighting Fat, Fighting Fit
Eat for Life Diet
The ABC of Healthy Eating for Babies and Toddlers

JANETTE MARSHALL

EAT TO BEAT YOUR AGE

Look Younger
Feel Fitter
Lose Weight

Hodder & Stoughton

Copyright © 2000 by Janette Marshall

First published in Great Britain in 2000 by Hodder and Stoughton
A division of Hodder Headline
The right of Janette Marshall to be identified as the Author of the Work has been asserted by her in accordance with the Copyright, Designs and Patents Act 1988.

1 3 5 7 9 10 8 6 4 2

British Library Cataloguing in Publication Data
Marshall, Janette
Eat to beat your age
1. Cookery – Health aspects   2. Nutrition   3. Aging – Nutritional aspects
I. Title
641.5'63
ISBN 0 340 76812 6

Typeset by Phoenix Typesetting,
Ilkley, West Yorkshire

Printed and bound in Great Britain by
Clays Ltd, St Ives plc

Hodder and Stoughton
A division of Hodder Headline
338 Euston Road
London NW1 3BH

Here is a powder conceal'd in this paper which . . . is the powder that made Venus a goddess (given her by Apollo,) that kept her perpetually young, clear'd her wrinkles, firm'd her gums, fill'd her skin, colour'd her hair; from her derived to Helen and at the sack of Troy unfortunately lost; til now, in this our age, it was as happily recovered, by a studious antiquary, out of some ruins of Asia, who sent a moiety of it to the court of France, (but much sophisticated,) wherewith the ladies there, now, colour their hair. The rest, at this present, remains with me; extracted to a quintessence; so that, wherever it but touches, in youth it perpetually preserves, in age restores the complexion; seats your teeth, did they dance like virginal jacks, firm as a wall; makes them white as ivory, that were black as (a crow).

Scoto of Mantua, the mountebank doctor
Volpone, Ben Jonson, 1607

Contents

Introduction

Every one of us started to age from before we were born. From the moment we are born we grow older. To begin with, this is an attractive proposition. Children want to grow up so that they can do all the things they are not yet capable of. Adolescents often appear to their parents not to want to grow up, yet they claim their advance in age should allow them to do all the things they should not yet be doing.

Throughout our twenties we continue to age without giving the matter much thought, but sooner or later all adults feel they would really rather not grow up any more! Even though we laugh at people who are ridiculous in their attempts to be younger than they are, many of us would like to be younger. The moment of truth – when we start wishing not to grow any older – is different for everyone. For some it is finding a few grey hairs or realising they have gained weight over time. For others a reunion can also be a revelation that they (and their contemporaries) are not as young as they thought, or felt, they were.

What was that moment for you? Was it having to give up a sport for lack of fitness, feeling that fashionable clothes look ridiculous on you, embarking on expensive dental work to retain your teeth, finding you have to train harder to maintain the same level of fitness – or realising you are holding the newspaper at arm's length to read the small print?

Whatever the trigger for you NOW is the time to do something about it. And the good news is that there is lots you can do to maintain the fitness of youth, the optimism and the vigour, the good health and the energy.

Wanting to be as young as you can is *not* a selfish concern but a responsible attitude to the serious problem that faces the world today: an unfit ageing population. You need not become part of that if you choose to make diet and lifestyle changes now.

You can slow down the ageing process and even achieve the potential to live longer. But living longer is only an attractive proposition if the extra years are healthy and active. *Eat to Beat Your Age* therefore focuses on preventing or delaying the onset of diseases associated with ageing so that as short a period of your life as possible – ideally none – is lived with age-related disability or discomfort.

Life expectancy has risen sharply this century, and is expected to continue to rise, in virtually all populations throughout the world. The number of people reaching old age is therefore increasing. There are currently 580 million people in the world who are aged sixty or older. This figure is expected to rise to 1,000 million by 2020 – a 75 per cent increase compared with 50 per cent for population rise as a whole.

In the UK the number of people aged sixty and over is projected to increase from 20 per cent of the population (12 million) at the turn of the twenty-first century to 30 per cent, or 18.6 million by 2031.

The maximum lifespan potential of man is, amazingly, between 115 and 125 years. In Britain the average life expectancy is seventy-six years. To give you an idea of how young this is, the American astronaut John H. Glenn, Jr. was seventy-seven years old when he recently went into space for a second time as part of a scientific experiment to explore the secrets of ageing.

Although the majority of older people will never go into space, they enjoy sound health, lead very active and fulfilling lives, and can muster intellectual, emotional and social reserves often unavailable to younger people. But the number of old people with chronic diseases and disabilities will increase two- to threefold as the percentage of old people in the population rises.

Health is vital to maintain well-being and quality of life for as long as possible, and is essential if you are to continue making active contributions to family, friends and society as you age.

Why Do We Age?

One of the hardest things to do when meeting someone for the first time can be to guess how old they are. And among friends of the same age there are big differences in the rate at which they will display the signs of ageing. This could be so for any of the following reasons:

Genetic clock theory   assumes that the body has an internal 'genetic clock' that determines when senescence (the process of growing old) starts. One genetic clock theory is that we each have a predetermined number of cell divisions before our cells lose their ability to replicate or divide effectively. Another genetic clock theory maintains that we have a finite number of heartbeats or a fixed amount of metabolic activity, which can be expended carefully over a long time (the health-conscious, non-smoking exerciser) or maximally over a shortened time (the sex- and drugs-crazed rock and roll star).

Somatic mutation theory   says that spontaneous damage to chromosomes and to the DNA that they contain can accumulate and cause age-related disruption of body tissues, organs and systems, resulting in a higher frequency of cancer in the elderly, or the gradual breakdown of the immune system with ageing. DNA carries information that directs cell and enzyme activities in the body. When cells divide, DNA replicates itself and errors or damage can occur spontaneously. The build-up of these mistakes results in an accumulation of errors in the body's enzyme systems, tissues and organs. By this theory ageing is a progressive loss of function.

Catastrophe theory   combines cell and enzyme disruption caused by DNA replication errors (as in the mutation theory above) with further cell damage caused by free radicals. Free radicals are produced as the body uses oxygen and when it is exposed to certain environmental pollutants such as cigarette smoke. Free radicals are highly reactive and unstable and need to be quenched by anti-oxidants – hence the need to eat more foods rich in antioxidants to beat your age.

Unquenched free radicals cause DNA damage that interferes with the function of cells and changes the characteristics of major constituents of body organs, such as collagen and elastin, which become less elastic. This results in hardening of the arteries, changes in bones and muscles, and in protein changes of the lens of the eye leading to the formation of cataracts. The effect can also be seen in age-associated changes in the skin. As these DNA replication errors accumulate, so the process of ageing accelerates.

Wear and tear theories   say that ageing is a symptom of how the body reacts to environmental toxins, cosmic rays, gravity and pollution. The differing lifespans of populations in a variety of different environmental situations are held up as evidence to support this theory, as are studies of identical twins that show a large variation in longevity when the twins live in different environments. This suggests that environmental factors may be as important as or more important than genetic factors in determining lifespan.

Sex or gender theory   Your sex is also an important predictor of mortality. At any age, the death rates for men are up to 80 per cent higher than those for women. Until middle age blood pressure levels are lower in women than in men, as are blood sugar levels, blood cholesterol levels and body-weight gain. Differences in longevity are also due to poverty and socio-economic and cultural factors.

Cybernetic theory   suggests that the central nervous system is automatically responsible for the rate at which the body ages. According to this theory, changes in the endocrine system of hormone-producing glands and in the hypothalamus (the control centre in the brain) result in the ageing of organs. Changes in the levels of dopamine (a neurotransmitter that acts on the brain) may cause age-associated illnesses such as Parkinson's disease.

Foetal programming theory says that longevity and health are determined before you are born by conditions in the uterus. The nutritional quality of 'womb service' and the efficiency of the body in delivering nutrients to the foetus and providing stimuli or deflecting insults at critical or sensitive periods in foetal development are said to determine the baby's susceptibility to a whole range of diseases in adult life, such as coronary heart disease, stroke, high blood pressure, diabetes, obesity and maybe even depression and schizophrenia. Body size and proportion at birth are indicators of future health susceptibilities and longevity. Critics say that studies supporting the hypothesis are flawed and that post-natal rather than pre-natal factors may explain some of the links between body size at birth and later disease.

How to Make a Real Difference to the Rate at which you Age

Whatever genetic hand you were dealt, *Eat to Beat Your Age* shows that if you play your cards right there are many practical steps you can take to improve your chances of a longer and healthier life. These are:

- eating a well-balanced diet (Chapter 1, Eat Right)
- eating plenty of anti-ageing foods (Chapter 2, Eat Me)
- becoming more active (Chapter 3, Be Active, Feel Fitter)
- keeping your weight under control (Chapter 4, Don't Gain Weight, Lose Weight)
- having more fun and a healthy attitude to life (Chapter 5, Mind Over Matter)

If you follow these steps, you can make a real difference to the rate at which you age.

CHAPTER ONE

Eat Right, Age More Slowly

The greatest impact of ageing on diet is that **as your calorie needs go down with age, so your nutrient needs go up**. Unless you are very active you will lose lean muscle tissue as you age and in its place gain fat. Preventing weight gain and keeping fit, healthy and as young as possible means choosing lower-fat foods that also give you the highest proportion of nutrients to calories.

Luckily **one diet fits all your anti-ageing requirements** so that your body can run at peak fitness whether you are 35 or 105. It will also help you avoid some of the subclinical deficiencies, i.e., ones not serious enough to produce diseases, such as scurvy, or even symptoms, but which have a direct impact on how you feel, look and function.

Eating to beat your age aims to help you reduce your risks and achieve a higher quality of life for longer. The basis of this successful anti-ageing eating plan is to:

- eat a variety of foods, choosing most foods from plant sources
- eat five or more servings of fruit and vegetables each day
- eat six or more servings of bread, cereals, pasta, rice or other starchy foods each day
- eat high-fat foods sparingly, particularly those from animal sources
- keep your intake of sugars and salt to a minimum
- regulate the amount of alcohol you drink

Enjoying a variety of foods is the key to a well-balanced eating plan. It ensures that you benefit from a wide range of nutrients and also that you enjoy an exciting, colourful and tasty diet.

There are four main food groups:

— starchy foods
— vegetables and fruit
— dairy foods
— meat, fish, vegetarian alternatives

Eating foods from these groups in the right proportion provides the essential components for long-term optimum health and vitality.

Eat 6 or more Servings of Starchy Carbohydrate Foods a Day to Beat Your Age

Starchy foods should make up around one-third of your anti-ageing diet. This food group includes pasta, bread, rice and other cereals, potatoes and other starchy vegetables. Starchy carbohydrates are the best food source of **energy**. They also contain **B vitamins** to release that energy and aid healthy nerves and digestion.

What is a serving of starchy food?

- 3 tbsp breakfast cereal
- 2 tbsp muesli
- 1 slice of bread or toast
- 1 bread roll, bap or bun
- 1 small pitta bread, naan bread or chapatti
- 3 crackers or crispbreads
- 1 medium potato
- 2 heaped tbsp boiled rice
- 3 heaped tbsp boiled pasta
- 1 medium plantain or small sweet potato

Which types of starchy food to choose

Eat and enjoy all types of starchy food, but choose high-fibre kinds whenever you can. These are wholemeal, wholegrain, brown or high-fibre varieties of bread, breakfast cereal, pasta and rice. Because the grains are 'whole', they have not had the fibre or vitamins and minerals refined out of them. Choose lower-fat sauces for pasta and rice.

Start the day the starchy way

A breakfast based on cereal (with milk) and bread is a good way to start the day. People who regularly eat breakfast are slimmer, happier and healthier. Those who regularly miss the first meal of the day eat more fat and consume larger meals throughout the day. They perform less well during the morning – and are less cheerful. The mood of breakfast eaters improves throughout the morning . . .

For fibre, read NSP

Everyone is familiar with the importance of fibre in their diet, but fibre is now referred to as non-starch polysaccharide, or NSP for short. This is because fibre is not just the part of food that isn't digested (as was previously thought). Fibre consists of many different types of polysaccharides, and these have a life of their own! Although they may not be initially digested, they are fermented farther along the gut where they provide a life-support system for the friendly bacteria associated with longevity.

The Anti-Ageing Powers of Starchy Foods

Preventing constipation   is the best-known role of NSP, which absorbs water to bulk and soften food waste as it passes through the gut. Preventing constipation also helps avoid **haemorrhoids** and **varicose veins**.

Reducing the risk of heart disease is achieved by NSP lowering the levels of harmful blood cholesterol. NSP also seems to help regulate blood pressure. High blood pressure is a risk factor for heart disease.

Helping prevent gallstones is another consequence of NSP's role in removing harmful blood cholesterol. Its effect on the way the body uses bile acid may also help in this area.

Helping the gut function better can prevent diverticular disease and help control some types of irritable bowel syndrome.

Reducing the risk of cancer is another effect of a diet rich in NSPs, which dilute, absorb or transport carcinogens out of the body in the faeces. NSP also reduces the pH in the colon, allowing beneficial gut bacteria to thrive and to increase their output of substances such as butyrate, which causes cancer cells to commit suicide.

A healthy gut flora is stimulated by a diet with a large proportion of starchy foods, vegetables and fruit, and a smaller proportion of protein, dairy foods and sugar.

- Eating too much protein results in the bacterial fermentation of toxic products such as ammonia, hydrogen sulphide and carcinogens.
- Eating too much sugar results in more bacteriodes (potentially harmful gut bacteria) in the flora. By swapping as little as 15g (3 tsp) of sugar a day in the diet for 15g a day of NSP oligosaccharides (a type of polysaccharide obtained from the non-digestible part of vegetables such as onions, garlic, artichokes, asparagus and bananas) scientists have shown a dramatic and beneficial change in the gut flora; within seven or eight days beneficial bifido bacteria become dominant over harmful strains of bacteria.

Slower release of energy   is another benefit of starchy foods. The effect of different foods on blood sugar levels is emerging as an important nutritional factor. This effect is measured by the Glycaemic Index (GI) which is a ranking of foods based on their effect on blood sugar levels and the demands made on insulin production.

Low-GI status belongs to a food that breaks down slowly during digestion, releasing energy gradually into the bloodstream which results in a smaller rise in blood sugar. High-GI foods result in a larger rise of blood sugar. Low-GI is more desirable because it can help control hunger, appetite and weight and can lower raised blood fats; it can improve sensitivity to insulin; it can help control diabetes or help prevent maturity-onset diabetes (the type that starts in middle age or later). Of all the starchy staples, pasta has the lowest GI score, both fresh and dried. The GI score of potatoes and rice varies between varieties. Regardless of their GI score, bread, potatoes, pasta and rice are all very valuable foods.

Can fibre protect middle-aged women against colon cancer?

Despite all the benefits of NSP a major recent study of more than 88,000 female nurses aged between thirty-four and fifty-nine over a period of sixteen years failed to find definitive proof (which even so may exist) that dietary fibre protects against cancer of the colon. The report has been criticised for not differentiating between the types of NSP or fibre eaten, which could be critical.

And in fact the report concludes that fibre may be helpful in other respects. For example, it could protect against breast cancer, either directly or indirectly, by speeding the excretion of oestrogen from the body; oestrogen is implicated in hormone-dependent breast cancer.

Other substances in complex carbohydrate foods, such as lignans (naturally occurring plant oestrogens or phyto-oestrogens), may prove to be more important in protecting against breast cancer by weakening the effect of the body's own oestrogen on breast tissue and therefore reducing the risk of hormone-dependent cancers.

How much NSP do you need?

The average person eats about 12g of fibre a day. Around 18g or more, specifically 16g for women and 20g for men, would be better. But don't go mad: 24g per day is top whack for most people, and above 32g per day no further benefits are seen.

The best way to eat NSPs is where they occur naturally in food, e.g. starchy foods, vegetables and fruit (including dried fruit), wholemeal and wholegrain breads, wholemeal pasta, brown rice, pulses (lentils and beans), nuts and seeds, wholemeal flour, soya flour, rye flour, oats and oatmeal, oatcakes, breakfast cereals, millet, barley.

Quick NSP fixes

1. A bowl of wholegrain cereal for breakfast, a serving of wholemeal pasta for lunch, two servings of vegetables with one meal of the day and an orange.
2. Wholegrain cereal for breakfast, a slice of wholemeal bread or toast, a small packet of nuts, a serving of brown rice and an apple.
3. A generous serving of All-Bran or equivalent and a snack of three or four prunes or dried apricots.
4. The 'HRT' cakes and biscuit recipes on page 242.

Skip the bran

For most people, there is no need to eat raw bran or bran-enriched foods. Avoid sprinkling wheat bran onto food because unprocessed (or raw) bran contains high levels of phytic acid which can reduce the absorption of minerals such as iron and zinc. The phytic acid in wholemeal bread, however, is broken down by yeast and so the fibre in wholemeal bread is far more beneficial than in bran.

Eat at least 5 Servings of (Preferably Organic) Vegetables and Fruit a Day to Beat Your Age

Vegetables and fruit contain carbohydrates to give you **energy** and they are the source of many important **antioxidant nutrients** such as vitamin C and E and beta-carotene. **Vitamin C** is found mainly in citrus fruit, but is widespread in fruit and vegetables. **Beta-carotene** is the pigment that gives orange, yellow and red fruit their colour. Beta-carotene is a vitamin A precursor, which means it can be turned into vitamin A in the body, if needed. Beta-carotene is found only in plant foods, whereas vitamin A is a fat-soluble vitamin found in dairy foods and oily fish. **Vitamin E** is found in some fruit, vegetables and seeds, but mainly in vegetable oils. These, and other substances in this food group, prevent or delay oxidation, the process that produces ageing free radicals. Reversing or preventing oxidative damage caused by free radicals is a major priority if you want to add years to your life and life to your years.

Free radicals: the ageing foe

Free radicals are a highly reactive oxygen species formed in the body as a normal by-product of breathing oxygen. Other sources include pollution such as radiation and cigarette smoke. Although free radicals are harmless in small amounts, if there are too many they can oxidise the polyunsaturated fats in cell walls, or damage DNA and other proteins, leading to the development of heart disease, cancer, cataracts and other age-related diseases. People who eat a lot of fruit and vegetables rich in antioxidant nutrients (see chapter 2 for examples) such as vitamin C, beta-carotene and vitamin E seem less prone to some forms of cancer, probably because the antioxidants in their diet destroy free radicals. Antioxidant vitamins and other similar substances are the body's natural defence against the harmful effects of highly reactive oxygen.

Because most fruit, and many vegetables, can be eaten raw or lightly cooked, it is possible to retain maximum vitamins and minerals, which would otherwise be depleted or destroyed by cooking.

What is a serving of vegetables or fruit?

All fresh, frozen, chilled and canned vegetables and fruit count, with the exception of starchy vegetables such as potatoes. Also included are dried fruits and fruit juice, but not fruit *drinks* which contain very little, if any, juice, and are bulked out with water, added sugars or sweeteners and other non-nutritious ingredients.

A serving is:

- 1 medium portion of vegetables (125g/4½oz), or/including salad
- 1 piece of fresh fruit
- 6 tbsp stewed or canned fruit (140g/5oz)
- 1 small glass of fruit juice (100ml/3½fl oz)

Why eat organic?

I would rather ask you 'Why not eat organic?' I have not come across one convincing argument that non-organic food is in any way superior to organically produced food since I first started researching and writing about the relationship between diet, nutrition and health in the 1980s. Organic food is better for you and better for the planet. We could digress and discuss this for the rest of the book, but we are not going to do that – please read further about it elsewhere. Or you could join the Soil Association (tel: 0117 9290661) or the Henry Doubleday Research Association (tel: 01203 303517).

In a nutshell:

- Organic food will not be genetically modified food with all its associated risks and dangers (for further information contact Greenpeace True Food Campaign tel: 0171 865 8222).

- Organic food is produced without pesticides and other agro-chemicals or artificial fertilisers.
- It minimises damage to the soil, to plants and to wildlife, and to the animals that feed on plants – including humans.
- The organic system of agriculture limits global environmental damage.
- It is a sustainable system (not a finite system like conventional farming) that will not result in the ultimate horror of the Silent Spring depicted in Rachel Carson's seminal book.
- Some studies show that organically produced food is nutritionally superior to non-organic food.
- Organic agriculture does not contribute to low sperm counts and other fertility problems and to some types of cancers that have been associated with the noxious chemicals used in modern farming.
- Organic vegetables and fruits are not subjected to post-harvest fungicides, waxes and other sprays and chemicals that leave harmful residues.
- Most organic produce tastes better than the non-organic.

The Anti-Ageing Powers of Vegetables and Fruit

Reducing the risk of heart disease and cancer   This reduction is attributed to vegetables and fruit because they are our main food source of the antioxidant vitamins C and E and beta-carotene. Working together with the different types of NSP and other natural plant chemicals, antioxidants neutralise free radicals. The products of free-radical reactions are responsible for the gradual accumulation of physical changes over time which are now thought to be the root causes of coronary heart disease and cancer, the two major causes of premature death and disability in Britain.

Cutting down on cell damage   This is damage caused by free radicals attacking the polyunsaturated fatty acids that make up cell walls. Unless they are neutralised free radicals can cause considerable damage to the structure and functions of cell membranes. Vitamin E terminates free-radical chain reactions, inhibiting the production of additional free radicals, and also limits the damage. Selenium is an antioxidant mineral (in nuts, cereals, fish, offal) and an ingredient of important enzymes that destroy free radical peroxides before they can damage cell membranes.

Protecting against arthritis   Vegetables and fruit reduce the inflammation caused by free-radical damage characteristic of many joint problems that affect the quality of life in later years, producing major or minor disabilities.

Boosting immunity and speeding healing   This is another role of vitamin C in fruit and vegetables.

Breathing new life into your lungs   People with the highest intakes of vitamins C and E and beta-carotene have better lung function than people with a low intake of vegetables and fruit. The scientific measure of lung power, or how much 'puff' is in the lungs, is forced expiratory volume (FEV). In a study of more than 3,000 middle-aged men in Finland, the Netherlands and Italy, those with greatest FEV had above-average intakes of antioxidant vitamins. In Finland, vitamin E intake was above average, where the main source was vegetable oils and forest berries. In Italy, the link was with vitamin C and fruit, while in the Netherlands it was beta-carotene from red and yellow fruit and vegetables, as well as vitamin C from potatoes. Closer to home, a study of more than 2,500 men living in Wales and aged 45 to 59 years showed that those who ate five apples a week had a greater lung capacity than those who did not eat fruit. (Vitamin E in their diet from other sources also had a beneficial effect on their lung power.)

• Potatoes are not a rich source of vitamin C but because they are eaten in quantity in the Netherlands, as they are in the UK, they make a significant contribution to the diet. In all the countries studied, eating more bread was also associated with putting more puff in the lungs.

Preventing respiratory illnesses   The high intakes of the antioxidant vitamins C and E and beta-carotene associated with eating a lot of vegetables and fruit keep the airways clear by reducing inflammation. Antioxidant nutrients mop up free radicals, the by-products of oxidation and pollution, preventing them from irritating the airways and causing inflammation. Vitamin C may also help fight the bacteria present in some respiratory illnesses. In addition it encourages the production of a natural bronchodilator (airway-widening substance) that makes breathing easier.

Strengthening blood capillary walls   is a function of vitamin E that is protective against age-associated problems as diverse as wrinkles and heart disease.

Providing potassium to reduce the risk of stroke   Potassium works in the body to counteract the harmful side-effects of eating too much sodium (salt). Potassium reduces the risk of stroke by helping prevent the high blood pressure that occurs with age due to excessive salt intake over time.

Providing tasty NSP   NSP (fibre) occurs in many different forms in fruit and vegetables. Eating fruit without peeling it, and eating the skins of vegetables where appropriate, increases NSP intake.

Providing nutrient-dense energy   This is particularly true of bananas, dates and pears, and starchy vegetables such as potatoes, sweet potatoes and parsnips.

Helping to lower raised levels of homocysteine   The active substance is folates, found mainly in green vegetables. A raised level of homocysteine is an independent risk factor for heart disease, stroke and other vascular disease. But that's another story (below, if you have time to digress a little).

The Homocysteine Story
(or Why Eating More B Vitamins Combats Heart Disease)

Ask most people what puts them at greatest risk of a heart attack and they will probably say 'cholesterol'. But a raised level of homocysteine seems to be more closely associated with increased risk of heart disease – and particularly stroke and vascular disease – than raised blood cholesterol levels.

Homocysteine is converted in the body by folic acid to methionine, one of the body's essential building blocks of protein, and to other substances essential for brain function and making DNA. So, like cholesterol, homocysteine is essential for normal body function and structure. Problems occur when the diet does not provide enough folic acid and two other B vitamins, B_6 and B_{12}, to convert raised levels of homocysteine to methionine.

Unlike raised blood cholesterol levels, which are quite hard to reduce through weight loss, diet and exercise, homocysteine levels can be lowered quickly and easily by taking an extra 200 micrograms (mcg) of folic acid a day – that is 200mcg more than the RNI which is also 200mcg a day for everyone aged eleven and over (except pregnant and pre-conceptual women, who are recommended to take supplements of 400mcg/0.4mg daily to reduce the risk of spina bifida in their unborn babies).

Note RNI stands for Reference Nutrient Intake. This is the amount of a vitamin or mineral thought to be sufficient per day, even for people with high requirements. RNIs are set by the UK government. For a table of nutrients, see page 105.

Folic acid pills to beat ageing

As half the population probably has raised homocysteine levels, this begs the question: should everyone take folic acid supplements as an anti-ageing measure? This is probably not necessary because studies have shown that eating just two standard (30g) servings a day of a breakfast cereal fortified with folic acid is sufficient to achieve beneficial blood levels within eight weeks. There is no need to take higher levels of folic acid because a supplementation of 4–5mg per day or above runs the risk of masking any cases of (pernicious) anaemia. And this supplementation will not further reduce homocysteine levels.

Foods that are fortified with folic acid (mainly breads and breakfast cereals) are marked with a large blue F symbol. Foods labelled 'contains extra folic acid' contain 100mcg of food per portion and those labelled 'contains folic acid' contain 33mcg per portion.

Time to fortify more foods?

In the US all flour has to be fortified with folic acid by law. American studies have shown that fortifying grain products with folic acid significantly increases folate values and decreases homocysteine concentrations in middle-aged and older adults. However, it has not been proved that taking folic acid supplements can prevent heart disease. And some scientists warn that high homocysteine levels may reflect another as yet unknown process that harms blood vessel walls and increases the risk of heart disease. Others are calling for randomised trials of folate supplements in the UK to test the benefits of reducing high serum concentrations of homocysteine. While the benefits of folic acid to protect against heart disease continue to be debated in the UK, the Committee on Medical Aspects of Food and Nutrition Policy (COMA), which advises the British government, recommended in January 2000 that folic acid should be added to all flour to prevent the birth of babies handicapped by spina bifida and related conditions. Fortification would involve adding 240 micrograms (μg) of folic acid to every 100g of food products to produce an estimated 41 per cent reduction in risk of all neural tube defects.

There is no danger of overdosing on folates, so foods rich in them can be enjoyed regularly, even if folic acid supplements are taken e.g. during pregnancy.

Good sources of folates

50–100µg folates per average serving (all foods are listed in order of folic acid content per serving): cooked black-eye beans, Brussels sprouts, beef and yeast extracts, cooked kidney, kale, spinach, spring greens, broccoli and green beans.

15–50µg folates per serving cooked soya beans, cauliflower, cooked chickpeas, potatoes, iceberg lettuce, oranges, peas, orange juice, parsnips, baked beans, wholemeal bread, cabbage, yogurt, white bread, eggs, brown rice, wholegrain pasta.

Many breads and breakfast cereals are fortified with folic acid.

Eat 2–3 Servings of Lower-Fat Dairy Foods a Day to Beat Your Age

Milk, cheese, yogurt and fromage frais are all good sources of **calcium** for strong bones and teeth; lower-fat versions are best. And it's not just children who need calcium. Bones and teeth are living structures with a regular turnover of calcium, so people of all ages – and particularly women around the menopause – have constant calcium needs. Dairy foods also provide **protein** for growth and repair, and **vitamins A and D** for eyes and teeth.

What is a serving of dairy foods?

* 1 medium glass of milk (200ml/7fl oz)
* 1 matchbox-sized piece of cheddar-type cheese (40g/1 ½oz)
* 1 small pot of yogurt, cottage cheese or fromage frais (125g/4½oz)

Try lower-fat milk

If you have always used whole milk, semi-skimmed does not take much adjusting to because it tastes like whole milk. Skimmed milk has a much thinner taste and takes longer to get used to. Both contain as much calcium and protein as whole milk, but less fat.

Full-fat milk contains 22g of fat per pint
Semi-skimmed milk contains 9g of fat per pint
Skimmed milk contains 0.6g of fat per pint

If you really cannot get used to the taste of skimmed milk for use throughout the day, you could use it in cooking and in drinks, where the difference in flavour should go unnoticed.

Vegetarian sources of calcium

- broccoli and other greens
- beans (e.g. red kidney, baked beans)
- fortified foods such as white bread
- tofu and some other soya foods (e.g. 'milks' and 'yogurts')
- sesame seeds
- tahini
- some mineral water (e.g. Evian)
- calcium-enriched foods (e.g. orange juice with added calcium)
- breakfast-replacement cereal bars.

The Anti-Ageing Powers of Lower-Fat Dairy Foods

Dairy foods do not contribute as much fat to most diets as meat, but over time swapping to low-fat milk, yogurt, cheese, fromage frais and desserts will still reduce the fat in your diet, especially saturated fat. Too much fat, and saturated fats in particular, increase the risk of heart disease and some cancers. Too much fat also contributes to being overweight and all its associated health problems.

Eat 2–4 Servings of Meat, Fish or Vegetarian Alternatives a Day to Beat Your Age

Meat, fish and vegetarian alternatives are needed for **protein** for growth and repair, not just for children and adolescents, but for all ages. Meat, poultry, shellfish and fish also provide the minerals **iron** and **zinc** (most in red meat, less in poultry and fish) and **vitamin B12**, which prevents anaemia. These minerals, plus another, **magnesium**, are also needed for growth, healthy bones and skin.

What is a serving of meat and meat alternatives?

Two daily servings of these foods is adequate for most people, but the very active, growing adolescents and vegetarians may need three or four:

- 3 medium slices beef, pork, ham, lamb, liver, kidney, chicken or oily fish (70g/3oz)
- 115–150g/4–5oz white fish (not fried in batter)
- 3 fish fingers
- 2 eggs (up to 4 a week, see page 30!)
- 5 tbsp baked beans or other cooked pulses, lentils, dhal (200g/7oz)
- 2 tbsp nuts, peanut butter or other nut products (60g/12¼oz)
- 115–150g/4–5oz tofu or other soya product

What types of meat and alternatives should you eat?

Eat whatever type you enjoy most, but quantity and quality are especially important issues to your health and your finances. By quality I do not mean purchasing only from 'high-class butchers', although you will probably do very well if you do, particularly if they know their suppliers and they stock organic and free-range meat. Quality is more about buying and eating **lean meat,** because while meat can be nutritious, it contains a lot of fat, especially saturated fat. Meat eaters get a hefty whack of their fat intake from meat products, which provide 25 per cent of the fat in the typical UK diet.

Fatty meat and fatty meat products include sausages, pâté, meat pies and pasties, burgers, koftas, keemas, black and white pudding, faggots, frankfurters, haggis, luncheon meat, meat paste, polony, salami, sausages, saveloy. All of these are poor value both nutritionally – because they are composed mainly of unhealthy saturated fats and fillers – and economically in terms of value for money.

Meat that is organic, free range or from other systems of farming that grass-feed their livestock has a healthier fat profile with a greater proportion of unsaturated to saturated fat (see the box on page 24).

Eat less meat to reduce your cancer risk

Two authoritative reports on diet and cancer recommend that people who eat between twelve and fourteen portions a week, or 140g/5oz a day, of red meat such as beef, lamb, pork and veal, should eat less to reduce their risk of cancers of the colon and rectum. There are also possible links between meat eating and other cancers: breast, prostate, pancreas and kidney. People who eat an 'average' amount, i.e. eight to ten portions a week or 90g/3½oz a day, are advised not to eat any more than this.

Eat more vegetables with your meat

Heavy meat eaters, whose consumption has been linked with increased risk of colon and bowel cancers, tend not to eat many – if any – vegetables. If you do eat meat regularly, make sure that you also eat mountains of vegetables and fruit because they contain substances that can offset some of the potentially harmful effects of a higher intake of meat. As many cancers occur later in life, a diet heavy in meat is one that can be said to be very ageing.

**Tip   Taking enough exercise (see Chapter 3)
also reduces the risk of colon cancer.**

Avoid the burnt bits

The charred and burnt bits that form on the surface of meat that
has been cooked by grilling/char-grilling, roasting, frying, and
barbecuing contain substances (heterocyclic amines or HCAs for
short) that have provoked cancer in animal-feed trials and have
damaged human DNA in test-tube studies. People are either fast
or slow metabolisers of these substances; which type is determined
genetically. It seems that individuals who are fast metabolisers are
at increased risk of developing polyps and large-bowel cancer, but
research in this area continues. So avoid the burnt bits, or eat them
infrequently, until more is known.

Eat less meat to protect your gut bacteria

The amount of meat you eat also influences the bacteria that live
in your gut and that ferment undigested food residues to produce
healthy – or toxic – by-products. Heavy meat consumption
increases the proportion of the harmful bacteria that produce
potential toxins.

Limit cured meat

Cured, salted and smoked meats and fish can contain preservatives
such as sodium nitrate which can be turned into potentially
carcinogenic nitrosamines in the gut. The more cured or processed
meat you eat, the more of these substances your body will absorb
and the greater the risk of colorectal and possibly stomach cancers,
particularly if your diet is not rich in the antioxidant fruit and
vegetables that can block nitrosamine formation.

The Anti-Ageing Power of Alternatives to Meat

Eat more fish to beat your age

Fish is an excellent **low-fat protein** food. And the type of fat that fish contains is beneficial polyunsaturated fat, as opposed to the harmful saturated fat found in meat.

White fish (e.g. cod, haddock, plaice) is especially low in fat and rich in minerals including **iodine**. Oily fish (mackerel, salmon, sardines, herring, pilchards) is rich in essential polyunsaturates and contains the fat-soluble **vitamins A** and **D** which are not found in white fish. Canned oily fish (e.g. sardines, pilchards) is rich in **calcium, phosphorus** and **fluoride** because the bones are eaten.

To benefit from fish, you need to make it a regular part of your diet. Substituting two meat meals a week with fish, and making at least one of them oily fish, will definitely have an anti-ageing effect. The advice is based on the beneficial effects of the omega-3 fatty acids found in fish oils.

What are fatty acids?

Fatty acids are the building blocks for fats. They can be saturated, monounsaturated or polyunsaturated.

There are two families of polyunsaturated fatty acids:

- omega-3, derived from alpha-linolenic acid
- omega-6, derived from linoleic acid

These two types of fatty acid are called 'essential' fatty acids (EFAs) because they cannot be made in the body and must be obtained from food.

Omega-3 and omega-6 fatty acids cannot be interconverted but they are changed by the body into important long chain fatty acids (long chain means they are literally made physically longer by being metabolised in the body):

- eicosapentaenoic acid or EHA
- docosahexaenoic acid or DHA
- docosapentaenoic acid or DPA

EPA, DHA and DPA occur as omega-3 fatty acids in oily fish, or they can be converted in the body from omega-6 alpha linolenic fatty acids, if the right conditions (such as the correct balance of fats in the diet) exist.

Reducing the risk of heart disease especially the risk of dying as a result of a coronary event, is a function of omega-3 fatty acids. They probably do this by making the blood less likely to clot and cause a heart attack; by reducing blood pressure and irregular heart rhythms; by improving insulin sensitivity and the response to blood fats after a (large) meal. The omega-6 fatty acids reduce the risk of heart disease in a different way, by helping to lower the level of harmful types of blood cholesterol.

Relieving the symptoms of arthritis Fish oils can also help relieve the symptoms of age-related inflammatory diseases such as osteoarthritis, and swollen and tender joints. They improve mobility in some people and reduce associated tiredness.

Helping to prevent diabetes You probably would not, in your wildest dreams, associate eating fish with preventing diabetes. But life is full of surprises, and there is growing evidence that omega-3 fatty acids can help prevent the development of maturity-onset (or non-insulin-dependent – NIDDM) diabetes – particularly if caught in the early stages. If you have a low intake of omega-3 fatty acids you are probably more likely to develop insulin resistance, the first step in the development of NIDDM. In some trials regular fish eaters have been shown to have half the risk of NIDDM. This is because the omega-3 fatty acids in fish oil improve the body's uptake of glucose and its sensitivity to insulin. The omega-3 fatty acids also lower the levels of triglycerides, which improve glucose uptake, and they make the membranes of cells more permeable to insulin uptake.

Insulin and Diabetes (in a nutshell)

Insulin is a hormone produced by the pancreas in response to the amount of glucose (sugar) in the blood. When starchy foods are broken down into glucose, they enter the bloodstream. Insulin is needed for the glucose to be taken up in the liver and muscle cells where it is converted to energy. Diabetes occurs when the pancreas produces little or no insulin, so insulin has to be given by injection. In NIDDM (the type that occurs later in life and is often related to obesity and lack of physical exercise), the body can still produce some insulin but not enough for its needs; or the body becomes resistant to insulin so that it does not work properly. NIDDM may be controlled by diet (and lifestyle) plus tablets or sometimes by diet plus insulin injections.

Getting the balance right

The balance between omega-3 and omega-6 fatty acids is important if you are to get enough EPA, DHA and DPA. Both omega-6 and omega-3 fats compete for the same enzymes to make their longer chain derivatives EPA, DHA and DPA. Because we eat a lot of omega-6 fats, the ratio of omega-6 to omega-3 fats in our diet is skewed. We need to shift from the current ratio of 7:1 omega-6 to omega-3, which puts us at risk of not getting as much EPA and DHA as we need, to a ratio of 6:1. The best way to correct the balance is to eat more oily fish. (See also information on fish oils and arthritis, page 80.)

How has the ratio gone wrong?

Thirty years ago we had a healthier ratio. The reasons for today's intake of more omega-6 than omega-3 is that people are eating less oily fish; there is increased use of polyunsaturated oils and spreads;

food manufacturers are adding more vegetable oils to processed foods; and livestock from intensively farmed meat does not contain as much omega-3 as that from organic or free-range, grass-fed livestock.

How much fish should you eat?

For fish to have an anti-ageing effect you need to eat between 200g and 400g of oily fish, which is a minimum of two servings a week. This will provide 4–5g of omega-3 fatty acids, enough to have a protective anti-ageing effect. And if you think that sounds a lot, be thankful you are not an Eskimo. Their traditional diet includes 250g a day which provides them with 2.5g of EPA per day and protects them against heart disease – but this high intake makes their blood so thin that they bleed for twice as long as people in the West before their blood forms a clot.

The jury is still out on which type of omega-3 fatty acid is the more beneficial – EPA or DHA. And differing amounts of each are found in different fish. Here are a few random examples of amounts found in various foods. Information is scant as most analyses of the omega-3 fatty acid content of food lump together EPA and DHA for total omega-3 content, although the non-fish ones all contain much less EPA and DHA.

Typical omega-3 fatty acid content of fish

Food	Average UK portion grams (g)	EPA	DPA	DHA	Total omega-3 per portion
		g/100g food			
Cod	120	0.08	0.01	0.16	0.30
Haddock	120	0.05	0.01	0.10	0.19
Plaice	130	0.16	0.04	0.10	0.42
Herring	119	0.51	0.11	0.69	2.18
Mackerel	160	0.71	0.12	1.10	4.46
Pilchards, canned in tomato sauce	110	1.17	0.23	1.20	3.16

Food	Average UK portion grams (g)	EPA	DPA	DHA	Total omega-3 per portion
		g/100g food			
Sardines, canned in tomato sauce	100	0.89	0.10	0.68	2.02
Salmon, canned in brine	100	0.55	0.14	0.86	1.85
Salmon	100	0.5	0.4	1.3	2.5
Trout	230	0.23	0.09	0.83	2.92
Prawns, frozen raw	60	0.06	trace	0.04	0.91
Cod liver oil	5ml/1tsp	10.8	1.40	8.30	1.19

Source: n-3 Fatty Acids and Health report, British Nutrition Foundation

How vegetarians can eat more omega-3 fatty acids

The richest sources of omega-3 fatty acids are oil-rich fish, but do not worry if you are a vegetarian or cannot eat fish. The omega-6 fatty acids in green leafy vegetables, some nuts, some vegetable oils and some margarines/spreads can be turned into DHA and DPA, provided that your diet does not contain too much saturated or trans fat (see pages 33–4).

Eating more vegetables (particularly dark green leafy types) and walnuts, and using rapeseed or soybean oils for cooking or in salad dressings because they have a high alpha-linolenic acid content, is the non-fish way to increase your omega-3 intake.

Another food with a relatively high omega-3 to omega-6 ratio is linseed oil. Some foods are also fortified with omega-3 fatty acids.

Farmed fish is not so healthy

As demand for fish increases, fish farming will also increase to make up the shortfall from declining fish stocks. Fish from intensive mass-production fish farms do not have the same fat composition as wild fish. Farmed fish have a higher total fat content and contain a lower ratio of omega-3 to omega-6 fatty acids than wild fish. So farmed fish are less beneficial, due to their lack of exercise and their poorer diet. Fish farmers will need to manipulate the diet of farmed fish if their fat composition is to match the composition needed to help prevent diseases of unhealthy ageing! There are also many harmful environmental aspects to fish farming that need to be addressed. Even so, fish is still a lower-fat and lower-saturated-fat alternative to many meat products.

Eat More Beans to Beat Your Age

Beans provide **B vitamins** for healthy nerves and digestion. They are low in fat, high in protein and **NSP** (meat and fish are devoid of fibre), plus minerals such as iron (see page 31). Pulses are also a good source of phytochemicals (natural chemicals that occur in plants), in particular phyto-oestrogens (plant hormones) which have recently been found to make an important contribution to health (see linseed, soya, Chapter 2). In particular they protect against age-associated heart disease, breast cancer, osteoporosis and menopausal problems in women. Substituting some of your meat or meat-product meals with beans, or extending meat dishes with pulses, nuts or seeds will have anti-ageing effects.

Beans are fantastically versatile and tasty ethnic dishes are often the most delicious ways to enjoy them: Indian, Middle Eastern, Chinese, Japanese and, nearer home, traditional Mediterranean foods – get those cookbooks out.

Everyone is recommended to eat at least 30g/1oz of beans per day. Combined with cereals (bread and pasta) and grains (rice etc.), beans provide amino acids (the building blocks of protein) in the right proportion to make them an excellent **vegetarian protein** alternative to meat.

What are pulses?

Pulses are beans, peas (including chickpeas) and lentils. They can be fresh, frozen, canned or dried. Examples include: aduki beans, baked beans, bean burgers, gram dhal, black-eye beans, butter beans, chickpeas, haricot beans, hummus, kidney beans, lentils, maser dhal, mung beans, pease pudding, pigeon peas, pinto beans, soya beans, tofu, split peas and tempeh. There are also products made from beans such as some vegetable 'roasts' and burgers.

Eat More Nuts to Beat Your Age

Nuts are concentrated sources of **energy** (calories), **vitamins** and **minerals**, providing all the nourishment needed by a new plant. Most nuts are a good source of **NSP** and the fat they contain is **unsaturated** (except for coconuts and macadamias). While salted nuts are not good news for people with high blood pressure and their high calorie content may be problematic for those who are overweight, when eaten as part of a balanced diet nuts are super nutrient-dense foods.

Protection from heart disease   Two major studies have shown that people who eat nuts frequently have a far lower risk of heart disease than those who do not eat nuts; intermediate nut consumers have an intermediate risk.

It could be that the unsaturated fats in nuts help to lower blood cholesterol levels, and/or that the omega-3 fatty acids prevent blood clotting and disruptions to heart rhythms.

Nuts are a rich source of arginine, an amino acid that stimulates production of nitric oxide. This in turn relaxes the cells that line arteries and it also helps make blood less likely to be sticky and to clot and cause a heart attack.

Nuts contain a lot of magnesium, copper, folic acid, potassium, fibre and vitamin E, which are all anti-ageing and protective in their own ways.

Clever on eggs

Current advice to eat no more than four eggs a week is based on their high cholesterol content. Raised blood cholesterol levels are

---

associated with heart disease. Although advice in the UK is to cut down on total fat and saturated fat consumption rather than to single out cholesterol for avoidance, a recommended limit has been put on eggs. However, recent studies of a possible link between egg consumption and heart disease, each covering about ten years, have shown that healthy people do not increase their risk of heart disease or stroke by eating one egg a day.

Apparently it is not the eggs but the lifestyle of frequent egg consumers that is the problem. People who eat more eggs are more likely to smoke, less likely to take enough physical activity and generally have unhealthy eating habits! So, if you really must eat an egg every day, that's OK, provided the rest of your diet and lifestyle is healthy. However, a better balance would be to eat a variety of protein foods because other foods have different nutrients to contribute to your anti-ageing armoury.

Tips on iron for vegetarians

Iron in meat and fish is more easily used by the body than iron from plant foods. The same is true for zinc. So care needs to be taken in a vegetarian diet. Here are some ways to improve iron uptake.

- **Orange juice** and other drinks and foods rich in vitamin C, when taken with vegetarian sources of iron such as whole grains, pulses, dried apricots and dark green vegetables, will help improve absorption of the mineral.
- **Tea** drunk less than 30 minutes before or after a meal results in the tannin in tea binding up the iron and making it unavailable to the body.
- **Eggs** and milk products are a useful source of zinc and vitamin B_{12} in a vegetarian diet. They can also improve zinc absorption from plant foods at the same meal.

- **Iron cooking pots** can improve uptake, if findings from a Third World study can be extrapolated to the West. Ethiopian children who are given food cooked in iron pots have lower rates of anaemia and better growth than children whose food is cooked in aluminium pots. So if your cast-iron pots are going a little rusty, or you find them a bit too heavy, do not throw them away: carry on cooking and literally pump iron (weight train) with them to gain strength to handle them for longer . . . and absorb the iron they add to your food.

Limit Foods Containing Fat to 1–5 Servings a Day to Beat Your Age

Fat, as we have seen, is essential for health when it comes in the form of essential omega-3 and omega-6 fatty acids, but we need only a small amount (around 30g/1oz) of unsaturated fats each day. Fat makes food palatable, but the trouble is that most of us eat too much fat, and too much of the wrong sort – saturated fat.

The maximum daily amount of fat you need depends on your age, size and how active you are. But for most sedentary adults trying not to gain weight, the ceiling on fats should be no more than 70g a day for women and 90g a day for men.

What is a serving of fats?

A serving of spreading fats and cooking oils is probably a lot less than you think so it is very easy to eat too much fat:

- 5g or 1 tsp margarine or butter
- 10g or 2 tsp low-fat spread
- 5ml or 1 tsp cooking oil, fat or ghee

What is a serving of fatty foods?

- 15g or 1 tbsp mayonnaise or vinaigrette (salad dressing)
- 15ml or 1 tbsp cream
- 1 packet of crisps

Other fatty foods include pastry, meat products, sausages, pâté and fried foods.

Why fats are limited in a balanced diet

Too much fat, and saturated fat in particular, increases the risk of heart disease by raising the level of harmful blood cholesterol. If there are not enough antioxidants in the diet to prevent free-radical damage to arteries and to prevent oxidation of cholesterol, then cholesterol can build up in the arteries, slowing down the blood supply to the heart – or even cutting it off completely, causing a heart attack.

The Anti-Ageing Fats of Life

All fats should be eaten in moderation. In a well-balanced diet, fat should provide no more than 30–35 per cent (not the current 40 per cent) of total energy.

We have seen that too much fat, and saturated fat in particular, increases the risk of heart disease. It may increase your risk of cancers of the prostate, endometrium, breast, colon, rectum and lung. Excessive amounts of polyunsaturated fats may also be harmful, particularly if your diet lacks antioxidants (see Chapter 2) which neutralise the harmful free radicals that are generated when these unstable fats are oxidised.

Saturated fats – the ones we should be cutting down on – are found mainly in animal foods such as meat and dairy produce. They are solid at room temperature (butter, lard, creamed coconut). Saturated fats are found mainly in hard and some soft margarines, cooking fats, cakes, biscuits, savoury snacks and other processed foods, confectionery and chocolate.

Your anti-ageing target
• No more than 10 per cent of your total fat intake should be saturated fats. Too much saturated fat raises levels of blood cholesterol, particularly the harmful type LDL (low-density lipoprotein).

Trans fats   these are produced when vegetable and fish oils are hydrogenated or partially hydrogenated to turn them into margarine and shortening. They also occur naturally in some dairy foods. Like saturated fat from animal food, they raise blood levels of harmful low-density lipoprotein (LDL) cholesterol, thus increasing the risk of heart disease. They block the conversion of essential omega-6 fatty acids into omega-3 fatty acids, which is important if you do not eat oily fish.

Your anti-ageing target
• No more than 2 per cent of your total calories should come from trans fats, and ideally less.

Monounsaturated fats   these are found mainly in olive, rape-seed and groundnut oils, avocados, most nuts and some spreads. Monounsaturates should replace saturated fats in the diet because they reduce harmful types of cholesterol (LDL) without also reducing levels of beneficial HDL (high-density lipoprotein) cholesterol.

Your anti-ageing target
• No more than 12 per cent of fat in the diet should be monounsaturated.

Polyunsaturated fats   these are found mainly in vegetable oils (except palm and coconut which are saturated). Replacing satu-rated fat in the diet with polyunsaturated fats lowers blood cholesterol levels. Polyunsaturates are also vital to maintaining health and longevity because they contain the essential fatty acids (EFAs) that the body cannot make and must obtain from food. There are two types of EFA: omega-6, from the linoleic acid in vegetable oils such as sunflower, and omega-3, from the linolenic acid in other vegetable oils, e.g. soya and rapeseed, in walnuts, and in oily fish, e.g. mackerel, herring, sardines, salmon (but not canned tuna).

Your anti-ageing target
- 6–10 per cent of your total energy intake (calories) should come from polyunsaturated fats.

Of that:
- 0.2–0.5 per cent should be omega-3 EFAs. We only need 1–2g of omega-3 fatty acids a day to maintain the membranes in the brain and eyes and to produce vital hormone-like substances. Your risk of heart attack is also reduced by these fatty acids which decrease the tendency of the blood to clot. Their anti-inflammatory action also helps in arthritis.
- 6 per cent should be omega-6 EFAs. We need a minimum of 4g of omega-6 fatty acids a day and no more than 30g. Amounts between these two figures offer protection from heart disease: more than that risks production of too many free radicals.

Eat 0–2 Servings of Foods Containing Sugar Per Day to Beat Your Age

On average men eat about 115g/4oz of sugar a day and women eat about 90g/3¼oz which accounts for around 20 per cent of total calories. In an ideal anti-ageing diet this intake would be halved to make room for more nutritious, and possibly lower-calorie, foods.

Most of us think of sugar in terms of white or brown, but there are many more forms: cane sugar, raw cane sugar, muscovado sugar, honey, treacle, syrup, molasses, dextrose, glucose, fructose, maltose, corn syrup, concentrated fruit juice, glucose syrup and other industrial sugars which are added to processed foods. Reading labels to avoid these hidden sugars is one way of cutting down. Another is to try to stick to the recommended number of servings a day.

What is a serving of sugar or sugary foods?

- 15g or 1tbsp sugar
- 1 rounded tsp jam/honey
- 2 biscuits
- half a slice of cake or a doughnut or a Danish pastry
- 1 small bar of chocolate
- 1 small tube or bag of sweets

Why sugar is problematic

As we have seen, we should be eating more carbohydrates. Sugar, on the other hand, is a refined carbohydrate and it is complex unrefined carbohydrates that are good for us. Unlike starchy carbohydrates (bread, rice, pasta, potatoes), sugar contains pure calories and no anti-ageing vitamins, minerals or NSP.

However, sugar makes some foods taste nicer, and most people enjoy some sugary food, even if they do not put sugar in their tea or coffee or on their breakfast cereal. While it's not necessary to give up sugar altogether (even if this were possible), it is a good idea to limit your intake.

Indeed, people without weight problems are more likely to eat a moderate amount of sweet foods than none at all. This makes sense when you consider that sweet foods seem to be better and quicker at switching off appetite than fatty foods. Fatty foods are therefore easier to overeat and as they are a more concentrated form of calories they have a greater potential to contribute to weight problems than sugary foods.

So stop thinking that sugar is 'bad'. You can enjoy everything in moderation (to borrow an old adage) as part of a well-balanced, anti-ageing diet.

Foods that contain 'intrinsic' sugars, where the sugars are locked into the structure of the food as in fruit or milk, are the least harmful to teeth and unlike the 'extrinsic' sugars (those listed above) in confectionery or sticky foods, they do not adhere to the teeth and cause dental caries (holes) that need filling by the dentist.

How sugar feeds tooth decay

Sugar causes problems for teeth by feeding the bacteria that live in dental plaque. These bacteria produce acid that attacks the tooth, causing caries. Between-meal snacks and late-night sweets and bedtime biscuits are particularly bad for teeth as the flow of saliva reduces during sleep. Saliva has a natural tooth-cleaning effect and without it sugars can ferment all night in the mouth. The more frequently sugary foods and drinks are taken, the greater the risk of dental decay – hence the advice to eat confectionery as part of a meal, if eaten at all. Sugary drinks that are slowly sipped have the same effect. Acid drinks, such as colas and other fizzy drinks, are even worse because the acid attacks the enamel of the teeth. This kind of decay is far more difficult for the dentist to fix than caries.

Invest in less sugar to pay dividends as you age

If you think you eat more sugary food than you should, try to make small changes over time. I am talking here, in particular, to the 45 per cent of you (dear readers) who add sugar to coffee, the 38 per cent of you who add it to tea and the 46 per cent of you who put sugar on breakfast cereal. Consider cutting out sugar in drinks and on cereal as an investment, because over the years, changing these small habits will save you thousands of empty calories that could be better spent on more nutrient-dense, anti-ageing foods.

Habitually grazing on sugary foods can also lead to a vicious circle of craving sweet foods. These cravings are caused by low blood sugar levels, a result, in part, of not eating regularly or of eating lots of sugary snacks. Such cravings seem only to be satisfied by eating even more sugary foods, which results in a blood sugar slump lower than the original low that caused the craving. These highs and lows of blood sugar levels can make concentration difficult and they can affect mood. Swings in blood sugar do not happen when complex carbohydrate foods (starchy foods such as potatoes, pasta, bread and rice) are eaten, even though they are broken down into simple sugars during digestion. Starchy foods provide a steady and sustaining stream of energy without the highs and lows caused by sugar.

Eat Less Salt to Beat Your Age

At the moment we eat about 13g/ ½oz of salt a day which is equivalent to 2½ teaspoons of salt. Around 1 teaspoon (6g) a day or less would be better.

All the sodium that most people need is naturally present in the foods that make up a well-balanced diet. The effect of eating too much salt, in combination with a low potassium intake (from eating too few fresh foods), and being overweight, is rising blood pressure with age. High blood pressure increases the risk of stroke, heart disease and other circulatory diseases.

Is salt the same as sodium?

Confusingly, nutrition panels on food labels give only the sodium content. The chemical name for salt is sodium chloride. Some foods claim to be 'reduced salt', 'low salt' and so on, but this is pretty meaningless when the nutrition panel talks only in terms of sodium. The wording of the panel is governed by labelling regulations which stipulate that the sodium content must be shown but some manufacturers and retailers add a salt equivalent. To work out for yourself how much salt and sodium is in your food (should you need to know exactly) multiply the sodium content figure by 2.5.

How much salt and sodium should you eat?

Salt	Men – less than 7g per day
	Women – less than 5g per day
Sodium	Men – less than 2.5g per day
	Women – less than 2g per day

Learn to love less salt

It is possible to like less salty food. Taste buds respond rapidly to salt – the more you have, the more you want and vice versa. Gradually cutting down results in what used to be tasty becoming unpleasantly salty. This is simple to do, and if done gradually it is less noticeable. Patients in high blood pressure clinics say that it takes about eight to twelve weeks of gradually cutting down on salt to 're-educate' their taste buds to appreciate the true flavour of real foods. After this they find many ready meals and food in restaurants, for example, unpleasantly salty.

Are substitutes worth their salt?

Most salt substitutes mix ordinary salt (i.e. sodium chloride) with potassium chloride and/or magnesium sulphate (and other ingredients such as anti-caking agents), so do not be fooled into thinking that you are avoiding salt altogether if you use them. These products vary widely in the amount of sodium they contain.

Reduced sodium 'salts' can contain 50 per cent salt, but very low sodium products may contain only 0.9g per 100g of sodium compared with 38.9g of sodium in ordinary salt. Some people detect a bitter aftertaste with potassium products in particular.

Another option is low-sodium sea salt which is evaporated by a process that reduces the sodium content by 60 per cent and leaves the remaining grains with the same mineral balance as standard sea salt. If you use these products shake them well to mix the salts.

Sea salt – the anti-ageing gourmet's choice!

Alternatively you could just make modest use of sea salt which has more flavour and aroma than common table salt, making it possible to use less. It should also be free from the additives found in table, cooking and kitchen salts, which are made by evaporation from brine or are ground from rock salt, then purified and refined. Sea salt is produced more naturally by being sun- or wind-dried from shallow sea water. It also contains traces of desirable minerals such as potassium, iron, manganese, zinc and copper – all lost in the refining of ordinary salt.

The Anti-Ageing Power of Eating Less Salt

The more salt you eat, the greater the likelihood that your blood pressure will rise as you age. The higher your blood pressure, the greater the risk of strokes and heart attacks that can reduce the quality of your life, or cut it short prematurely.

One recent major analysis of the most important studies into salt says that there is a strong argument for everyone to cut their salt intake, while another says there is only real benefit for those with raised blood pressure. However, eating less salt will not do you any harm (unless you are an athlete or a coal miner or you sweat profusely and lose body salts for any other reason).

The food and drink industry has a vested interest in adding as much salt as possible to food (or at least in not cutting down the amount of salt in processed foods). Salt is a cheap flavour enhancer and it allows water to be added to foods (greater profit for less outlay). Salt also makes you thirsty, so you buy more soft drinks. Many food companies sell you both the salty snacks and the drinks you need to quench your salt-induced thirst.

Eat more potassium to beat your age and counter excess salt

Food processing removes the potassium that is found naturally in foods and that is needed by the body to keep sodium in balance. The best sources of potassium are vegetables, fruit, fish and lean meat. Eat more of these fresh foods and there will be less room on your plate for high-salt, processed foods.

How much salt is there in common foods?

High-salt foods
- table/cooking salt
- cured and smoked meat
- smoked fish
- canned meat
- cottage cheese
- salted butter and margarine/spreads – unless low-salt
- savoury crackers
- crisps
- salted nuts
- other savoury snacks
- some sweet biscuits
- baked beans and canned vegetables
- olives
- sauces (ketchup, brown sauce, soya sauce, Worcestershire sauce
- stock cubes – unless salt-free

Moderate–low-salt foods
- fresh fruit and vegetables
- Wholemeal flour and pasta
- brown rice

- breakfast cereals without added salt (puffed wheat, shredded wheat, porridge oats)
- unsalted butter and low-salt spreads
- nuts
- dried fruit
- pulses
- oatmeal and oats
- milk
- fresh fish
- poultry
- game
- meat
- eggs

Salty exceptions the following foods are relatively high-salt foods but they should not be avoided (unless on doctor's orders) as they provide other important and protective nutrients:

- bread
- many breakfast cereals (especially cornflakes)
- hard cheese
- some oily fish (e.g. kippers, smoked mackerel and canned fish, especially in brine); choose lower-salt if possible

Despite its salt content, which varies widely, bread (e.g. in the form of sandwiches) is better in a lunch box than high-fat sausage rolls or pie. And sandwiches or toast can be a more nutritious snack than crisps or confectionery.

How many calories are there in your food?	
Fat	9 calories per gram
Alcohol	7 calories per gram
Protein	4 calories per gram
Carbohydrates (starchy foods)	3.75 calories per gram

Enjoying Alcohol
(in the Hope of Beating Your Age . . .)

Alcohol, like sugar, is one of life's sweeteners and many people enjoy a drink. Wine with food has been one of the world's greatest pleasures since the days of the ancient Greeks. Most societies have found ways of fermenting grain, milk, fruit or other staple foods to produce alcoholic drinks.

Several studies suggest that moderate drinking may even be beneficial to health. Moderate drinking is 1–3 units of alcohol per day for women and 3–4 units per day for men, but not every day. This equates to no more than 21 units a week for women and 28 for men. While these are the 'official' figures for low-risk drinking, many in the medical profession are less comfortable with them than the previous recommendations of a maximum of 14 units a week for women and 21 for men. Taking into account the disadvantages of drinking for women in particular (see page 49), and considering the politics behind the last increase in the recommended limits, I am more inclined to go with the lower limit for low-risk drinking.

Further evidence to support a lower level is trickling in as more recent studies suggest that any health benefit for women is likely to be derived from the equivalent of only one glass of wine a day – and two for men. And the benefits are not universal: reduced risk of heart disease and stroke is only really seen among women who are moderate drinkers and aged over forty-five.

People who currently derive about 8 per cent of their total calories from alcohol are advised to cut down to 4 per cent and to spend the 4 per cent on nutrient-dense foods. Alcohol also robs the body of minerals and of vitamins B and C which are needed to detoxify alcohol. However, most of us can live with that, especially if we are eating a nutrient-dense diet.

Alcohol units

1 unit of alcohol = 8g (or 10ml) of alcohol which is found in
- half a pint/284ml (10fl oz) normal-strength beer, lager or cider
- 1 small glass (95ml/3fl oz) of wine
- 1 pub measure (25ml/^{1}/$_{6}$ gill) of spirits
- 1 pub measure (50ml/^{1}/$_{3}$ gill) of fortified wine (e.g. sherry, martini)

Alcohol strength   is measured as ABV (alcohol by volume). This appears on drinks labels as %alcohol or %vol or %ABV. The higher the percentage, the stronger the drink.

The Supposed Anti-Ageing Power of Alcohol

Moderate drinkers have a significantly lower death rate from all causes than abstainers, those who take only the very occasional drink, or heavy drinkers. High consumers show the highest mortality risk, and the rate for non-drinkers falls somewhere between that for moderate and high consumers. (However, the apparent increased risk of mortality among non-drinkers may be because people who are ill frequently give up alcohol and so 'skew' the figures.) These findings are remarkably consistent when other factors such as the amount of saturated fat in the diet, exercise and smoking are also taken into consideration. Typical of the results is one study by the American Cancer Society of men aged between forty and fifty-nine which showed less heart disease in moderate drinkers than non-drinkers, with the most beneficial alcohol consumption rate at one or two drinks a day.

How might alcohol protect you?

Take heart disease, as an example. Studies that show a positive link between moderate drinking and reduced risk of heart disease attribute the benefits to the effects of ethanol in alcoholic drinks, which:

* raises levels of the beneficial type of cholesterol, HDL (high-density lipoprotein). HDL is good because it takes cholesterol from the bloodstream, where it is a risk, to the liver for disposal
* lowers levels of fibrinogen, which is associated with the formation of blood clots that can lead to heart attacks
* slightly decreases LDL (low-density lipoprotein), the harmful type of cholesterol. LDL is bad because it is the type of cholesterol that is modified by free-radical damage to form arterial plaque, a risk in coronary heart disease

The greatest benefits are found among people who are moderate consumers of alcohol and who drink wine regularly in small quantities with food.

Why wine is the anti-ageing choice of alcoholic drink

If it's an anti-ageing effect you are after, then your best choice of alcoholic tipple would seem to be red wine. This is because red wine contains more beneficial antioxidants and other substances than other alcoholic drinks. It is also because the pattern of drinking associated with wine – regularly in smallish quantities and with food – is healthier. Beers and spirits are more often associated with binge drinking, and this pattern of drinking, even if it is within the low-risk consumption range, is more harmful. Beers and spirits are not great sources of antioxidants.

It is the polyphenols, a particular type of antioxidant found in wine, but not in significant quantity in other alcoholic drinks, that have led to the assumption that wine is more protective than other drinks. To recap, antioxidants protect you from ageing by mopping up or neutralising harmful free radicals that could otherwise trigger cancer and heart disease. Red wines contain more polyphenols than white wines. The antioxidants in red wine are thought to work by dilating blood vessels and encouraging the production in the cells of nitric oxide, both of which reduce high blood pressure and therefore the risk of stroke and heart attacks.

One study that involved getting rats ratted showed that only red wine, with or without its alcohol content, had the beneficial effect (via an increased nitric oxide production) of:

- making the blood less likely to clot
- working against arterial plaque formation
- making any blood clots that did form smaller

Drink wine, live longer, live happier

Wine drinkers are happier with their health and their lives than those who drink the equivalent amount of alcohol in beer or spirits. In one study, beer and spirit drinkers felt no better about their health than teetotallers, and lovers of beer alone were more likely to be ill. If you think the explanation is that wine drinkers are more likely to be middle class and well-off, and therefore happier and healthier, the researchers claim to have taken this socio-economic factor into account. However, they had no answer as to why the wine drinkers perceived themselves to be healthier.

Wine and longevity and the French paradox

It is the antioxidant effect of red wine in the diet of the French (and their greater consumption of antioxidant-rich fruit and vegetables) that has been touted as an explanation for their longevity in comparison with non-wine-drinking populations who, like the French, eat a high-fat diet. Hence the so-called French paradox, which attributes the protective effect of drinking wine to the fact that the French, who eat more fat and take less exercise than many other nationalities, have half the number of fatal or disabling heart attacks. It claims that phenols, such as resveratrol in red wine, inhibit the oxidation of LDLs through their antioxidant properties, thus helping to prevent heart disease.

The paradox debunked?

Of late, however, the French paradox theory has taken some knocks from 'rival' medical researchers who claim that the high consumption of alcohol in France, and of red wine in particular, fails to explain why heart disease among French people aged between fifty-five and sixty-four is about a quarter of that in Britain, despite the major risk factors being the same. The paradox-debunkers propose the time lag theory, which attributes the difference to the time lag between the increase in consumption of animal fat and raised blood cholesterol levels and the resulting increase in deaths from heart disease (similar to the recognised time lag between smoking and lung cancer). They argue that consumption of animal fat and serum cholesterol concentrations increased only recently in France but did so thirty or more years ago in Britain. If this is right, then in a few years the French will have the same high death rate from heart disease as the British.

Critics of the time lag theory, who have not hit the headlines, suggest that red wine may still explain a large part of the French paradox (which extends to most of southern Europe including Italy, Spain and Greece) and in addition that other dietary differences such as a greater intake of folates, cereal fibre, nuts, linolenic acid and a different GI loading of the diet (see page 10) might all be playing a crucial part and need further investigation. Living in warm, sunnier climates with a strong sense of family and place, and a more relaxed attitude to life, could also be a non-scientific explanation!

Whether the time lag theory eventually gains more favour than the French paradox hypothesis remains to be seen. In the meantime most of us are happy to continue drinking red wine (consumption of which is gaining ground on white wine) in the belief that it is helping to keep us young and vital.

- Alcohol-free days, avoiding getting drunk and eating a diet rich in the vitamins and minerals needed to detoxify alcohol are conditional to any benefit you might receive from drinking moderately.

Reasons not to drink

Despite the potential benefits of moderate drinking, a recommendation to take up alcohol, especially in the over forty-fives, is unlikely ever to become official public health policy for many reasons, not least that:

- one in four men and one in twelve women in the UK drinks too much alcohol
- 3 per cent of cancers are probably caused by alcohol
- men who drink more than 35 units a week double their risk of death from stroke

The health risks of drinking more than a moderate amount (not even as much as heavy drinking) include increased risk of:

- hepatitis
- gastritis
- pancreatitis
- gout
- irregular heart rhythms
- accidents
- strokes
- failure to take prescribed medicine
- impotence
- foetal damage

The risks for heavy drinkers (for men, anywhere between 28 to 50 units a week, for women 22 to 35) are far too depressing to go into here, and they are not directly related to ageing, but if you need to know, they include cancers of the mouth, throat and liver.

How to get a buzz without booze

Most social occasions seem to revolve around alcohol. 'What can I get you to drink?' is usually the first thing your host(ess) asks (well, all right, after they have asked if they can hang up your Pashmina). If you feel naked without a drink, accept one so that you have the requisite glass in your hand at a cocktail party, or a glass full of wine in front of you at a dinner party. But don't drink it! Or make it last all night and drink from the water instead.

What else can you do?

- If you want to make a point of not having alcohol, ask for anything else that is fizzy – even non-alcoholic bubbles seem to engender a party mood.
- Try some sparkling conversation – if you have time beforehand, do your homework and mentally prepare some questions to ask, or topics that will interest other guests, particularly if you know who is going to be there.
- Wear clothes that you feel flatter you and that you are happiest and most relaxed wearing.
- Make sure your hair is looking how you like it.
- Relax and give yourself plenty of time before you go to an event . . . or leave it to the last minute; whichever makes you feel buzziest.
- Wear a favourite piece of jewellery.
- If you have time during the day, make sure you take your 30 minutes of exercise or do 50 sit-ups – that way you will feel more inclined to relax.

Women beware – alcohol affects you more than men

A drink a day might cut the risk of heart disease in post-menopausal women. But any potential benefits for women over forty-five need to be weighed against the potential harm caused by alcohol.

Alcohol has a more potent, quicker and longer-lasting effect on women, simply because women are smaller than men and they have less body fluid, making the alcohol, and its effects, more concentrated. Women's bodies also contain more fat than men's, and fat does not absorb alcohol, so it stays in the bloodstream for longer, which is why women feel the effects for longer. Women's livers are also less efficient at breaking down and excreting alcohol so they are more likely to get cirrhosis. This used to be a predominantly male disease, but now 40 per cent of cases are female.

Alcohol increases the risk of breast cancer

Studies on more than 320,000 women in the US, Canada, Sweden and the Netherlands by the Harvard School of Public Health conclude that drinking two to five alcoholic drinks a day increases a woman's risk of breast cancer by more than 40 per cent. Women who take one to two drinks a day increase their risk by 16 per cent and lighter drinkers (up to one drink a day) by 6 per cent. Over a lifetime most women's risk of developing breast cancer is 1 in 8; for those women who have more than two drinks a day, it increases to 1 in 6. The harmful effect comes from liver enzymes metabolising alcohol to produce carcinogens.

Other risk factors include:

* family history of breast cancer
* early onset of menstruation
* no pregnancies
* history of benign breast disease

And finally, before I forget . . .

Another theory on the benefit of red wine is that it improves the memory and protects against diseases of ageing such as Alzheimer's and Parkinson's. The resveratrol in it increases the activity and effectiveness of an important enzyme that stimulates the nerve cells to rebuild and regenerate. Laboratory experiments with human nerve cells show that resveratrol makes the cells grow small extensions through which nerve cells can connect to their neighbours. In neuro-degenerative diseases such as Alzheimer's and Parkinson's the contacts between nerve cells are broken.

Drink Water, and Lots of it

Drink plenty of water each day. You need at least eight cups/five or six tumblers or 1.5 litres/2¾ pints of liquid every day. This is needed to replenish natural losses of up to two litres a day. It is said that once you are feeling thirsty you are already becoming dehydrated. If you do not drink enough you will suffer poor concentration, headaches and stomach upsets. Make plenty of your drinks water and limit tea and coffee to three or four cups a day in total. Try to find lots of other caffeine-free (and calorie-free, if necessary) drinks that you enjoy.

Fruit juice or diluted juice are suitable. Fruit juice *drinks* are often an expensive 'con' in this respect, particularly when they are promoted to imitate fresh fruit juice. Try some of the better-quality squashes and cordials (even though these are only around 5 per cent juice, plus water and sugar – check labels for additives). There is also a wide range of herb and fruit teas available which are not in fact tea, but just use the name generically as they are infused in hot water.

The reason you should limit tea and coffee is that they contain stimulants (e.g. caffeine) and are diuretic (or dehydrating). A couple of hours after drinking a cup of coffee or tea, you will urinate about half of what you took in. (It's a common misconception that you lose more than the volume of tea or coffee, but even half can be ill-afforded in the anti-ageing stakes.) Of course you lose a percentage of everything you drink in this way, which is why it is important to replenish fluids throughout the day.

Be aware that many types of sweetened fizzy drinks also contain caffeine and sugar or artificial sweeteners and other non-nutritional additives. Water is the best drink for quenching thirst and hydrating the body to help prevent dry skin and wrinkles.

Proof that Eating Foods in the Right Proportions is Anti-Ageing

If you are still unsure that eating food in the proportions I have described can help keep you young (and prevent middle-age spread), consider this. On average young adults gain 500g/1lb of weight per year resulting in a significant number of middle-aged people who are overweight. But it need not be like that, as a recent real life study proved with 300 volunteers from five European countries.

The object was to allow the volunteers to choose their food freely from what was normally available to them in supermarkets and shops in their own culture or society. The volunteers, whose average age was thirty-nine and whose average body mass index (BMI) was 30 (overweight), were split into three groups. (For more on working out your BMI, see page 149.)

Group 1 aimed for a diet with 30 per cent energy from fat (10 per cent less than we normally eat in the West) and 10 per cent more energy than their usual diets derived from starchy foods, i.e. potatoes, pasta, bread, rice, etc. Group 2 aimed for 30 per cent energy from fat but replaced the lost calories with 5 per cent energy from starchy foods and the other 5 per cent from sugar and sugar-containing foods. Group 3 acted as a 'control' by eating their usual diet, which gave them 40 per cent of energy from fat.

Starchy foods help weight loss

Groups 1 and 2 lost weight and similar amounts of body fat by the end of the six-month study; they also maintained their weight loss. Group 1 and Group 2 lost the same amount of weight. Group 3, who ate the standard British diet from which 40 per cent of calories is obtained from fat, had continued to put on weight. Certainly this supports other studies that show for many people the presence of sugar is a factor that helps them stick to a slimming diet and helps them maintain their weight loss – once they can allow themselves to get over the idea that all sugar/chocolate is 'naughty' and avoid it until they are forced to binge!

The important thing to remember about this study (called CARMEN for Carbohydrate Ration Management in European National Diets) is that the volunteers, who came from England, Germany, Denmark, Spain and the Netherlands, were ordinary sedentary people from a variety of cultural and geographical backgrounds. It proves that if you choose the correct proportion of fat and carbohydrate in your diet, you can control your weight without calorie counting, without buying expensive slimmer's foods, and without restricting your enjoyment of a variety of 'normal' foods. *All* of which is very anti-ageing.

CHAPTER TWO

Eat Me, Look Younger!

I'd like to invite you to dinner. If you were able to come, we might eat any of the following menus that I have recently cooked for friends:

Rocket salad
with figs and parma ham
· · ·

Seared salmon
on spinach mash
with ratatouille
· · ·

Fresh strawberries
with pistachio biscotti

Crab, lemon, parsley
and bulgur salad
· · ·

Guinea fowl, roast pumpkin and
pak choi, stir-fried with ginger, garlic
and hot beetroot in horseradish sauce
· · ·

Chocolate soufflé
with vanilla ice-cream

Caramelised shallot tartlets
with watercress salad
· · ·

Venison with potatoes dauphinoise
and braised red cabbage
· · ·

Winter fruit compote on lemon polenta cake

Of course we do not eat like this every day. I have just highlighted these menus to make the point to you that Eating to Beat Your Age is far from drab. It can be as exciting as you want it to be. It shows that you can enjoy a varied and colourful diet. But these foods are not simply plucked out of the air, or selected because I just happen to like them. They are also included for good scientific reasons.

How some foods can help you look younger

Without exception, people who eat large quantities of fruit and vegetables and starchy foods have a greater potential for a longer healthier life. The vitamins, minerals and the 500 or so phytochemicals (naturally occurring chemicals in plants) contained in these foods play an important role in keeping you young and healthy.

Scientists have exhaustively researched what vitamins and minerals can do for you – and there are many examples of anti-ageing foods, packed full of vitamins and minerals, included in this chapter. But now research is concentrated on the phytochemicals in fruits and vegetables, which are also unlocking some secrets of better nutrition, health and vitality. It is these phytomedical components of food that you will learn most about in the following catalogue of anti-ageing foods.

Unlike vitamins and minerals, phytochemicals are not essential for life. A lack will not lead to deficiency diseases such as anaemia (lack of the mineral iron and the B vitamins) or scurvy (vitamin C deficiency). But they are essential for a healthy long life because they can help slow down ageing and prevent many diseases.

The main group of phytochemicals that have been investigated are flavonoids. These are also the most widespread in fruit and vegetables, beans, pulses and cereals. More than five thousand flavonoids are known and practically all have antioxidant effects.

Flavonoids take their name from the Latin word *flavus*, meaning yellow because their pigments are responsible for most of the yellow colour, and red and blue, in food. Flavonoids are also sometimes called bioflavonoids.

There are many different sub-groups of flavonoids, including the following which all have varying degrees of phyto-oestrogenic (plant hormone) properties in addition to their antioxidant powers: flavones, flavonols, flavanones, isoflavones, coumestans, lignans, chalcones. For more details about the role of phyto-oestrogens see soya, page 89.

Do you eat enough phytochemicals to benefit from their anti-ageing properties?

According to Ministry of Agriculture, Fisheries and Food (MAFF) studies, we eat 10–100mg of flavonoids a day. Although only a few flavonoids have been identified and studied in depth, you do not have to wait until scientists have completed more research to benefit. From what is known already, eating more vegetables and fruit, nuts, seeds, beans and pulses and starchy foods on a daily basis will add vitality and years to your life. Eating more fish and yogurt will pay dividends, as will choosing lean meat.

Top Foods for Antioxidant Nutrients

Antioxidants, as you will have realised, are one of the most important ingredients in foods to protect your body against free-radical damage, which speeds up the process of ageing. All the antioxidants in the food list are needed for the body's defences against free radicals. Vitamin E helps break the chemical chain reaction through which free radicals multiply and get out of hand. Vitamin E also scavenges for free radicals, as do vitamin C and beta-carotene. Although vitamin A is more effective as an anti-oxidant in its precursor form as beta-carotene, it can scavenge a type of oxygen involved in free-radical damage. The minerals listed below are needed for the enzyme systems that fight free radicals, and selenium is also an active antioxidant in its own right.

In their role as antioxidants phytochemicals protect your cells from free-radical damage.

- Some are even more active antioxidants than vitamins C and E. Some increase the activity of the enzymes that protect cells against carcinogens (cancer-causing substances or agents).

- Some block receptor sites for cancer-causing hormones.
- Some enhance the activity of vitamins and minerals.
- Some are needed for the production of enzymes that remove carcinogens from the body.
- Some bind up substances that would otherwise convert to carcinogens.

Vitamin C in fruit and vegetables, particularly citrus fruit and juice, blackcurrants, broccoli, cherries, kiwi fruit, mangoes, peppers, passion fruit, strawberries, green leafy vegetables.

Beta-carotene in yellow and orange fruits, particularly apricots, broccoli, cabbage, cantaloupe melon, carrots, mangoes, peaches, pumpkin, red peppers, spinach, sweet potatoes, tomatoes, watercress – and prunes.

Vitamin E in vegetable oils, particularly sunflower-seed oils and products made from them, almonds, brazil nuts, avocados, dark green leafy vegetables, hazelnuts, olives, peanuts, sunflower oil, sunflower seeds, sweet potatoes, wheatgerm, whole grains, blackberries, blackcurrants.

Folic Acid in asparagus, beans and pulses, breakfast cereals, broad beans, broccoli, liver, spinach, sweetcorn, watercress, wholegrain cereals and foods fortified with folic acid.

Vitamin A in liver, kidney, dairy products, oily fish, fortified margarine.

Copper in wholegrain cereals, meat, vegetables.

Manganese in wholegrain cereals, nuts, tea.

Selenium in brazil nuts, cereals (especially bread), fish, shellfish, liver and other offal, broccoli, pork, cheese, eggs, walnuts, vegetables, fruit.

Zinc in meat, milk and milk products, bread and other cereal products.

What do 100-year-olds eat?

Studies of centenarians have found that they have high levels of vitamins C and E in their bodies, presumably protecting them against the oxidative damage that is a major feature of ageing. Trials in which nursing-home patients aged between sixty and a hundred years received supplements of vitamins C and E showed improvement in their general health and mental well-being.

Supplementation with antioxidant nutrients among older people (from their mid-fifties to a hundred) have also shown a slowing down of the progression of Alzheimer's disease, improved immunity and a reduced risk of cataract and macular degeneration.

Centenarians also, invariably, have a healthy attitude to life – see Chapter 5.

Add colour to your diet

Feast your eyes on the reds, greens, yellows, golds and purples of a vegetable display and then make your meals as colourful as possible. Eat vegetables as a meal in their own right or as a side dish to complement and enhance fish, poultry and meat dishes. They go well with nuts, grains, seeds and pulses. Without vegetables food would be very boring. Whatever the season vegetables are an inspiration, for salads, soups, starters, side dishes and main courses; in risottos, in pasta sauces, on pizzas and with traditional roasts.

Your best friend will tell you but will you listen?

I have put a lot of emphasis on vegetables because we British still seem to need cajoling by Nanny to eat them. Grown-ups and children alike need less encouragement to eat fruit than to eat vegetables. Even if our best friends and colleagues tell us of the advantages of vegetables (and other foods), we are not likely to eat more of them. An expensive and extensive programme of 'peer education' in the US recruited teams of trusted workers to tell their friends and colleagues to eat better – but it resulted only in half an extra portion of fruit or vegetables a day being eaten. I hope you will do better than that for me, and protect yourself against the ravages of ageing.

Anti-Ageing Superfoods

Chocolate, cherries, red wine, strawberries, salmon and seafood, mangoes and game are just some of the fabulous foods that you can tuck into to keep the years at bay.

All fruit and vegetables are good for you but some contain more nutrients than others. The following assemblage of anti-ageing foods highlights specific areas in which certain foods can influence good health in one way or another. The list is by no means exhaustive and our knowledge about these foods is being added to continually.

Apples   It is said that an apple a day keeps the doctor away, but now we know that a couple might keep the specialist away . . . Apples are **anti-ageing because** apples are one of the richest food sources of flavonols in the British diet, contributing up to 10 per cent of your total intake. Quercetin, the main flavonol in apples, is associated with lower risk of blood clotting and strokes. Quercetin deactivates harmful free radicals and helps prevent blood clotting and narrowing of the arteries. Apples also contain pectin (the gummy substance that sets jam), which helps lower blood cholesterol levels and remove potentially carcinogenic (cancer-causing) toxins from the body.

Apricots   (and other orange or yellow fruit such as **peaches, mangoes, papayas, persimmons, carambolas or star fruit and tamarillos**) are **good sources** of the antioxidant beta-carotene, the natural plant pigment that gives these fruits their colour. The body can also turn beta-carotene into vitamin A (although most people get enough vitamin A from animal foods), which is needed by the immune system and for healthy eyes. An average serving of three or four dried apricots will give you one third of your daily NSP (fibre) and provide around one-fifth of the RNI (reference nutrient intake or suggested daily amount) for vitamins A and C, plus some iron.

- The peach is a symbol of longevity carried by the Chinese god of longevity, Shou-Hsing. He also has tablets on which are inscribed the dates of everyone's death to come, but if you treat him well he can be persuaded to favourably change the date. Should you not have much luck with Shou-Hsing you could always try following the advice in this book.

Organic fruit and veg are best

Organic farming does not allow the use of pesticides, herbicides, artificial fertilisers and other agro-chemicals that end up as residues in non-organic fruit and vegetables (and other foods: non-organic milk, cheese, yogurt, meat, fruit juices, tea, coffee, chocolate and so on). You can safely eat the skins of organic fruit and vegetables, where appropriate, such as tomatoes or jacket potatoes, knowing that they have not been sprayed with post-harvest chemicals such as fungicides or anti-sprouting agents. You can use the rind or zest of organic citrus fruit in baking and other recipes, knowing that they have not been treated with waxes and fungicides.

If you want a priority list of non-organic vegetables in which pesticides and other residues are most commonly found at the highest levels, these include: lettuce, spinach, pears, carrots, apples and apple juice; but these residues are found across the board.

A government warning is in force on carrots in particular. Non-organic carrots should be topped, tailed and peeled to remove pesticide concentrations, especially when being given to babies, toddlers and young children. Wash or scrub *all* produce thoroughly before use.

Asparagus   A good source of vitamin E for a vegetable. While there is no British RNI for vitamin E, a modest serving of five spears of asparagus would provide 30 per cent of the American recommended daily amount (RDA) and 75 per cent of the UK recommended nutrient intake (RNI) of vitamin C, plus some beta-carotene and folic acid. The green, unblanched varieties contain marginally more nutrients.

- Asparagus has long been known as a potent diuretic that may help with fluid retention.

Avocados   are **anti-ageing** because they have a 'healthy' fats profile, containing mainly monounsaturated fats. This is useful in replacing saturated fat in the diet. Avocados are also **a good source** of several vitamins that are not usually found in vegetables (probably because avocados are technically fruits). For example, avocados contain vitamin E (more commonly found in nuts and vegetable oils), vitamin B6 and folic acid, plus a small amount of other B vitamins, including thiamine and riboflavin needed for using energy, proteins and fats.

Bananas   are **anti-ageing** because they are a useful source of potassium to fight rising blood pressure with age. They are also packed with slow-release energy, making them better than sugary drinks and confectionery for a quick energy boost. Bananas are unusual among fruit because they are **a good source** of vitamin B6 (35 per cent of your RNI is in a medium fruit, plus 11 per cent RNI of folic acid) and they contain a small amount of vitamin E. B vitamins and minerals are needed for releasing energy from food during digestion, and for healthy nerves.

Beans, Peas and Lentils   including **chickpeas, soya beans** (see separate entry), **mung beans, sprouted seeds** (see separate entry), **kidney beans, butter beans, haricot beans** and **runner beans** are **anti-ageing** because they contain a lot of phytochemicals, including:

- protease inhibitors to suppress enzyme production in cancer cells, which slows tumour growth. Legumes seem to provide the greatest benefit if you eat them regularly throughout your life from as young an age as possible
- plant sterols to help prevent colon cancer by hindering cell reproduction in the large intestine
- saponins to prevent cancer cells multiplying by interfering with DNA replication
- plant sterols and saponins (also found in garden peas and spinach) help lower blood cholesterol levels. Plant sterols are physically similar to cholesterol and they inhibit absorption of cholesterol by replacing it to prevent arteries becoming clogged
- isoflavones to prevent heart disease, some cancers and osteoporosis (see soya, page 89).

Beetroot   The humble beetroot has recently become de rigueur in fashionable restaurants. Beetroot juice has long been available in health food shops but it is an acquired taste. Beetroot has not attracted much scientific investigation – but its arresting purple colour indicates **a good source** of anthocyanins, a type of anti-oxidant flavonoid that gives beetroot its colour and is also found in black grapes (see page 72) and dark cherries. Beetroot contains modest amounts of folates.

Berries   that are coloured **purple**, **dark red** and **blue**, and **dark cherries**, are **anti-ageing** because they too get their colour from the antioxidant flavonoid anthocyanin, which in studies on bilberries (below) shows that berries may help strengthen the walls of small blood vessels, helping prevent unsightly thread veins that occur with age.

Blueberries, bilberries and huckleberries   are **anti-ageing** because they contain flavonoids, that seem capable of strengthening collagen, which maintains the structure and plump-ness of the skin. Herbalists advise eating these fruits to stop deep wrinkles forming. In fact blueberries are among the fruits richest in antioxidants (see table, page 87). Animal studies by the US Department of Agriculture have shown that blueberries in the diet protect the brains of rats against free-radical damage. The results point to possible improved memory and motor functions in humans. Other experiments have also shown wild blueberry extracts to be capable of inhibiting one of the enzymes that promotes the development of cancer in living cells. Bilberry dietary supplements are also available to assist visual function and provide relief for tired eyes. The theory is that the antioxidant anthocyanins that give these fruits their deep purple-blue colour help the body produce retinal, which forms visual pigment and improves night vision.

Blackberries   are the **richest fruit source** of vitamin E, containing 3.5mg in a small 100g/3½oz serving, and are a good source of vitamin C. They also contain a significant amount of iron.

Blackcurrants   are an **outstanding source** of vitamin C, containing around five times the RNI in a small 100g/3½oz portion. The same portion also provides around half your daily NSP (fibre) needs, plus calcium, magnesium and potassium. Blackcurrants are **anti-ageing** because they contain significant amounts of the antioxidants beta-carotene and vitamin E.

Brazil nuts   are **anti-ageing** because they are the **richest food source** of selenium (see pages 57, 112 for other sources). In the British diet, **cereals** and cereal products, **meat, fish, eggs, vegetables** and **fruit** are the main contributors of selenium in the order listed. Selenium, in the antioxidant enzyme gluthaione peroxidase, neutralises free radicals and is regarded as an anti-cancer agent. Selenium is also needed by the thyroid gland for the use of iodine and to help control hormone metabolism. Sperm production requires selenium.

Broccoli   **and its relatives from the cabbage patch** are **anti-ageing** because broccoli is consistently associated with lower risk of cancer in diets where it is eaten frequently. Broccoli and other brassica vegetables contain a variety of phytochemicals:

- Some stimulate enzymes that make the hormone oestrogen less effective, possibly reducing the risk of breast cancer.

- Some fight cancers by blocking the carcinogens before they reach their target sites or by snatching the cancer-causing agents out of the cells before they multiply and wreak havoc (particularly in breast and ovarian cancers).

- Some persuade precancerous cells to commit suicide, a process with the wonderful scientific name of apoptosis (can't you just hear those cells going pop!)

- Some stimulate the production of enzymes of the body's natural defence system, which detoxifies cancer-causing chemicals in the liver.

Brassicas are a **good source** of folates (the naturally occurring version of folic acid), with **broccoli**, **Brussels sprouts**, **kale** and **spring greens** being among the richest food sources. Brassicas also contribute the antioxidants beta-carotene and vitamin C and the minerals calcium, iron and zinc, plus in broccoli some vitamin E. Dark green leafy greens such as broccoli and kale contain a lot of chlorophyll, the pigment that allows green plants to photo-synthesise (make energy from sunlight) and that may protect people who eat a lot of them against the DNA damage that can lead to cancer. **Kale** has the distinction of being the most powerful antioxidant vegetable (prunes took the title for being the most active antioxidant fruit) in one league table of antioxidants (see page 87).

Carrots as you know, help you see in the dark, because they are a **good source** of beta-carotene and other carotenoids that

---

Breeding super-vegetables

The ability of the cabbage family to block cancer cells rather than just suppress them interests scientists, who are using traditional methods and genetic modification (GM) techniques to breed new varieties of broccoli with between ten and a hundred times the natural amount of the phytochemicals normally found in the greatest concentration in Brussels sprouts. Because many people do not like the taste of Brussels sprouts, plant breeders are experimenting with putting the phytochemical into broccoli, which is more popular.

---

are turned by the body into vitamin A, which is essential for night vision. They are also especially **anti-ageing** because two types of carotene in carrots – lutein and zeaxanthin – may help prevent ultraviolet light damaging the lens of the eye, thus reducing the risk of age-related cataracts. Studies show that people who eat carrots regularly also have a reduced risk of cancers of the lungs, stomach, bladder and other sites. Carrots contain another powerful antioxidant enzyme called alpha-lipoic acid that re-invigorates the antioxidant vitamins C and E, and vitamin A allowing them to repeatedly quench free radicals. Alpha-lipoic acid is also an antioxidant in its own right. It is made naturally in the body and has an important role in the Krebs cycle (the chemical conversion of food to energy). Its small chemical structure allows it to pass through cell membranes that other antioxidants cannot get through, therefore offering protection inside cells as well as outside. Apart from carrots, it is found in **potatoes, yams** and **sweet potatoes**.

- Trials to see whether smokers were less at risk of lung cancer if they took beta-carotene supplements were halted when it was realised that supplements actually increased the risk. However, eating beta-carotene as a natural food, as in carrots, is protective.

65

Cooks' tips for minimising vitamin loss

1. Cook vegetables and fruit for the shortest possible time.
2. Cook in the minimum amount of water. Better still, steam or microwave them or use a waterless cooker.
3. Prepare immediately before cooking.
4. Don't chop fruit and vegetables too small because that exposes more surfaces for nutrient loss.

Celery is **anti-ageing** because it is higher in sodium than most vegetables, so it contributes a salt-like flavour to recipes without adding salt. It also contains potassium, which counterbalances sodium in the body cells to help prevent high blood pressure. Celery is **a good source** of the antioxidants lutein and zeaxanthin (see carrots above).

- Perhaps it is no coincidence that celery seeds are used in traditional herbal medicine to reduce blood pressure – which as we know can rise due to excessive salt intake.

Cooks' tips for minimising mineral loss

Cooking doesn't destroy minerals (as it does vitamins). The minerals just leach out into the cooking water.

1. Use cooking water for soups, sauces and so on.
2. Cook in hard water, if you can, because losses are greatest in soft water.

And, of course, serve food immediately after cooking as more losses occur if food is kept warm or reheated.

Cereal-rich diets are **anti-ageing** because they help prevent development of the type of diabetes associated with ageing. A recent study shows that women who eat diets high in cereal fibre and low in sugary carbohydrates have a significantly lower risk of developing maturity-onset (or non-insulin-dependent) diabetes. Complex carbohydrates from cereals offer this protection because they break down slowly during digestion, releasing energy gradually into the bloodstream and resulting in a smaller rise of blood sugar. This improves sensitivity to insulin and helps prevent insulin resistance, which can occur with age, particularly if you take insufficient exercise and are overweight.

The slow release of energy is due in part to the NSP (non-starch polysaccharide) content of cereals such as wholemeal bread and pasta, brown rice and unrefined breakfast cereals. The NSP is also fermented by gut bacteria for a healthy digestive and immune system.

Cereals are also **a good source** of phytonutrients such as lignans, coumarins and other phyto-oestrogens (see soya). And the moral of that is . . . (as the rather disagreeable Duchess said to Alice in Wonderland) that you should snack on an anti-ageing sandwich, toast or bowl of cereal rather than a sticky white iced bun or a confectionery bar! (See also grains.)

Chocolate is not only one of life's pleasures, but people who eat it one to three times a month cut their risk of early death by one third. This **anti-ageing effect** was illustrated in an eighty-year study of 7,800 male Harvard graduates, which suggests that regular chocolate eaters (those who eat chocolates three times a week or more) live on average one extra year. Once-a-week chocolate eaters had a 15 per cent reduced risk of mortality compared with a 25 per cent reduced risk in the higher consumers. The possible longevity link may be due to phenols (a type of antioxidant) found in chocolate; 40g/1 ½oz contains as much as a glass of red wine. Phenols' antioxidant properties inhibit cancer and cholesterol build-up.

However, there is a sting in the tail – chocolate contains mainly saturated fat which has the potential to cause your blood cholesterol level to rise, thereby increasing the risk of heart disease. Claims that stearic acid, the main type of saturated fat in plain chocolate (slightly less in milk chocolate), is less damaging to arteries than the saturated fat in meat and butter have been disproved by new medical data. But then, if you follow the *Eat to Beat Your Age* principles you will not be eating it in large enough quantities to cause a problem.

Chocolate and the pleasure principle

Pleasure can also strengthen your immune system; enjoying chocolate probably contributed in this way to the health of those who took part in the longevity study. When you eat foods that you like, your brain releases endorphins which have a mild opiate effect, reinforcing the pleasure and improving your mood. Even if you are dieting you need not give up chocolate. Diets that incorporate some sugar are easier to stick to and more successful. And studies show that people with a slightly higher sugar intake usually eat less fat and are slimmer than those who deny themselves sweet foods.

Chocolate vs. tea over antioxidants

A Dutch study of chocolate reveals its catechin (an antioxidant flavonoid) level to be four times that of tea. In the Dutch diet chocolate contributes 20 per cent of the catechin intake; tea contributes 55 per cent. The point of comparing the catechin contents of tea and chocolate is that catechins are the main flavonoid component of tea. Their beneficial effects on the immune system and in helping prevent blood clots are usually attributed only to tea, whereas chocolate may also be benefiting the Dutch.

Dark chocolate has the highest total catechin content: 53mg per 100g compared with a paltry 15mg per 100g in milk chocolate; but both are higher than tea at 14mg per 100ml.

More reasons not to give up chocolate

- Chocolate is often lumped together with coffee as a demon stimulant. In fact as a stimulant chocolate is pretty pathetic. You would need to eat eight 100g bars (not recommended) to get the equivalent of the caffeine content of a cup of coffee.

- Chocolate is more nutritious than many other types of confectionery – it contains reasonable amounts of iron. If you buy high-quality chocolate with a cocoa solids content of around 70 per cent, the taste is so concentrated and satisfying that a little goes a long way. In fact a small amount eaten soon after you fancy it prevents binges for so-called chocoholics who unnecessarily try to deny themselves (a course of action that is bound to end in a binge).

- Incidentally, self-diagnosed 'chocoholics' cannot be addicted to chocolate. Being a chocoholic is a state of mind, not a true physiological addiction. You just crave chocolate because its sweet taste and fatty texture give a melting sensation and a unique flavour.

Jelly babies – at fifty

If you are aged between forty and fifty you probably eat more toffees, Licorice Allsorts and jelly babies than children. Sadly, eating jelly babies does not make middle-aged people younger, even if it does evoke memories of childhood and youth . . .

Chillies are **anti-ageing** because they contain capsaicin, the source of their 'heat' which stimulates digestion – useful as an anti-ageing tool if you suffer depleted gastric juice production. Capsaicin also has an antioxidant role. If enough is eaten – e.g. in a Mexican or Indian diet – chillies (like their relatives, peppers) can also make a significant contribution of vitamin C and beta-carotene. Their temperature-raising effect also temporarily raises the rate at which you burn off calories. And in some animal studies they have stimulated the burning of body fat. What next, the chilli slimming diet?

Cranberries are **anti-ageing** because cranberry juice has a reputation for the treatment and prevention of urinary tract infections (UTIs) such as cystitis, which can occur more frequently with age. Scientific trials back up the folk use of the cranberry, a native berry of North America, for urinary infections. The juice stops the bacteria which cause cystitis from attaching themselves to the walls of the urinary tract. If the bacteria cannot attach and multiply, they cannot cause an infection. As cranberry juice is available in the form of very palatable drinks it is a great addition to the eight or more glasses of water (or equivalent) that you should be drinking each day . . .

Dried fruit   such as **apricots, dates, peaches, prunes**, and **raisins** are **a good source** of NSP (fibre) and potassium. Most Western diets contain too little potassium and too much sodium (i.e. table salt). Potassium maintains the sodium balance in cells, helping to prevent high blood pressure. Dried apricots are one of the **richest fruit sources** of iron, a mineral lacking in many women's diets, and essential to prevent tiredness, poor immunity and anaemia.

Fennel   is chiefly of interest because it contains more phyto-oestrogens than most vegetables, although it is not eaten frequently or in quantity in the UK. But you could change that . . . Enjoy it raw in salads or braised. Its aniseed flavour goes well with fish. Fennel is also **a good source** of potassium.

* In herbal medicine fennel is used to alleviate indigestion and relieve flatulence.

Fortified margarine   as well as **pilchards, sardines, tuna, herrings, kippers, mackerel, breakfast cereals, eggs** and **butter** are all **a good source** of vitamin D, essential for the absorption of calcium to keep bones healthy and help prevent osteoporosis as you age. The action of sunlight on the skin converts inactive vitamin D into active vitamin D. This does not mean you have to sunbathe – you get enough sun from April to September in Britain to make enough active vitamin D to last through the winter. Only the housebound or those whose clothing always covers their entire bodies, hands and faces need to take supplements.

Fruit juice is **anti-ageing** because a daily glass of orange or grapefruit juice reduces the risk of stroke. Fruit (and vegetable) juice is an easy way to increase your consumption of fruit (and vegetables). However, five glasses of juice a day is not as beneficial as five servings of fruit and vegetables because many of the phytochemicals attached to the 'body' of the fruit and vegetables are removed in making juice.

Gooseberries are a great treat in the early British summer. They are **a good source** of NSP (fibre), are rich in potassium and an excellent source of vitamin C.

Grains are **anti-ageing** because they contain lignans, a type of phyto-oestrogen. In the UK diet they are important because we eat more cereals than soya which is the richest food source of phyto-oestrogens. Legumes, vegetables and fruit also provide isoflavones in the traditional British diet.

- Grains contain up to 7mg of lignans per 100g.
- Fruit and vegetables contain up to 6mg per 100g.
- Linseed is exceptionally high in lignans, with levels of around 60mg per 100g.

During digestion, lignans are broken down by friendly gut bacteria into structures that are interchangeable in the body for the female sex hormone oestrogen, except that they have both weak oestrogenic and anti-oestrogenic properties that protect against hormone-dependent cancers. (For more sources of lignans, see page 92.) Grains are also **an excellent source** of NSP (fibre).

Grapefruit is **a good source** of vitamin C and beta-carotene. It is **anti-ageing** because it contains flavonoids that work with vitamin C to enhance the vitamin's antioxidant effects. Pink grapefruit also contains lycopene (see tomatoes for its anti-cancer effect).

And grapefruit, like other citrus fruit, also contains terpenes, another type of antioxidant.

Grapes   You might think that grapes would be anti-ageing because wine is, and wine is made from grapes. But the varieties of grapes grown for table grapes do not have the same antioxidant benefits against heart disease as those used to make wine, and the concentration of flavonoids in the skin of table grapes is lower. However, they are **a good source** of potassium and 'intrinsic' sugars – and there is no good reason why you should not continue to enjoy them!

Green salad   eaten as a starter can have an **anti-ageing effect**. The nitrates it contains are transformed in the mouth to antibacterial nitric oxide, which can kill a bacterium called *Helicobacter pylori* that could otherwise cause stomach ulcers. People who carry large numbers of *Helicobacter pylori* also seem to be more susceptible to heart disease, but the reason why is not yet understood. Of more immediate effect, the nitric oxide can also kill food poisoning bacteria in the stomach. Until recently all nitrates were considered harmful and potentially carcinogenic. However, this recent research suggests that some nitrates are protective.

Green soya beans   or young 'wet' beans are **anti-ageing** because they contain very high levels of isoflavones, up to 1g per kilogram. In America green soya beans are a fashionable but expensive commodity enjoyed by the gourmand health food cognoscenti. In the UK you will probably have to make do with TVP and tofu.

Look after your vegetables and they will look after you . . .

Try to shop for fresh produce on a regular basis and store it in a cool dark place, or the fridge.

Prepare as close to cooking/eating as possible and avoid soaking in water.

Do not chop fruit or vegetables too small because that exposes more surfaces to nutrient loss.

Tear the leaves of green leafy vegetables rather than cutting them with a knife.

Dress cut vegetables and fruit in lemon juice, or a light vinaigrette if they are to be eaten raw, to prevent vitamin C loss by oxidation.

Use vegetables unpeeled where appropriate (if they are organic), e.g. potatoes and carrots, parsnips, courgettes and cucumbers, because much of the vitamins and minerals are just under the skin. There is also fibre in the skin.

Cook vegetables for the shortest time possible and in the minimum amount of water.

Use water in which vegetables have been cooked for soups, sauces and so on because cooking does not destroy minerals (as it does vitamins) – they just leach out into the cooking water.

Add vegetables to boiling water – bringing them to the boil in cold water prolongs cooking time and nutrient loss. Better still, steam them, microwave them or use a waterless cooker.

If you are preparing vegetables for a dish, instead of sautéing, 'sweat' them in a covered pan where they will cook in their own juices. This avoids the addition of unwanted fats.

Use puréed vegetables and fruits to thicken savoury and sweet sauces instead of egg yolks, cream or a roux (flour and fat paste).

How cooking affects antioxidant vitamins

Eat raw fruits and vegetables regularly to help boost your nutrient intake and to benefit from the enzymes and other ingredients that might be destroyed by cooking.

Vitamin A and **beta-carotene** are stable during mild heating, but losses occur at high temperatures.

> **Vitamin C** leaches out during cooking because it is water-soluble. So if you throw the cooking water down the sink you will lose some of the nutrients.
>
> **Vitamin E** is destroyed gradually by heat.

Guavas   contain three times more vitamin C than kiwis and are rich in carotenoids.

Herbs and spices   are in general **good sources** of antioxidants. Rosemary claims greater antioxidant activity than many herbs, but not far behind are sesame seeds, oregano, pepper, chilli pepper and ginger. Having read this far you will realise that any food has to be eaten in quantity and regularly to have any effect on your health. So stop using the salt and from now on flavour your food with herbs and spices!

Honey   may be 'yucky, sticky stuff' to Tiggers (and dentists) but it is 'the best thing' to Pooh. Try some . . . as you meditate over your honey pot, honey can feed the spirit and take you far away from the grown-up world that Christopher Robin had to enter each time he left the 'Bisy Bakson' note on his door to the enchanted place at the top of the forest. Hang about long enough doing nothing and you will fall into idle therapoohtic chat with the ageless Winnie the Pooh.

Kiwis   contain twice the vitamin C of oranges and as much vitamin E as avocados. They are also rich in potassium and contain some folic acid.

Leeks   are **a good source** of vitamin C if you eat the green part of the leaves. They also make a reasonable NSP (fibre) contribution. As members of the onion family they share many of its healthy attributes, but they have not been the subject of extensive studies.

Lentils are **anti-ageing** because they are **a very good source** of lignans (see grains and cereals). They are also **a good source** of protein, NSP (fibre) to regulate cholesterol and blood sugar, some iron, potassium, magnesium and B vitamins (but not B_{12}). Red lentils are **a good source** of selenium.

Lettuce is **a good source** of antioxidant flavonols, with red-leaved varieties such as lollo rosso containing one hundred times more than limp round (cabbage) lettuce. The greener the lettuce leaves, the more vitamin C, beta-carotene, folic acid and iron they contain. To prepare, pull out the heart and tear off the leaves because this reduces the vitamin content less than cutting with a knife. For the same reason buy whole lettuce rather than pre-washed and torn pre-packed lettuce leaves, (but pre-packed and pre-torn is better than none).

Linseed contains exceptionally high levels of lignans, which makes it **anti-ageing**. Lignans have similar benefits to the phyto-oestrogens in soya, but they are weaker plant oestrogens. However, as they are eaten in greater quantity in the UK than soya foods, they have more relevance and practical benefit. Speciality breads contain linseed, as do cereals. Some products containing linseed are manufactured and marketed for menopausal women for their anti-ageing benefits. Packets of linseed can also be bought from health food stores and added to salads, cereals and baking. Try some of the HRT baking recipes (pages 242–45).

Marmalade is **anti-ageing** because it contains antioxidant terpenes and flavonoids such as liminoids found in the pith of citrus fruits (which is eaten in marmalade). These help strengthen blood capillaries and enhance the effects of vitamin C. Pectin, which sets marmalade (and other preserves), has cholesterol-lowering abilities.

Marmite is a British nursery food that has become an institution (and a puzzle to those foreigners not weaned on it). It is **a good source** of the B vitamins, and B vitamins feed your ageing memory. So if you are going to follow the rest of the advice in this book and look and feel younger, you had better not become forgetful (the hallmark of the old, along with spectacles hanging round the neck, sloppy cardigans and slippers).

Milk is **a good source** of calcium to build strong bones (and teeth) and prevent osteoporosis, the demineralisation of the bones in which more calcium is lost than is replaced. It affects one in three women, mainly those over sixty, causing 150,000 bone fractures a year. While that might sound totally irrelevant to younger people, prevention should begin early. Demineralisation of bones starts in women in their mid-thirties and increases dramatically at the menopause when the production of oestrogen, which has a bone-saving facility, stops. Strong bones rely on adequate calcium, vitamin D intake and weight-bearing exercise (i.e. ones in which you put pressure on the bones).

The best sources of calcium

Food	Milligrams (mg) of calcium
milk per pint: skimmed	708mg
semi-skimmed	693mg
whole milk	675mg
cheddar per 25g/1oz	207mg
yogurt 150ml/individual pot	240mg
tofu 100g/4oz	510mg
sardines 56g/2oz	220mg
shelled prawns 85g/3oz	126mg
sesame seeds 1 tbsp	102mg
tahini paste 1 tbsp	102mg
red kidney beans 115g/4oz	100mg
broccoli 115g/4oz	85mg
baked beans 150g/5oz	80mg
bread 2 slices	60mg
Evian mineral water 500ml/18fl oz	39mg

Vegetarian sources of calcium include:

- muesli
- oatmeal
- other pulses
- nuts
- dark green vegetables
- dried fruit

Drink low-fat milk to save your teeth
Milk and milk-flavoured drinks are better for you than fizzy drinks, which have a high acidity that can erode dental enamel, a far more difficult thing for your dentist to fix than caries. Milk and yogurt drinks also contribute a lot more nutrients than colas and their equivalents. There is more protein and A and B vitamins in milk than in carbonated drinks such as cola; and in plain milk there is no cariogenic (caries-inducing) added sugar or artificial sweeteners. Fruit juice (not fruit drinks) has the advantage over milk of containing useful amounts of vitamin C, but it lacks the calcium. Enjoy both but limit colas etc. to special occasions.

Nuts are seriously **anti-ageing** because regularly eating nuts can decrease your risk of having a heart attack or dying from it.

In a study of 27,000 Seventh-Day Adventists in California, the influence of sixty-five different foods on coronary heart disease was compared. Of all the foods studied, nuts had the strongest effect on decreasing heart disease. People eating nuts more than five times a week decreased their risk by more than 50 per cent; eating nuts one to four times a week cut the risk by 27 per cent.

Walnuts – the polyunsaturates of the nut world
A 'walnut diet' trial, in which eighteen men aged between twenty-one and forty-three ate 84g/3oz of unsalted and unroasted walnuts each day as a substitute for other high-fat foods in a typical American diet, resulted in lower cholesterol levels. There was a reduction in LDL (the harmful cholesterol) of 16.3 per cent

and in HDL (the beneficial cholesterol) of only 4.9 per cent and in the ratio of LDL to HDL of 12 per cent. Although the trial was based on an intake of 84g a day, as little as 28g/1oz of walnuts per day has been shown to have a beneficial effect within one month.

- A thirteen-year study of vegetarians has also revealed a 23 per cent lower-than-average death rate among those who ate nuts regularly.

Peanuts on a par with walnuts and red wine

Similar studies with peanuts have also shown that they provide protection against heart disease. The NSP (fibre) and fatty acids in peanuts make the blood less sticky and therefore less likely to clot and cause a heart attack. Peanuts are a reasonable source of the phenol resveratrol, best known for its effect in red wine of reducing the risk of heart disease.

- Nuts are also **a good source** of the antioxidant vitamin E (amounts differ between nuts but peanuts and walnuts provide around 25 per cent of the US RDA for just 25g/1oz), folates and other B vitamins, iron, selenium, zinc and phytochemicals.

Nuts to the French paradox . . .

Heart disease experts, who are sceptical about both the French paradox and the time lag theories (Chapter 1, pages 46–47) as an explanation for why the French, who eat a high-fat diet, still suffer less heart disease, suggest that the greater intake of nuts in France, which has been two to three times higher than the intake in the UK for more than thirty years, is more likely to be protective than wine.

We have seen that nuts have an impact on total blood cholesterol, and in some studies they increase HDL levels (the beneficial form) a little. But, it is suggested, they could be exhibiting a benefit disproportionate to these smaller measurable effects.

The Lyon Heart Study illustrates the point. Patients who had survived a heart attack were randomly put either on a normal diet or on a Mediterranean-style diet – rich in fruits, vegetables, monounsaturated fat and linolenic acid derived from olive oil, nuts and vegetables. Alcohol consumption was similar in both groups. Blood cholesterol levels, and blood pressures, were similar in the two groups during the two-year study and yet those who ate the Mediterranean diet had 70 per cent less chance of dying from a subsequent heart attack. Other studies show peanuts and peanut butter are as effective at beneficially influencing blood cholesterol levels as more expensive olive oil, but olive oil has additional benefits too, see page 84.

Oats   rose to nutritional fame when oat products were permitted to make claims that their soluble-fibre content can help reduce blood cholesterol if eaten on a regular basis as part of a well-balanced diet. The minimum you could get away with for an **anti-ageing** effect is around 35–45g a day, found in a medium bowl of porridge (low sugar and fat) or a large flapjack (high sugar and fat). But some studies have found 150g a day a more effective amount. Oats reduce both total cholesterol and levels of harmful LDL without reducing HDL levels. It is important to keep HDL levels high to protect against heart disease.

Oats are **a good source** of calcium and provide slow-release energy that avoids the rapid rises and falls of blood sugar associated with sugary carbohydrate foods.

Oily fish   such as **mackerel, herring, sardines, pilchards, salmon,** and **trout** are one of the **richest sources** of omega-3 fatty acids.

You need to eat between 200g and 400g, or two oily fish meals, a week for **anti-ageing** benefits, which include lowering blood cholesterol and making blood less likely to clot to protect against heart disease and stroke.

Fish cuts risk of fatal heart attacks
The risk of sudden death from a fatal heart attack is lower in people who eat fish compared with people who eat no fish. And the risk

of a second heart attack being fatal is also reduced if you eat fish or take a daily fish oil supplement providing 1g of omega-3. As well as thinning the blood, omega-3 fatty acids in fish also:

- increase the production of nitric oxide, which relaxes the blood vessel walls and improves their elasticity
- stabilise heart rhythms and help prevent irregular heartbeats associated with heart attacks
- slow down the blood clotting process

Cooking tip
Steaming oily fish retains more omega-3 fatty acids than grilling, baking and frying – although together with canned oily fish (except tuna which contains only a minuscule amount of omega-3 fatty acids after processing) these are all still valuable foods and methods of cooking.

Fish oils help joint problems and arthritis
The oils in fish also have anti-inflammatory properties.

Getting the ratio of omega-6 to omega-3 fats right is important (as we saw to prevent heart disease, page 26), but it is also vital to treat or prevent other health problems because omega-6 fatty acids can be pro-inflammatory. This means they can, in some people, trigger inflammatory diseases such as rheumatoid arthritis, joint problems, asthma, eczema, Crohn's disease, irritable bowel syndrome and psoriasis.

Inflammatory diseases occur when the body has an allergic reaction to its own tissues. Some allergy responses are caused by the important chemical messengers, prostaglandins (and other substances) that are produced when the omega-6 fatty acid linoleic acid, found in sunflower oil, is broken down to arachidonic acid. If the omega-6 polyunsaturated fats in the diet are replaced by omega-3 fatty acids, i.e. fish oils, then the substances that trigger inflammatory reactions are less likely to be produced. In addition omega-3 fatty acids produce different types of prostaglandin that are less anti-inflammatory. Fish oils also dampen down the effects of damage to joints. Several trials have shown 3–4g of omega-3 a day (or 10–15g of fish oil or 100g portion of oily fish) helps ease rheumatoid arthritis.

Bad news for vegetarians
Alpha-linolenic acid (the omega-3 fatty acids from plant foods such as linseed and soya oil) is less effective than fish oils in treating the symptoms of arthritis etc. Trials that have used alpha-linolenic acid, the fatty acid found in linseed, show that 14g per day over four weeks is needed to get only half the effect of 2.5g a day of fish oils containing EPA/DHA. Then larger amounts of alpha-linolenic acid are probably required because the enzymes in the body have to modify alpha-linolenic acid into longer-chain versions (literally physically longer fatty acids) to match the naturally long-chain fish oils in omega-3 fatty acids.

Fish oils to stop dry skin and wrinkles
Skin cells need omega-3 fatty acids for strong membranes to hold in moisture and give good flexibility. Omega-3 fatty acids help strengthen the collagen and elastin fibres in the skin that keep the skin looking younger for longer and prevent or slow wrinkling and sagging.

As omega-3 fatty acids improve blood flow, by thinning the blood and improving the elasticity of red blood cells, they can carry

---

Dry skin tips

Feeding the skin from within brings benefits, but external skin care is also important. Soap and detergents can turn normal skin into dry skin and provoke eczema by breaking down the natural barrier of lipids on the surface of the skin. The skin barrier becomes damaged and the skin underneath becomes cracked and dries out more. Emollients, lotions and creams can restore the barrier by plumping out dry surface skin cells and by creating a film of lipids on the surface to prevent more moisture being lost.

more oxygen to the skin surface to give you a healthy glowing complexion.

Deficiency in essential fatty acids in your diet can result in dry, scaly and itchy skin. People with dry skin have fewer natural lipids (natural oils) to act as a barrier and trap water in the skin.

Be a happy fish

Adequate omega-3 fatty acids may also protect against depression, as well as cognitive decline (thinking, reasoning, etc.) associated with ageing. Patients with depression have consistently been shown to have depleted levels of omega-3 fatty acids in their bodies. The severity of the depression has been linked with the degree of deficiency. Patients with dementia who have been given omega-3 supplements had longer periods of remission than patients given an olive oil supplement.

This is not to criticise olive oil because olive oil-rich 'Mediterranean' diets have also been associated with better memory in older age. The monounsaturated fatty acids in olive oil help maintain the structural integrity of nerve membranes.

Anti-ageing supplement tip

Omega-3 fish oil supplements

Although eating a well-balanced diet is your first line of defence against ageing, sometimes it is justified to take a dietary supplement to offset the effects of ageing. In the case of omega-3 fatty acids, a dietary supplement of fish oils or cod liver oil (or linseed/flaxseed oil for vegetarians) may be justified to:

- try to redress the balance and get a healthier ratio of omega-6 to omega-3 levels
- offset the fact that the body is not always efficient at converting alpha-linolenic acid to EPA and DHA

- benefit from the anti-ageing effects of omega-3 fatty acids that protect against heart disease, stroke and some cancers
- benefit from the anti-ageing effects of omega-3 fatty acids, which are therapeutic for arthritis, skin conditions (eczema, psoriasis), depression and mildly raised blood pressure

How much to take

For general good health and to benefit the skin, take 150–200mg daily of omega-3 fish oil or cod liver oil supplements. For heart disease prevention, take 400mg daily. Relief from arthritis etc. varies from individual to individual. Amounts that have given results in trials are high, at 2.6–3g (2600–3000mg) daily.

- If you take fish oil (or evening primrose or sunflower, see page 95) capsules, they are best taken with a general multivitamin tablet (if you take one) at mealtimes because they need other nutrients to be utilised.

Diet or pills: both take time

As nutrients in foods and in supplements work from the inside out, both take time to have an effect. In general a nutritional supplement will probably take up to twelve weeks to have any real or visible effect. This is particularly true with the skin. Skin takes about six weeks to grow from the deepest layers to the surface so any nutritional approach to improving your skin will take a month or two. This is also true for diet and if you are taking fish oil or evening primrose oil (see sunflower oil, page 95) supplements for an anti-ageing effect on your skin or to help dry (or eczematous) skin, results will not be seen overnight.

Olive oil   has tended to be over-shadowed by recent discoveries about the benefits of fish oils. But olive oil has long enjoyed an anti-ageing reputation because it contains a higher percentage of monounsaturated fatty acids than other vegetable oils and animal fats. The monounsaturated fats and the vitamin E in olive oil have been associated (in part) with its protective effects against heart disease, which is comparatively low among southern European countries where a traditional Mediterranean-style diet is consumed. Monounsaturates, as we have seen, are as effective as polyunsaturates in lowering cholesterol levels and they help keep a healthy balance of beneficial types of cholesterol. In addition olive oil, in particular extra-virgin olive oil, has recently been found to contain pinoresinols, a type of phenol that cancer researchers report aggressively scavenges free radicals, helping to prevent cancer (and heart disease).

Using olive oil in cooking may also prevent the development of bowel cancer. A Spanish team of researchers variously fed rats a diet rich in olive, fish or safflower oil. The rats were then given a cancer-causing agent. Four months later the rats on the olive oil diet had less pre-cancerous tissue and fewer tumours than those fed the other diets. The fish oil diet also had a positive impact on reducing cancerous tissue.

Onions   and the other members of the allium family are **anti-ageing** because they provide up to one-third of the antioxidant intake in the diet of northern Europeans and North Americans. Heart disease protection comes from the antioxidant flavonoid quercetin, also associated with lower rates of stroke. To benefit, onions have to be eaten regularly. **Red onions** are a richer source of flavonols than yellow-skinned or white onions.

Protection also comes from the sulphur compounds, found in **garlic**, **onions**, **shallots**, **leeks**, **spring onions** and **chives**, which help prevent blood clotting. Allium compounds also help lower blood cholesterol levels, and when taken in the form of garlic dietary supplements, they can lower blood pressure, although not all trials have shown protective effects.

The antioxidant flavonols may also reduce the risk of cancers among regular onion eaters. In addition flavonols can help reduce inflammation and allergic reactions. And the sulphur compounds are antibacterial, helping to prevent infections.

Onions are **a good source** of NSP (fibre), in particular oligosaccharides, the non-digestible part of the vegetable that passes into the large intestine where it is metabolised by beneficial bacteria such as bifido bacteria and lactobacilli to produce substances that protect against cancer and boost immunity. When oligosaccharides are extracted from vegetables and used as a food supplement to increase the number of beneficial bacteria in the gut (and therefore to decrease the dominance of potentially harmful gut bacteria), they are called 'probiotics'. This is a term you may see on food wrappers and supplements.

Orange juice and oranges are **good sources** of the antioxidant vitamin C that also boosts immunity. One medium-to-large orange provides 80mg of vitamin C, twice the RNI (daily recommended amount) for all adults. Oranges also supply a reasonable amount of folic acid to prevent heart disease. The **anti-ageing** effect also comes from flavonoids in citrus fruit that work with vitamin C to boost immunity, to strengthen blood capillaries and to act as anti-inflammatory antioxidants. Another group of flavonoids called limonoids also increases the production of enzymes that help the body dispose of carcinogens (cancer-inducing substances).

Peas fresh from the garden taste best, but frozen peas must be among the world's most nutritious convenience foods. Frozen peas can be **a better source** of vitamin C than fresh when they are frozen (as many are) within a few hours of harvesting. An average 70g portion of peas provides nearly half an adult's RNI of vitamin C. They also contain the carotenes lutein and zeaxanthin (see spinach). Unusually for a vegetable, peas make a good contribution of the B vitamins, in particular thiamine, as well as providing protein and a useful amount of folates. Peas even contain a fair amount of iron and zinc for a vegetable. The NSP (fibre) in peas has been associated with lowering cholesterol levels. Along with carrots and sweetcorn, peas – both fresh and frozen – share the distinction of having a low GI or Glycaemic Index (see Chapter 1, page 10). This means they release energy slowly and do not disrupt blood sugar levels, keeping you on an even keel and helping prevent maturity-onset diabetes.

Peppers are **an excellent source** of vitamin C, and red peppers are a particularly good source of **anti-ageing** carotenes – including lutein and zeaxanthin – to help prevent cancer and heart disease (see spinach). All peppers also contain a small amount of vitamin E and capsaicin, the phytonutrient found in chillies.

• Green peppers change from green to red as they ripen. Orange, yellow, purple and black are the result of colourful plant breeding and do not share the chameleon characteristic of green peppers.

Pomegranate extracts are superior, in terms of antioxidant flavonoids, to red wine in test-tube experiments, but they are not as potent as green tea extracts. However their **anti-ageing** effect is strictly limited in the UK where they are eaten very little. Their antioxidant, anti-inflammatory properties and phyto-oestrogen content are no doubt of benefit to people who eat a traditional Turkish and Middle Eastern diet in which pomegranates and their products feature regularly. Track down a few good recipe books and try these fantastic cuisines for yourself.

• The drink grenadine, the 'rising sun' part of the cocktail Tequila Sunrise, is also made from pomegranates. To make a Tequila Sunrise, you need 1 measure of tequila, 120ml/4fl oz orange juice and 15ml/ ½floz grenadine. Pour the orange juice and the tequila over some ice cubes and stir. Slowly add the grenadine and allow it to settle at the bottom.

Prunes are full of surprises! They are **anti-ageing** because they contain double the level of antioxidants of fruits and vegetables more commonly associated with a high antioxidant content, such as mangoes, apricots, spinach and broccoli. They have great potential to eradicate damaging free radicals – and you probably do not need me to mention the laxative effect of their NSP (fibre) content.

Top-scoring* antioxidant fruits and vegetables

Fruit	Score	Vegetable	Score
Prunes	5,770	Kale	1,770
Raisins	2,830	Spinach	1,260
Blueberries	2,400	Brussels sprouts	980
Blackberries	2,036	Alfalfa sprouts	930
Strawberries	1,540	Broccoli	890
Raspberries	1,220	Beets	840
Plums	949	Red peppers	710
Oranges	750	Onions	450
Red grapes	739	Sweetcorn	400
Cherries	670	Aubergines	390
Kiwi fruit	602		
Pink grapefruit	483		

*   The ORAC (or Oxygen Radical Absorbance Capacity) score is a test-tube analysis that measures the total antioxidant power of food. The amounts are ORAC units per 100g/3½oz food. Source: Human Nutrition Research Center on Aging, Tufts University, Boston, US.

Pumpkins   and other varieties of **squash**, particularly those with bright orange flesh, are **good sources** of antioxidant carotenes. Population studies from several countries show that people who eat squash regularly, i.e. a few times a week, have a lower risk of diet-related cancers.

Radishes   contain a phytochemical called glucosinolate that the body converts to anti-cancer compounds.

Red or purple grape juice   is **anti-ageing** because it contains similar levels of flavonols to many red wines, enabling it to dilate blood vessels and prevent blood clots. It can also trigger the release of nitric oxide (the substance that widens blood vessels and inhibits clotting). Drinking a large glass of purple grape juice is as effective as drinking two glasses of red wine in preventing heart disease – and it doesn't give you a hangover, or other side-effects. The quercetin in the juice also inhibits the clumping of platelets in the blood which can cause the clots that lead to heart attacks.

Red wines are **anti-ageing** (for all the reasons outlined in Chapter 1, page 44). But which wines are most beneficial? Red wines made from the grape varieties Cabernet Sauvignon, Merlot and Pinot Noir contain 40–50mg of polyphenols a litre when produced in Chile; significantly more than wines grown from the same grape varieties in Spain (25mg), California (10–15mg), France (10mg), Romania (10mg) and Bulgaria (5mg). The very hot sunny conditions in Chile result in there being more polyphenols in Chilean wine, because these substances act as UV protectants (sunscreens) to the fruit, and so greater concentrations of polyphenols are found in the skins of grapes grown in the hotter climates. Methods of vinification (winemaking) in Chile also result in more of the skin extracts being retained in the wines, which gives them their wonderful deep ruby and purple colours and higher polyphenol content. Unlike, for example, lighter coloured less full-bodied Beaujolais where the grape skins are removed quickly, as they are in Bulgarian wine where the skins are taken for brandy production.

As research into the phenol content of wine has only recently started there is only limited information available, and there is not yet a comprehensive list of which wines and grape varieties around the world contain the most phenols making them, theoretically, the most beneficial.

As a general rule of thumb drink red wines from hot countries. The ageing of wine does not seem to deplete their levels of polyphenols much – although old vintages have not been analysed. However, they are hardly everyday quaffing wines that could make a significant contribution to the polyphenol content of your diet – unless you are a privileged wine connoisseur with an exceptional cellar.

Soya foods and soya milk are **anti-ageing** because they contain isoflavones. These plant hormones are physically identical to the female sex hormone oestradiol made by the ovaries and adrenal glands. By replacing oestradiol in the body, studies suggest, they may allow you to capitalise on the benefits of oestrogen – protection against heart disease and osteoporosis – without unwanted side-effects such as the triggering or the supporting of sex-hormone-related breast and prostate cancers.

How they work
The isoflavones in soya and to a lesser extent in legumes (peas, beans, etc.) are fermented during digestion by friendly gut bacteria to make 'phenolic hormones' which are weak oestrogens and anti-oestrogens. The products of these plant oestrogens seem to have several beneficial anti-ageing effects in that they:

*   act as weak oestrogens so they can do the job of oestradiol without being powerful enough to also have harmful effects
*   include anti-oestrogens which work against the harmful side-effects of normal oestrogens
*   inhibit oestrogen production in fat tissue. Oestrogen can also be produced in fat deposits in the body and too much is a bad thing, so turning off production is helpful
*   inhibit the production of enzymes such as aromatase that are involved in maintaining cancer cell growth
*   cut off the blood supply to cancerous cells, starving them of oxygen and nutrients
*   inhibit the production of the enzymes required for prostate cancer growth
*   act as antioxidants, destroying free radicals
*   cause cancer cells to commit suicide (a process called apoptosis). Healthy cells have a finite lifetime and apoptosis ensures that they die off when they need to be replaced. Cancer cells do not know when to die off so they multiply out of control to cause tumours.

Soya prevents heart disease

Before the menopause, oestrogen protects women against heart disease by keeping their cholesterol levels low. Heart disease is still the biggest killer in the UK, claiming more than 148,000 lives a year and accounting for the deaths of one in five women.

Soya isoflavones protect against heart disease by:

- their action as antioxidants, preventing harmful LDL cholesterol from being deposited in the arteries
- decreasing the tendency of the blood to form clots or thromboses
- clearing the blood vessels of plaque

Soya protein also decreases the level of harmful LDL blood cholesterol and triglycerides, while increasing the level of beneficial HDL cholesterol.

- In the US, health claims are allowed on foods that provide 25g of soya protein a day. The claims state that, taken in conjunction with a diet low in saturated fat and cholesterol, these foods can reduce the risk of a heart attack.

Soya prevents osteoporosis without the side-effects of HRT

In the West we are advised to eat lots of foods containing calcium to prevent osteoporosis – the demineralisation of bones that causes the 60,000 hip, 50,000 wrist, 40,000 vertebral and 50,000 other types of fracture each year in post-menopausal British women. However, the calcium content of your diet is not the be-all and end-all of bone health.

Oestrogen protects against osteoporosis in that it:

- discourages the cytokines (messengers) that stimulate osteoclasts (cells that break down bone)
- encourages other types of cytokine to stimulate osteoblasts (bone-building cells)

This is why oestrogen is given to women as hormone replacement therapy (HRT) around and after the menopause. However, oestrogen therapy is not trouble-free because the dosage needed to decrease the rate of bone breakdown may increase the risk of breast cancer and blood clots. Other unwanted side-effects such as abnormal bleeding, persistence of periods, breast pain and tenderness can also occur.

This is where phyto-oestrogens come in. The incidence of hip fractures is significantly lower in countries such as China and Japan where there is a relatively low intake of dietary calcium, but a high intake of isoflavones. Although plant oestrogens are only weakly oestrogenic, they still decrease bone loss without the potential for causing cancer.

Eating more foods rich in plant oestrogens becomes an alternative way to boost bone strength without unwanted side-effects (see HRT, Chapter 5).

How much phyto-oestrogen-rich food should you eat?

A study that added 60g a day of textured vegetable protein (TVP) to the diets of healthy British women lengthened the follicular (or first half) of their menstrual cycle so that the cycle increased from the average twenty-eight days in the West, to nearer thirty-two days, the average for women on traditional Oriental diets. The purpose of extending the follicular phase of the menstrual cycle is to reduce the second half, during which oestrogen levels are at their highest. Oestrogen makes breast cells divide at twice the normal rate, making them more vulnerable to cancer. Women on the trial who ate only 30g of TVP a day did not show the beneficial effects of those on 60g a day. The critical dosage must therefore be between the two amounts. The TVP that the women were given contained 45mg of isoflavones – the amount of isoflavone in TVP varies from 30mg to 70mg for an average 60g serving. The Japanese, the Koreans and Seventh-Day Adventists (who are strict vegetarians) eat between 30mg and 100mg of isoflavones a day, mainly from the soya foods and pulses in their diet.

What if you don't like soya foods?

Isoflavones are also found in chickpeas and in lentils. And lignans, which are similar to isoflavones but have not had as much research done on them yet, are found in **linseed**, **breakfast cereals**, **oat bran**, **oatmeal**, **wholemeal** and **rye breads**, **asparagus**, **carrots**, **lentils** and **pears**.

Some good food sources of phyto-oestrogens (micrograms per 100g of food)

TVP	1136
soya bean flakes*	366–501
soya bean dessert	232
soya milk	18–42 (some brands are fortified up to around 100)
chickpeas and lentils	approx 5mg per 100g (3½oz) portion

*   Soya bean oil and soya sauce do not contain any isoflavones.

Some good food sources of lignans (micrograms per 100g of food)

linseed meal	675–808
linseed flour	527
linseed oil	17
oat bran	7
oatmeal	2
wheat	5
rye	2–6
asparagus	3
carrots	4
lentils	18
pears	2

Should you take isoflavone tablets?

If you do not want to change your diet, but want to take advantage of the benefits of plant oestrogens, there are a variety of isoflavone or phyto-oestrogen dietary supplements on sale in health food shops and pharmacies. But some scientists question how beneficial these dietary supplements are, and wonder whether they might even promote hormone-dependent cancers in some high-risk people. Once the isoflavones are extracted from soya protein, they may not work in the same way as they do in food. Studies have shown that isoflavone extract supplements do not lower blood cholesterol so they do not have the same heart benefits as the soya protein in food. The same may be true for cancer. Supplement dosages differ, but recommendations are between 25mg and 50mg per day. However, some foods fortified with isoflavones contain up to 160mg per serving – and no one knows the effects of an over-dose (or even at what dose overdose might occur).

Eating more foods rich in soya protein and lignans is probably your best option at the moment. Some experts think that it is necessary for soya to have been a staple food over a lifetime in order to lower susceptibility to breast cancer.

Spinach – plus **chard, mustard greens, pak choi** and other **dark green leafy vegetables** such as **broccoli, kale** and **watercress** – are **good sources** of carotenoids, but unlike orange vegetables and fruit, the colour in them is masked by chlorophyll, the green pigment that allows plants to photosynthesise (make energy from sunlight).

Although **spinach** is associated with iron (and Popeye), it is not particularly rich in iron. However, its content of beta-carotene, vitamins C and E and folates more than maintains its excellent nutritional reputation. It is wonderfully versatile both cooked and raw in salads.

Spinach and dark green leafy vegetables (and **red peppers, maize, sweetcorn, peas, celery** and **tomato sauce**) are also **anti-ageing** because they contain the antioxidant carotenoids lutein and zeaxanthin that help prevent degenerative eye disease such as age-related macular degeneration and cataracts. The macular is the centre of the retina, which distinguishes fine detail at the centre of the field of vision. Lutein and zeaxanthin are the only carotenoids found in the lens of the eye and in the macular.

Higher than average intakes of lutein and zeaxanthin result in increased macular pigment density, which improves the ability to filter off harmful ultraviolet light to protect the eye against free-radical damage. Lutein and zeaxanthin may also protect against cataracts, a progressive fogging of the lens of the eye making it difficult to see.

- Age-related eye disease accounts for 80 per cent of visual impairment and blindness in the UK. You are most at risk if you smoke, or have a family history of macular degeneration. Excessive exposure to the sun, particularly in people with light-coloured eyes, can also contribute to the problem.

Sprouted seeds – such as mung beans, better known as **bean sprouts** in Chinese food – are a **good source** of coumestan, a type of flavonoid, as are other seeds such as alfalfa, clover and soya. Sprouted seeds also offer vitamin C, a little iron and B vitamins.

Sprout your own

Pick over the mung (or other) beans and wash. Put in a wide-mouthed jar and secure a piece of muslin over the top with an elastic band or string. Rinse the beans with cold water through the muslin and leave them to soak for twelve hours. Then rinse again and leave the jar on its side to drain. Keep the jar out of direct sunlight and rinse twice a day. The beans should have sprouted and grown enough to be harvested within six days, when they are ready to eat. They can be left in sunlight for the day before harvesting so the leaves become greener, which increases their chlorophyll content. Beans may also be sprouted on a plate and rinsed daily in a sieve. In addition to mung beans, try sprouting alfalfa seeds, aduki beans – and mustard and cress.

- Sprouted chickpeas and soya beans should be boiled, steamed or fried for 3–5 minutes before eating to destroy an enzyme that would cause digestive upsets.

Strawberries are **a good source** of vitamin C. Strawberries and raspberries also contain a lot of ellaic acid, a substance that seems to neutralise carcinogens before they attack a cell's DNA.

Sunflower oil is in danger of being overlooked these days in favour of olive oil, which is associated with healthy longevity in the popular Mediterranean diet. Like olive oil, sunflower oil is **a good source** of vitamin E. It is **anti-ageing** because it contains the omega-6 linoleic fatty acid, which protects against heart disease by decreasing total blood cholesterol and harmful LDL cholesterol while also raising levels of beneficial HDL cholesterol.

Linoleic acid is also turned in the body into gamma linoleic acid (GLA) which is essential for the basic structure of all cells, the maintenance of hormonal balance and the production of prostaglandins (chemical messengers). It is also anti-inflammatory.

As you age your body becomes less efficient at producing GLA, which needs the background of a well-balanced diet that does not contain too much saturated and trans fats for successful production. Other factors that prevent GLA production include too much alcohol, too much sugar, zinc deficiency, viral infections, allergic conditions, cancer and radiation. All of which adds up to more good reasons to eat a diet as you age that is rich in nutrients, low in fat and without excess alcohol. Lifestyle is important too (see Chapter 5), as stress can interfere with GLA production.

Anti-ageing supplement tip: evening primrose oil

Although a well-balanced diet is your first line of defence against ageing, sometimes it is justified to take a dietary supplement to offset the effects of ageing, and a dietary supplement of evening primrose oil is a case in point because it can ensure direct input of GLA.

- If you take evening primrose (or fish) oil capsules they are best taken with a general multivitamin tablet (if you take one) at mealtimes because they need other nutrients to be utilised.
- If the scientists and close readers among you are now questioning how GLA can be anti-inflammatory when pro-inflammatory

---

arachidonic acid is produced from GLA breakdown, the answer is that the GLA in evening primrose oil is used up before it can be turned into the arachidonic acid that produces pro-inflammatory prostaglandins.

How much to take

Advice will vary from product to product, depending on its potency, but the basic principle when taking GLA supplements is to take the highest dosage recommended for twelve weeks to fill up the body's reservoir (if that analogy may be used) and then reduce the dosage over time to a top-up dose.

Sweetcorn kernels   in cans (choose varieties with no added salt or sugar) or corn-on-the-cob are both **good sources** of the carotene lutein (see spinach) and of folic acid. An average corn-on-the-cob is a very good source of NSP (fibre) providing about one-third of your daily needs. The canned equivalent of 85g/3oz sweetcorn kernels provides just under one quarter.

Tea   is **anti-ageing** because regular tea drinkers have a reduced risk of heart disease. In one study, men and women who drank one or more cups of tea a day had a 44 per cent reduction in their risk of heart attack compared with non-tea drinkers. In another, men who drank three to four cups of tea a day had a 69 per cent lower risk than those drinking 2.5 cups a day. A study of more than 35,000 post-menopausal women in the US showed that those who drank two or more cups of tea a day had a 40–70 per cent lower risk of cancers of the digestive and urinary tract.

Tea contains the antioxidant flavonoids quercetin and catechin, which neutralise free radicals, thus helping to prevent atherosclerosis, which leads to strokes and heart disease.

Green (unfermented) tea, of the type popular in Japan, is more potent than black (fermented) tea, the type drunk in Britain.

Adding milk to tea has variously affected, and not affected, the uptake of antioxidants in different studies.

Specific claims for the health benefits of green tea rest on laboratory studies that show epigallocatechin gallate, a catechin found in green tea, can inhibit the growth of isolated cancer cells and block reactions specific to skin cancer. Plans are underway in the US for the gallate to be tested in topical creams for its ability to prevent cancer.

Drink your tea through a straw . . .
Tea is also **a good source** of natural fluoride, which protects teeth from decay – but the other side of this particular double-edged sword is that tea (and coffee) can also stain your teeth if not vigorously rinsed away immediately after every cup.

The US Academy of General Dentistry has come up with a suggestion to prevent this. But I have to say that the suggestion will be as enthusiastically received by cappuccino, *latte* and Darjeeling drinkers as a cup of their favourite brew from a vending machine. It is to drink tea and coffee through a straw so that your front teeth are not touched. They *cannot* be serious!

Tips on tea

Tea timing . . .

This is not a reference to the time at which you drink your tea, but to its timing in relation to meals. Because the tannin in tea binds with minerals, making them unavailable to the body, it is best to leave a thirty-minute gap after a meal before you drink a cup of tea.

. . . and pill popping

Taking vitamin pills with a cup of tea or coffee could also inhibit the effect of the minerals in the tablets. These drinks contain tannins which prevent the absorption of iron from the intestine. Tablets are best taken with water.

Tomatoes are **anti-ageing** because they contain lycopene, a powerful antioxidant carotene, which gives them their bright red colour. Cooking and processing releases lycopene from the skins so there are higher levels in cooked tomatoes and in foods such as **pasta sauce, tomato ketchup, canned tomatoes, passata, tomato soup** and **tomato purée** than in raw tomatoes. Cooking also makes the lycopene more readily absorbed. But beware – some of these products are high in salt; with home-made versions you can regulate the salt content. Alternatively, buy lower-salt versions.

Tomatoes to protect men's health
Men with a high intake of tomatoes (five to ten servings a week) are less at risk of prostate cancer than those who never eat tomatoes – other carotenoids do not show the same association. Protection may extend to other cancers: lung, stomach, pancreas, bowel, breast and cervix. Regular tomato eaters also halve their risk of heart attack. The lycopene in tomatoes is thought to prevent the formation of sticky plaques in the blood, reducing the risk of clots forming, which can block blood vessels and cause a heart attack.

Cherry tomatoes are the richest source of lycopene because there is a higher skin-to-flesh ratio. Cooking reduces their flavonol content to 75 per cent when fried, 40 per cent when microwaved and 30 per cent when boiled. (Boiled tomatoes? What do scientists eat?)

Tomatoes are also **a good source** of vitamin C and beta-carotene (cosmetics companies are investigating the sunscreen properties of the tomato). As in black (or red) grapes, the chemicals in the tomato skins act as a kind of sunscreen so current studies are investigating whether lycopene can help prevent ultraviolet radiation from ageing the skin. Lutein is also the subject of similar investigations (see sweetcorn).

- When you fancy a change from red wine, pour yourself the occasional Bloody Mary – for medicinal purposes . . .

Watercress is **a good source** of chlorophyll, the pigment that allows green plants to photosynthesise (make energy from sunlight) and which may protect you (if you eat it regularly) against the DNA damage that can lead to cancer. Watercress also owes some of the colour in its luxuriously deep green foliage to its high levels of beta-carotene and iron. It also contains some zinc, potassium and even calcium. Eating it raw retains its high levels of beta-carotene and vitamins C and E.

Watermelon is **a good source** of lycopene (see tomatoes). It's just so pretty too that you have to eat lots!

Yogurt It is almost 100 years since the Nobel prize-winning Russian scientist Mechnikov first published *The Prolongation of Life* in 1907, which linked longevity among Bulgarian peasants with their healthy gut flora, acquired from a daily dose of live yogurt.

It is still true that the efficiency of your digestive system at extracting nutrients from your food and eliminating the waste relies in large part on having a healthy gut flora – a term that describes the colony of 1kg of bacteria that live in your gut. Yogurt (and other fermented products) contain exactly those beneficial types of live bacteria – Lactobacillus and bifido bacteria – which are needed to ferment the undigested NSP (fibre) from carbohydrate foods (bread, cereal, rice, pasta, potatoes, beans and pulses, vegetables, fruit, other grains) that eventually reach the large intestine. There, the function of these bacteria is to:

- produce a 'biomass' which bulks up body waste (more than half stool weight is bacteria) to prevent constipation
- discourage the growth of potentially harmful bacteria by controlling levels of oxygen and acidity
- make anti-adhesives so that the harmful bacteria cannot get a grip in the gut
- neutralise and transport carcinogens out of the body
- produce anti-cancer chemicals such as butyrate, which causes cancer cells to commit suicide
- manufacture vitamin K (to prevent haemorrhages) and B vitamins
- stimulate the immune system

Looking after your gut flora is particularly important as you age because **the number of beneficial gut bacteria falls off dramatically after the age of fifty**.

Reducing the harm from antibiotics
Bacteria from yogurt and fermented milk drinks such as *lactobacillus acidophilus*, *lactobacillus casei* and bifido bacteria are very good at recolonising your gut during and after antibiotic treatment which indiscriminately reduces the numbers of beneficial and harmful gut bacteria. If yogurt is not eaten almost daily, any newly introduced bacteria are washed out of the gut within a couple of weeks. Eating yogurt regularly keeps up the numbers of bifido bacteria which are associated with good health.

What kills friendly gut bacteria
- ageing
- antibiotics
- gastroenteritis
- laxatives
- radiotherapy
- chemotherapy
- severe deficiency of B vitamins
- emotional stress
- excessive physical activity e.g. marathon running

Can Vitamin Pills Keep You Young?

We know that people who eat a lot of vegetables, fruits, beans, cereals, etc., are healthier and live longer.

We know that vitamins, antioxidants and phytonutrients have been credited with the protective anti-ageing effects of these foods.

So taking vitamin and mineral supplements may seem like a short cut to health, instead of eating a healthier diet. But it does not necessarily follow that the components that make these foods healthy will have the same effect (if any) or be safe when they are extracted and made into dietary supplements.

There is also the danger, when singling out one or more nutrients, that you will forget that it is your total diet – plus lifestyle and exercise – that need to be anti-ageing. An example of putting too much emphasis on one purified ingredient, while ignoring other factors, is oat bran. Several years ago, studies showed that the soluble fibre (as one type of NSP was then called) in oat bran was capable of lowering cholesterol levels. Since then it has been added to many foods. In the meantime wheat bran, which is mainly insoluble fibre, has been shown to work almost as well. However, the effect of the NSP in these foods cannot be separated from the rest of the diet. Putting oat bran in a high-fat cake or biscuit, or adding it to a high-fat (and high-sugar/salt) diet, will not prevent elevated levels of blood cholesterol. The whole diet has to be relatively low in fat for the oat bran to have a useful cholesterol-lowering effect.

The benefits and dangers of vitamin pills

Taking vitamin pills cannot be assumed to be risk-free. Too much of some nutrients can be harmful: vitamin A, niacin and iron can all be toxic if taken in excess. Vitamin pills can also increase the risk of cancer. While beta-carotene is a beneficial antioxidant nutrient when eaten in the form of fruit and vegetables, when taken as tablets by smokers it has increased, not decreased as expected, their risk of lung cancer, and also that of death from heart disease. The government has advised people against taking beta-carotene supplements because of this.

Vitamin pill trials

Having made a case for taking your vitamins and minerals in the form of food, I have to say that much of the research attributing the health benefits of certain foods to their component vitamins, minerals or phytonutrients relates to trials that have used dietary supplements to show or achieve the effects.

For example, according to the Cambridge Heart Antioxidant Study (CHAOS), in which more than 2,000 men and women who were diagnosed with atherosclerosis (hardening of the arteries, a risk factor of heart disease) took either vitamin E supplements (400 IU or 800 IU) or placebos (inactive pills) for seventeen months, the risk of non-fatal heart attack was reduced by 77 per cent in the vitamin E group. Another study reports a 40 per cent lower risk of developing heart disease among more than 125,000 men and women who took supplements with 100 IU or more vitamin E a day. These results were obtained with the 'natural' form of vitamin E, d-alpha-tocopherol, which is more effective than the synthetic version, dl-alpha-tocopherol.

Tip   If you decide to take vitamin E supplements, you will need to be aware of this subtle difference on the label.

Selenium has also been shown to be anti-ageing. In one placebo-controlled, double-blind trial of more than 1,300 people, those taking supplements of 200mcg (μg) of selenium a day had 63 per cent fewer cases of prostate cancer, 58 per cent fewer cases of colorectal cancer, 46 per cent fewer cases of lung cancer and a 50 per cent reduction in cancer mortality overall. This has prompted the recently started Prevention of Cancer Intervention with Selenium (PRECISE) trial of more than 52,000 people at a cost of £20 million. Selenium is a mineral found in all foods in very low concentrations, its content varying according to the levels of selenium in the soil in which the food is grown.

Currently the World Health Organisation guidelines on requirements for adults are 60μg per day for men, 50μg for women. In the UK, the average intake has fallen from 60μg a day in 1971 to 34μg in 1994. The Department of Health RNI is 75μg for men and 60μg for women. See also nuts (page 77).

Amounts for 'anti-ageing' nutrition

It is something of an open secret in the nutrition world that larger amounts of vitamins and minerals than the RNIs are probably required for optimal nutrition – and to combat the effects of ageing.

While RNI levels will adequately prevent subclinical malnutrition, larger quantities of the antioxidant vitamins (C and E and beta-carotene), for example, are needed by most people who eat a modern nutrient-depleted diet and live a sedentary lifestyle (**which means most of us**) for protection against heart disease and some cancers. Suggested intakes that are higher than RNIs, but well within safety margins, are as follows:

- Vitamin C, 200mg per day

- Vitamin E (natural), 100mg per day, which is equivalent to 67 IUs, (d-alpha-tocopherol on labels indicates a natural source of vitamin E, not *dl*)

- Beta-carotene, 8–10mg per day

In food terms you would need to eat the following to meet the anti-ageing effect of the above antioxidants. As you can see it is virtually impossible for vitamin E.

Vitamin C, 200mg per day
A normal day's healthy eating could easily provide the above amount if it included a generous glass of orange juice, 1 orange, a medium serving of broccoli and a medium portion of strawberries.

Vitamin E, 100mg per day
50mg a day, only half the amount recommended, is provided by the following menu which would not be easy to follow on a regular basis. To achieve the 50mg of vitamin E the food would have to be prepared with vegetable oils rich in vitamin E such as olive oil or sunflower oil.

Breakfast – nutty muesli and wholemeal toast, with a spread fortified with vitamin E.
Lunch – 100g tuna in oil with a large green mixed salad, dressed with an olive oil vinaigrette, 2 slices wholemeal bread, plus a spread fortified with vitamin E.
Afternoon snack – fruit cake.

Main meal – half an avocado followed by a meat-stuffed red pepper, with carrots and broccoli. *Pudding* – blackberry and apple pie.

Beta-carotene, 8–10mg per day
This is slightly easier to achieve as beta-carotene is widespread in fruit and vegetables. The following menu plan would provide 14mg of beta-carotene.
Breakfast – dried fruit compote (prunes, apricots, peaches, etc.,) and yogurt.
Lunch – poached salmon sandwiches with watercress, glass of orange juice.
Evening meal – lean meat with vegetables, including carrots and spinach. *Pudding* – large slice cantaloupe melon.

Are you older than fifty-one?

If you are, the American National Academy of Science's Institute of Medicine recommends that you consume a maximum of the new US recommended daily allowance of 2.4µg per day of vitamin B_{12} in its synthetic vitamin pill form rather than its food form. This is because surveys have found that up to 30 per cent of people aged fifty-one years and older have what is called protein-bound vitamin B malabsorption. In other words their digestive system is not grabbing the vitamin from foods such as meat. This is due to an age-related reduction in gastric acid secretion and digestive enzyme activity.

Who should take vitamin supplements?

This is an often asked question. The general medical view is that healthy adults eating a healthy diet do not need them, with the following exceptions:

- women planning a pregnancy and during the first trimester of their pregnancy – a daily folic acid supplement of 400μg or 0.4mg
- pregnancy – possibly iron and other nutrients
- vegans – vitamin B₁₂ supplements
- the housebound – possibly vitamin D
- alcoholics – thiamine

RNI: Your Daily Vitamin and Mineral Needs

The reference nutrient intake (RNI) is the amount of a vitamin or mineral thought to be sufficient for each day's needs, even for people with high requirements.

Reference nutrient intakes (adults aged 19–50)

mg = milligrams, μg = micrograms.
The figures in bold indicate the amount for women if requirement differs from men.

Vitamins

Vitamin A	700μg **(600 μg)**
Thiamine (vitamin B₁)	1mg **(0.8mg)**
Riboflavin (vitamin B₂)	1.3mg **(1.1mg)**
Niacin (vitamin B₃)	17mg **(13mg)**
Vitamin B₆	1.4mg **(1.2mg)**
Vitamin B₁₂	1.5μg
Folates	200μg
Vitamin C	40mg
Vitamin D	0 (dietary vitamin D not required)

Minerals

Calcium	700mg
Phosphorus	550mg
Magnesium	300mg **(270 mg)**
Potassium	3,500mg
Chloride	2,500mg
Iron	8.7mg **(14.8mg)**
Zinc	9.5mg **(7mg)**
Copper	1.2mg
Selenium	75µg **(60 µg)**
Iodine	140µg

Safe and adequate daily intakes

Where the government's expert panel felt there was not enough evidence available to set RNIs for other vitamins and minerals, they set a 'safe intake', one judged to be about right for most people's needs, but not so large as to cause undesirable effects.

Vitamins

Pantothenic acid (vitamin B5) – between 3 and 7mg; biotin (vitamin H) – between 10 and 200µg. Vitamin E does not have an RNI. The amount you need depends on the polyunsaturate content of your diet, because vitamin E is principally an antioxidant protecting those fats. Because polyunsaturate intake varies widely it was deemed impossible to set an amount that applied to an average person. However, if you consume the average UK intake of around 6 per cent of your total calories in the form of polyunsaturates, then a safe intake would be more than 4mg per day for men and more than 3mg for women.

The EU recommended daily amount for vitamin E, which applies to labelling laws, is 10mg. Our conservative anti-ageing recommendation is 10 times that amount at 100mg a day, yet still well within safety margins, as no side-effects have been noted in trials using dosages up to 3,200mg per day.

Minerals

Molybdenum – 50–400µg; manganese – more than 1.4mg; chromium – more than 25µg.

Engage brain before popping pills

There is concern among health professionals that those people who choose to treat themselves with vitamin preparations are probably the very people who already eat a good diet and who have the least need for extra nutrients. The vitamins they choose to take may not be those that are inadequate in their diet, and they may also overdose if they take megadosages. Toxic effects can occur with excesses of vitamins B6, A and D. So before you decide to take any supplements think it over carefully and check with a nutritionist or dietitian if possible. It's amazing what we don't know!

Dangers of overdosing

Any book that suggests that you might need to take supplements of vitamins or minerals or other nutrient pills has a responsibility to also let you know the downside (which I think I have done comprehensively!) You should check the amount or dosage of any tablets you are taking with this chart. It contains upper safe levels for daily supplementation. *These are not suggested amounts to take.*

Safety and toxicity chart

Nutrient	Long-term	Short-term
Vitamin A	2,300µg	7,500µg
Vitamin D	10µg	50µg (allowing for a contribution from sunlight)
Vitamin E	800mg	800mg*
Beta-carotene	20mg	20mg*
Thiamine (vitamin B1)	100mg*	100mg*
Riboflavin (vitamin B2)	200mg*	200mg*
Nicotinamide (vitamin B3)	450mg	1,500mg

Nutrient	Long-term	Short-term
Nicotinic acid (niacin)	150mg	500mg
Vitamin B6 (pyridoxine)	100mg	200mg
Folic acid	400µg	700µg
Vitamin B12	3,000µg*	3,000µg*
Biotin (vitamin H)	2,500µg*	2,500µg*
Pantothenic acid (vitamin B5)	1,000mg*	1,000mg*
Vitamin C	2,000mg	3,000mg*
Calcium	1,500mg	1,900mg
Phosphorus	1,500mg	1,500mg
Magnesium	300mg	400mg
Chromium	200µg	300µg*
Copper	5mg	8mg
Iodine	500mg	700mg*
Iron	15mg	80mg
Manganese	15mg	20mg*
Molybdenum	200µg	10,000µg
Selenium	200µg	700µg
Zinc	15mg	50mg**

*   Precautionary amount; no adverse effect has been established.

**   High levels of zinc should be combined with 5mg a day of copper.

Source: Council for Responsible Nutrition.

Pregnancy vitamin warning

Pregnant women should not take vitamin A supplements – in retinol form, beta-carotene is safe, but may not be necessary – because retinol is teratogenic (meaning a substance, agent or process that induces the formation of developmental abnormalities in a foetus) if taken in high amounts just before, or during the early stages of pregnancy. For the same reason, liver should not be eaten during pregnancy because it contains unacceptably high levels of vitamin A.

EU recommended daily amounts

Vitamin and mineral dietary supplements sold in the UK come under EU labelling regulations which stipulate RDAs (recommended daily amounts) for some nutrients. They differ from British RNIs and are considerably lower than the upper limits listed above.

Vitamin A (retinol)	800mg
Beta-carotene	Not established
Thiamine (vitamin B_1)	1.4mg
Riboflavin (vitamin B_2)	1.6mg
Niacin (vitamin B_3)	18mg
Pyridoxine (vitamin B_6)	2mg
Folates	200µg
Vitamin B_{12}	1µg
Biotin (vitamin H)	0.15mg
Pantothenic acid (vitamin B_5)	6mg
Vitamin C	60mg
Vitamin D	5µg
Vitamin E	10mg
Calcium	800mg
Copper	Not established
Iodine	150mg
Iron	14mg
Magnesium	300mg
Molybdenum	Not established
Phosphorus	800mg
Selenium	Not established
Zinc	15mg

Nutrients and their Major Food Sources

To re-emphasise the importance of diet, here are the main food sources for the nutrients you need:

Vitamins

Vitamin A (retinol) – liver, oily fish, offal, milk, butter, egg yolks, margarine, butter, full-fat milk.
Vitamin A is needed for healthy skin structure and mucus-secreting tissues, for eyesight, particularly night vision, healthy skin and growth in children.

Beta-carotene (pro-vitamin A) – orange, red, yellow and dark green vegetables and fruit. A few examples are spinach and broccoli, carrots, apricots, melon, pumpkin.
Beta-carotene can be converted to vitamin A in the body. It also acts as an antioxidant, protecting against cancers.

Vitamin B$_1$ (thiamine) – brown rice, peas, beans and other vegetables, fortified breakfast cereals, and wholemeal breads and cereals, pork, bacon and liver.
Thiamine is needed to transmit messages between brain and spinal cord. It is essential for enzymes that convert food into fuel for the body.

Vitamin B$_2$ (riboflavin) – liver, kidneys, fortified breakfast cereals, meat, milk, some green vegetables, eggs, cheese, yeast extracts.
Essential to make energy available in the body. Riboflavin works with iron, vitamin B$_6$ and folic acid. It is important for skin and eye health.

Vitamin B$_3$ (niacin/nicotinamide/nicotinic acid) – meat, oily fish, poultry, bread, potatoes, breakfast cereals, and can be synthesised from tryptophan (an essential amino acid), a good source of which is the protein in milk and eggs.
Vital for releasing energy from food and into tissues and cells. Helps to maintain a healthy nervous and digestive system. Essential for normal growth and for healthy skin.

Vitamin B$_6$ (pyridoxine) – wholemeal bread, meat (especially liver and pork), fish, bananas, wheat bran and fortified breakfast cereals.

Important in protein metabolism, promotes healthy skin and is essential for the nervous system. Needed for the formation of haemoglobin in red blood cells and for antibodies that help fight infection.

Folates (folic acid) – cooked black-eye beans, Brussels sprouts, beef and yeast extracts, cooked kidney, kale, spinach, spring greens, broccoli and green beans, cooked soya beans, cauliflower, cooked chickpeas, potatoes, iceberg lettuce, oranges, peas, orange juice, parsnips, baked beans, wholemeal bread, cabbage, yogurt, white bread, eggs, brown rice, wholegrain pasta.
Essential for neural tube development during the earliest parts of pregnancy, brain and spinal cord formation.

In addition, folic acid is essential for the formation of red blood cells and helps reduce the levels of an amino acid (homocysteine), to reduce the risk of heart disease.

Vitamin C (ascorbic acid) – oranges and other citrus fruit, blackcurrants, guavas, green peppers and other fruit and vegetables.
An antioxidant able to neutralise potentially damaging free radicals. Helps the white blood cells to fight infection and is essential for wound healing. Also needed for the formation of collagen, for healthy skin, and for the formation of other structural materials in bones, teeth and capillaries. Helps the absorption of iron from plant (non-animal) sources. Keeps the structure of connective tissue, such as that in the skin, healthy. **Bioflavonoids** such as rutin are also found in citrus fruits and blackcurrants.

Vitamin D (cholecalciferol) – cod liver oil, kippers, canned fish, dairy foods, butter and fortified margarine and spreads. Mainly made by the action of sunlight on the skin.
Helps the body absorb and use calcium and phosphorus for strong and healthy bones.

Vitamin E (tocopherol) – seeds and seed oils, fortified margarine, avocado, muesli, nuts, leafy green vegetables,

wheatgerm, wholemeal bread, egg yolks, wholegrain cereals.
An antioxidant vitamin that helps neutralise potentially damaging free radicals in the body. Vitamin E is particularly important for the protection of cell membranes where it prevents the fats being oxidised and giving rise to harmful free radicals, as well as maintaining healthy skin, heart and circulation, nerves, muscles and red blood cells.

Minerals

Calcium – milk, cheese, yogurt, broccoli and other greens, beans (e.g. red kidney beans, baked beans), fortified foods such as white bread, tofu and some other soya foods (e.g. 'milks' and 'yogurts'), sesame seeds, tahini, some mineral water.
Essential for building and maintaining healthy bones, muscle contraction and blood clotting mechanism. Calcium is also essential to build healthy teeth.

Iron – offal, red meat, beef, pork, canned pilchards/sardines, fish, shellfish, wholegrain cereals, eggs, spinach, chicken, leafy green vegetables, fortified breakfast cereals.
Iron deficiency results in anaemia, but before iron intake becomes that low, symptoms of tiredness, lack of concentration and poor mental performance can be attributed to lack of iron. Iron is essential for the daily formation of the haemoglobin that transports oxygen around the body in red blood cells.

Magnesium – green plants. Main dietary sources are unrefined cereals and vegetables, peanuts and wholemeal bread.
Needed for the formation of many enzymes in the body which release energy from food. Vital for the nervous system and muscle movement and for the formation of healthy bones and teeth.

Selenium – brazil nuts, cereals – especially bread, fish, shellfish, liver and other offal, broccoli, pork, cheese, eggs, walnuts, vegetables, fruit.
Provides antioxidant protection of the body cells in con-

junction with vitamin E. Helps maintain the body's defence system: also a component of many enzymes.

Zinc – red meat, liver, shellfish (particularly oysters), pulses, wholemeal bread and other wholegrain cereals, pumpkin seeds.
An important component of many enzymes including superoxide dismutase (a powerful antioxidant enzyme that neutralises potentially damaging free radicals). Required to aid growth, needed for immune cell function and for healthy hair, skin and nails.

CHAPTER THREE

Be Active, Feel Fitter

Psst, middle-aged? Would you like an extra five years' healthy living?

Now that is an offer you cannot refuse, particularly as it comes from a reliable scientific source . . . A survey that followed more than 1,700 men and women through middle age into old age found that those who took up healthy living habits, such as adequate exercise, enjoyed five years' more active life free from disabilities before they died.

The survey started at an average age of forty-three years and continued for thirty years. The researchers found that those who in middle age exercised vigorously for four hours a week, did not smoke and remained slender (fewer than 152 pounds for a man at a height of 5 feet 9 inches; fewer than 131 pounds for a woman at a height of 5 feet 4 inches) were 50 per cent more likely to live into their seventies than sedentary overweight smokers.

Hardly surprising, you may say, but what *is* notable is that those who had the healthy lifestyle habits did not develop minor disabilities such as difficulty with walking, stretching or mobility in general until they were seventy-four. This is compared with the start of disabilities for others in the trial as young as forty-nine!

So, however old you are, even if you have had bad health habits up to now, if you change them you can still reap benefits in the future.

DO something now

If you are really serious about keeping the years at bay, then you should start now. **Being active in combination with Eating to**

Beat your Age is THE key to a longer, healthier and happier life.

For years junk food has been blamed for our health and weight problems, and while it is a factor for some people, it could be that couch potatoes are as bad as French fries in terms of foreshortening an active life. The shocking fact is that only one-third of men and one-fifth of women in the UK are active enough to give themselves some protection against heart disease and stroke, osteoporosis and some types of cancer. The good news is that it is never too late (or too soon) to become more active and to reap the rewards, both now and in a longer, healthier future.

Don't be complacent

Most people just accept that fitness declines with age, but they are wrong. Older people can be as fit as people in their twenties, thirties or forties if they keep active because the old maxim is true: 'If you don't use it you will lose it.' However little you increase your level of physical activity, you will gain some benefit, but generally the more you do the more you will gain. This dose-related response to physical activity is true whether you are thirty or ninety. Whatever your age, regular physical activity at a moderate level (see page 123) improves cardio-respiratory (heart and lung) fitness which results in a lower death rate from all causes.

How being more active beats your age

Paradoxically, exercise rewards you with more energy and improves your stamina so that you can keep going for longer without feeling tired, whatever you are doing. There are many other rewards as well:

Exercise helps you lose weight

- it helps regulate appetite
- done vigorously or intensely enough, it can burn off fat

- it can prevent the gradual weight gain with age that results in middle-age spread
- it can prevent obesity
- it helps keep weight off after a diet
- it tones muscles, giving you a better shape
- it improves posture so that you also look slimmer

Exercise protects you against everyday and age-related health problems

- it improves resistance to infection by stimulating the immune system to produce more white blood cells to fight infections
- it helps build denser bones, preventing osteoporosis (the demineralisation of bones that leads to fracture and breaks, particularly among women older than fifty)
- it helps protect against heart disease, stroke, high blood pressure, maturity-onset diabetes (NIDDM) and some cancers (notably colon and probably breast)
- it improves the health of people who already suffer from heart disease, high blood pressure, mild depression, raised blood cholesterol and anxiety

Exercise makes life easier

- it improves physical strength, flexibility, mobility and suppleness so that you can do everyday activities such as carrying, lifting, cleaning – and partying – without getting so tired

Exercise improves your mood and reduces stress

- it makes you feel good because activity improves your mood and mental health and reduces depression and anxiety
- it combats stress and helps you sleep well, but you should avoid strenuous activity before bed as it may disrupt sleep; a gentle walk is better

How exercise delivers all those benefits

Exercise prevents coronary heart disease   by its effect on blood cholesterol levels. More than thirty major studies of men and women have shown that exercise training is associated with an increase in high density lipoprotein (HDL), the type of blood cholesterol (you will recall) that helps prevent heart disease. HDL transports cholesterol to the liver where it binds up bile and is then carried out of the body by NSP (fibre). This stops cholesterol building up in the arteries. The more regular physical activity you do, the higher your level of protective HDL. Endurance-trained male and female athletes have 20–30 per cent higher levels than healthy sedentary people. There are similar findings for blood pressure: regular physical activity prevents or delays the development of high blood pressure. Exercise reduces blood pressure in people who already have hypertension. And physical activity may also play a protective role against strokes.

Exercise reduces your risk of cancer   Studies consistently show that physical activity is associated with a reduced risk of colon cancer and breast cancer and probably also endometrial, ovarian, prostate and testicular cancers. It may be that physical activity in adolescence and early adulthood offers additional protection against later development of breast cancer. But taking up exercise at any age brings many benefits.

Exercise helps prevent diabetes   We are talking here specifically about the type that strikes in middle age and later. In general, physical activity helps prevent non-insulin-dependent diabetes (NIDDM for short) by increasing sensitivity to insulin. Insulin resistance, rather than not enough insulin, is usually the cause of maturity-onset diabetes.

Another way in which physical activity may prevent or delay the onset of NIDDM is by reducing total body fat and specifically abdominal fat, a known risk factor for insulin resistance. Recent studies have demonstrated that physical training can reduce body fat stores around the tummy (which are also a risk for heart disease).

If you already have NIDDM, becoming more active helps prevent the progression of the disease during the early stages and, in conjunction with diet and often weight loss, can help prevent the need for insulin therapy.

Tip   Even walking can help prevent age-related diabetes. The lowest risk is among the most vigorous exercisers, but women who do not take vigorous exercise but who do some brisk walking (more than three miles per hour) show a lower risk than women who walk at a leisurely pace (less than 2 miles per hour). Half an hour of brisk walking a day should do the trick.

Exercise maintains healthy joints and reduces the risk of osteoarthritis   It is an old wives' tale that taking exercise increases the risk of arthritis and harm to the joints as you age. The opposite is true: physical activity is essential for maintaining the health of joints and (with adequate pain control) appears to be beneficial for controlling the symptoms of arthritis. Perhaps the misunderstanding has arisen because injuries sustained during competitive sports do increase the risk of developing osteoarthritis.

Exercise reduces the risk of osteoporosis   Physical activity is particularly important for women in their thirties when bone demineralisation starts, and around the menopause when they are susceptible to the more rapid decline in bone mass that can lead to osteoporosis. (Taking enough exercise in childhood and early adolescence builds greater bone mass and helps to maintain peak bone mass in adulthood.)

Moderate exercise, in the form of both muscle-strengthening (resistance) and endurance activity, can help slow down bone loss and prevent osteoporosis. But the best activity is weight-bearing exercises such as walking, jogging or running. Although swimming is a good exercise, the water rather than your bones takes your weight, so it should be done in conjunction with other activities.

Osteoporosis, however, is not caused solely by ageing. The menopause, cigarette smoking, inadequate intake of calcium or phyto-oestrogens also have an effect.

Exercise lessens menopausal symptoms
Physical activity can also enhance the beneficial effects of hormone replacement therapy (HRT) in decreasing bone loss after the menopause. Regardless of bone status, physical activity such as muscle-strengthening (resistance) exercise helps protect against falls and fractures with age, probably by increasing muscle strength and improving balance.

Exercise helps you avoid weight gain and obesity   Evidence shows that if you want to lose weight – and keep that weight off – the best way to do it is by incorporating more physical activity into your dieting regime. The aim of many dieters is to improve their body shape, and physical activity will also favourably affect distribution of body fat.

Exercise helps you avoid weight gain with age   For lovers of good food, one of the great benefits of being more active is that it enables you to eat well and lose weight without crash dieting.

If you are fat, you can still be fit

Although obesity can aggravate many health problems and is a risk factor in others, it is more important to be fit than to be thin! Cardio-respiratory (heart and lung) fitness and body fatness were measured with the use of a treadmill in nearly 22,000 men aged between thirty and eighty-three, of whom 428 died over an eight-year follow-up period. All causes of death correlated with poor fitness, irrespective of body fatness, making fitness more important than leanness. Being fit as well as fat may therefore reduce some of the risks associated with obesity.

A Fitness After Forty-Five Program in Baltimore, USA, showed that both lean and obese men who took up exercise (cycling or rowing at moderate intensity for thirty to forty-five minutes three times a week) for six months could eat more (8 per cent and 5 per cent respectively) and not gain weight. The study illustrates that taking up regular exercise can offset the tendency to put on weight with age.

Exercise improves your brain power   A daily jog is also good for the brain as well as building muscles and increasing stamina. Studies show that animals that exercise on treadmills grow more new brain cells than their sedentary counterparts or animals that swim. It may be that vigorous weight-bearing exercise stimulates brain cell production in humans too.

You do need to exercise your brain in other ways, too. Reading and talking are good exercises for the brain! Join, or start, a book- or play-reading circle in your neighbourhood, or among friends to motivate you to do both activities. The extent to which the brain is exercised depends, of course, on what you read. A complex novel with a well-developed plot is more effective than a light romance. A non-fiction book about an area that you are unfamiliar with – genetics, a period in history, space, classical mythology – so long as it interests you, will keep you absorbing and memorising facts. Learning a foreign language is another idea. Memorising telephone numbers of friends or their car registrations are good exercises. Perhaps learn the Latin names of a few common garden plants or trees . . .

Enjoy the feel-good factor   This is not the same thing as the smug smirk often worn by Lycra-clad people leaving the gym with their kitbags slung over their shoulders (although you can rightly feel pleased with yourself if you do manage to fit regular exercise into your life). The feel-good factor is more to do with the biological effects of exercise.

Put yourself in a better mood   Taking exercise increases the concentrations of opiate-like endorphins produced in the brain.

These substances can help to lift your spirits and improve your mood.

Decrease muscle tension, aches and pains The increase in body temperature that results from physical activity may also decrease muscle tension and help you feel more relaxed. Because physical activity also boosts your energy levels and improves mood, it makes you less bothered by everyday aches and pains.

Better mental health Physical activity is known to help in the prevention and treatment of certain types of depression. Other metabolic, hormonal and cardio-respiratory changes that result from physical training are also being studied to see if they have any links with enhanced mental health.

Better quality of life You should also take into consideration the beneficial effect on mental health of just getting away from whatever causes daily stress in your life in order to do something for yourself, such as physical activity. In this way, becoming more active will improve your quality of life and in particular your health-related quality of life. Taking this holistic approach to physical activity shows that being active is just one way to improve your overall satisfaction with life. Activity therefore has a pivotal role in your psychological well-being.

Even if you are compromised by ill health, being a little more active will help you feel better.

Fit for late pregnancies

Keeping fit into their forties is particularly important for women today because they increasingly delay having children until what is technically middle age! In some cases pregnancies, not necessarily the first, are so late in life that women have to cope with babies during their menopause, when they need to be doubly fit. A good diet in pregnancy helps with a speedier return to fitness after the arrival of a baby when compensating for sleep deprivation and lack of energy. And, of

---

course, a well-nourished foetus is less likely to become an under-weight baby, low birth weight increasingly being associated with health problems later in life such as high blood pressure and heart disease.

- Putting off having children may result in a longer life. Studies of fruit flies have shown that reproduction triggers a genetic ageing process. Scientists postulate that it's possible that delaying parenthood may also delay setting off a similar ageing mechanism in people.

To summarise the fitness story so far

Doing any moderate activity for half an hour a day will keep you active for life and boost your energy and self-esteem. It will also help to:

- control body weight
- reduce stress
- develop strength and tone muscles
- improve mood
- prevent osteoporosis
- prevent heart disease
- prevent stroke
- control blood pressure
- improve diabetes
- offset arthritis symptoms
- assist healthy pregnancies among older mothers

Activate Your Fitness

For most of us our daily routine is now sedentary and no longer involves physical effort: most of us do not walk long distances, or carry heavy shopping or coal scuttles; we do not cycle or walk to work, we do not do heavy housework, or dig the allotment or garden, or mow the grass with a manual lawnmower, or scrub the floors, beat the carpets and so on . . . Cars, escalators, electric lawn-mowers and other labour-saving devices mean that we are physically far less active. Far fewer men do manual work. And it's thousands of years since we had to hunt, gather or farm our own food. So it has become necessary to compensate by setting aside time for activity that used to be part of everyday life.

How much exercise and how often?

Thirty minutes of moderate activity on at least five days a week, or half an hour a day, significantly improves your health and well-being.

What is moderate activity?

This means any activity that leaves you feeling warm and makes you breathe more heavily than usual. Examples of moderate activity are brisk walking, an energetic game of golf, lively dancing (salsa, jive, bhangra, ballroom – but not static line dancing), cycling, table tennis, aquacise (exercise class in a swimming pool), rollerblading (or roller skating), heavy DIY (mixing cement), heavy gardening (digging), heavy housework (spring cleaning). It also includes exercise classes and sports such as football, swimming, tennis, aerobics, badminton, volleyball and martial arts, if they are done so that you are not very out of breath or sweating profusely, as this constitutes vigorous activity.

Easy Ways to Become More Active

Make activity part of your everyday life, build it into your daily routine. It could involve:

- walking a couple of bus stops
- parking farther from your work or the shops

- walking instead of sitting in traffic jams
- using the stairs instead of the lift
- washing the car instead of using the car wash
- doing some gardening or some DIY instead of watching television
- spring cleaning the home
- taking a dog (even someone else's) for a walk
- cleaning the windows (instead of paying a window cleaner)
- cancelling the newspaper delivery or milkman and walking to the shops to fetch the paper or milk yourself

Take up a fitness activity

Be realistic about how much you can achieve. Do not join the Early Birds swimming club if you are not able to easily get to the pool between 6.30 and 7.30 a.m. Do not book a fitness class if it is going to be a real rush to get to it and you will miss the start or miss some classes completely. Do not set yourself impossible targets or you will become demotivated and give up. Try to choose activities that you – and your partner or family, if appropriate – will enjoy. Find something that appeals to you, that you think will be fun or will make you new friends or develop your interests. Vary your activities so you don't get bored.

Polish off the pounds

Do your housework with attitude to tone your muscles and improve your heart–lung fitness. If you know a bit about working out, and you are careful about your posture, you can adapt the housework routine to an exercise regime. Instead of bending to pick things up or to load and unload the washing machine or dishwasher, use squat movements to tone bottoms and thighs. Working trunk-twists and turns into wiping work surfaces, and upper arm rotations and flexes into dusting can tone triceps and biceps. Lunges and side leg raises while vacuuming will improve inner thigh and calves. A bit of carpet beating, scrubbing and running up and down stairs to tidy up will all do wonders for weight maintenance. Do your abdominal (tummy) exercises as you lie exhausted on the living room floor while waiting for the kettle to boil.

No Time?

There are lots of ways in everyday life that you can become more active. If you don't think you have time to set aside for exercise, don't despair. Over time, everyday habits can make you fitter and help you lose weight. If the very least you can do is a three-minute walk after every meal, it is still worth it because it amounts to four pounds less body fat annually. Walking up two flights of stairs a day burns off half a pound of body fat in a year. And so on . . . Stay active.

Getting Started with Exercise

Walking

Put your best foot forward and go for a walk. You can do it pretentiously in Lycra and trainers, wearing your personal stereo, or you can put on a pair of hiking boots to support the ankles and feel the training effect by walking up hill and down dale. Alternatively, try walking as though you are late for an appointment (or you can walk to the shops or to work).

Walking is aerobic, and among some of the keep-fit cognoscenti, jogging is seen as passé for its injurious joint-jarring of knees, hips, backs and ankles. While brisk walking is best for fitness and is necessary if you want to improve your stamina, any walking can promote weight loss and stronger bones, and can produce the same short- and long-term benefits as other aerobic sports, albeit to a lesser degree.

One study of London bus conductors and drivers showed that the conductors who walked up and down the bus all day had a significantly lower incidence of heart disease than the bus drivers. Similar studies between postmen and postal clerks who sat all day behind the counter found that the postmen had the healthier hearts.

And a group of septuagenarians, aged between seventy and seventy-nine, walked back to fitness. Those who took walks every day for six months gained the aerobic capacity of fifty-year-olds. Aerobic capacity is the amount of oxygen taken up during exercise; it declines about 1 per cent a year from the age of thirty.

The experiment proved the rejuvenating effects of moderate exercise: in this case, a forty-minute walk three times a week. By becoming more active the seventy-year-olds were able to turn back the clock and reverse their advancing age. But brisk walking, or power walking, is the only way to achieve noticeable training results. You do not have to wiggle your bottom and adopt the ridiculous posture of a race walker, but you do need to **put purpose into your stride** and pump your arms if you want to get fitter for a more fun-packed life.

Warm up for walking   You do not have to do any special stretching, bouncing or other contortions to warm up for walking. Simply walk at a reduced pace for five to eight minutes. This will increase your circulation and breathing and will raise the temperature of the muscles that are going to be worked and that could be damaged if you went into exercise while they were cold.

After five to eight minutes, speed up to the pace you enjoy. Most walkers cruise comfortably at 3½ miles an hour – the speed at which the body was designed to walk. You will even burn off fat if you keep on walking at that speed as a consistent daily physical activity. However, if you want to train your heart and go in for a little cardiovascular conditioning, you can step up the pace on some days to a brisk walk. Doing walks at different paces also adds variety and interest – as does varying the route.

To prevent foot problems regular walkers should invest in some well-cushioned walking shoes, or make sure that there is at least a thumb's width of space in front of the toes. Dust your feet with talcum powder before walking. Moisturise your feet before you go to bed and wear socks with a high cotton or wool content. If you are doing a day's hiking give your feet a breather during the day by taking off your boots and socks for some fresh air. Change your socks midway for extra comfort.

T'ai chi

Even if you are not up to walking any distance, light exercise, such as the Chinese discipline of t'ai chi, may have a beneficial anti-ageing effect. An American study randomly assigned sixty-two sedentary older adults to either moderately intense aerobic exercises or t'ai chi. Unusually for such trials, the majority of participants were women and 45 per cent were black; all had mild hypertension (high blood pressure). After twelve weeks, the t'ai chi and aerobic-exercise groups showed similar significant reductions in blood pressure. As the groups in the study were those that are often under-represented in such trials, it may be possible to draw more general conclusions from these findings than would otherwise be the case, even though the number of participants was small.

Active holidays

Holidays based around activities such as skiing and water sports may seem expensive, but if they are the main holiday of the year they need not be any more expensive than other holidays. Other alternatives are holidays based around tennis, golf, riding – whatever activity or sport you like. The family could take these more active holidays in the UK during the summer when the weather should be kinder to outdoor pursuits. Some holidays combine activity with learning skills, fresh air and friendship (and you do get days off!) For example, holidays centred around cycling, sailing, rambling, guided walking and trekking; or working holidays on farms or with organisations such as the National Trust, building dry stone walls or restoring paths and buildings. Conservation groups offer accommodation and meals in return for 'work' in a pleasant outdoor environment where new skills can be learned. These are all worth considering.

Want something more vigorous?

Vigorous regular exercise is best for weight control. People who take part in intense exercise are leaner than those who exercise at lower intensities. One reason is that they burn off more fat during exercise. They also burn off more calories and their raised metabolic rate continues to burn fat after exercise. Because vigorous exercisers have burned off more calories, they are also less likely to compensate fully for the energy they used than the moderate or low-intensity exercisers so they do not eat more and put on weight. Because they exercise regularly, they probably keep their energy output marginally above expenditure, which results in weight loss.

Check it out

If you have not exercised before, or are a man over forty or a woman over fifty and plan to start strenuous exercise, have a proper fitness assessment and a programme of suitable exercise worked out for you at a local authority class or private club. If you have any health problems, e.g. high blood pressure, back problems or joint pains, or are recovering from an operation/illness, it is definitely safest to check with your GP before you start.

Eating for Energy

Athletes are great starchy-food fans. Most elite athletes eat a high carbohydrate diet for a few days before an endurance event. This is called carbohydrate loading. They also eat a starchy pre-event meal to boost their energy and endurance. The body turns the starches into glucose for use by the brain and for storage in the muscles and as glycogen in the liver. No matter what advertisements linking sugary confectionery to sport say, starches are, as we have seen, a better source of energy than sugar because they contain the fibre, vitamins and minerals missing from sugars.

If you are wondering what relevance carbohydrate loading has for you (most of us are too sedentary to need to practise this), it does apply to everyone after exercise when a starchy snack, as opposed to sugary confectionery or drinks or fatty food, is better at replenishing depleted energy. A banana and some water is a lot less expensive than fashionable sports drinks – and does the job of re-hydrating and boosting energy just as efficiently.

Can snacking *make* you more active?

You have probably gathered by now that the more active you are, the more calories you burn. It has also been observed by scientists (and is also a matter of common sense) that people on very low calorie, crash diets become lethargic and are not very active. Reducing how much they move around is a natural way to preserve their low energy stores – like hibernation.

Interestingly, low levels of physical activity are also seen in 'restrained eaters' and 'gorgers'. And the opposite is seen in very active people. In one study, men who were physically active at work were frequent eaters, i.e. snackers. Putting all these observations together begs the question of whether a pattern of frequent eating or snacking increases activity levels spontaneously. If infrequent eaters and gorgers are physical sloths, then snackers might be seen as the role model for boosting the energy needed to increase physical activity.

When not to exercise

If you are unwell, or recovering from a viral illness such as a cold, or if you are taking painkillers, do not exercise vigorously. Stop straight-away if you ever experience pain in the chest, neck or upper left arm, joint pain, dizziness or faintness, severe breathlessness or exhaustion.

Beginners' Exercise Programme

Take it one step at a time and build up gently. Start slowly, particularly if you have not been active for some years, and stay motivated because even at the start of your new regime little changes can make big differences. Do not be concerned if your schedule does not allow all the time you would like for activity. If thirty minutes on five days a week is daunting, try fifteen minutes, then two lots of fifteen minutes a few times a week and build from there. But stick to the eventual goal of half an hour a day. Try to be a little more active each week. Invest in trainers or other suitable footwear and clothing for the activity you choose.

What are you aiming for?

For exercise to have a training effect on your heart and lungs, that is, to improve cardio-respiratory function which increases your level of fitness, it needs to be aerobic. A safe level at which to take aerobic exercise is to work at around 70 per cent of your maximum heart rate (and 40–60 per cent for moderate activity.) To work out your maximum heart rate, subtract your age in years from 220, which gives you the maximum heart rate in beats per minute for your aerobic sessions. Measure your maximum heart rate by taking your pulse at your neck or wrist. To start with, work to 50 per cent of your maximum capacity. Most modern gym equipment can monitor your heart rate as you work.

Workout programme

Starting out
To improve muscle tone, strength and increase flexibility by using weights or resistance equipment such as bands, tubes or rings:
2–3 x 20-minute sessions a week.

To improve cardiovascular fitness, either using the above workout equipment or skipping, brisk walking or jogging:
3 x 20–30-minute sessions a week.

Building on
To improve muscle tone, strength and increase flexibility by using weights or resistance equipment such as bands, tubes or rings:
3–4 x 20-minute sessions a week.

To improve cardiovascular fitness, either using the above workout equipment or skipping, brisk walking or jogging:
4 x 30–40-minute sessions a week.

When you are fit
To improve muscle tone, strength and increase flexibility by using weights or resistance equipment such as bands, tubes or rings:
4–5 x 30-minute sessions a week.

To improve cardiovascular fitness, either using the above workout equipment or skipping, brisk walking or jogging:
5 x 30–60-minute sessions a week.

The above times are rough guides only. Adjust them to how you feel and the time you have available. Stay at each level for at least twenty-eight days before moving on to the next.

Warm up and cool down

Protect yourself from injury by warming up for eight to ten minutes before beginning a workout or going for a jog. March or jog lightly on the spot or ride an exercise cycle or walk briskly on a running machine for five minutes. Stretch out the upper, middle and lower body after warming up. When you have finished, do not stop abruptly but march on the spot or walk around to cool down and follow this with stretching exercises to prevent sore muscles.

Tips

- Perform each exercise in a slow controlled manner, paying attention to posture and 'style'.
- Work each side of the body equally.
- Exhale through the exertion part of the movement; for example, when lifting weights or on the way up when doing abdominal lifts or on the way down when doing a press-up. Don't hold your breath and remember to breathe in again!
- Avoid locking knees and elbow joints during exercise and when stretching.
- Don't ever 'go for the burn' – work to the point of fatigue, not pain or collapse!

Mix it up

To maintain interest, mix and match pure aerobic sessions with weight or resistance training. This kind of cross-training will ensure overall fitness and that each group of muscles is worked out. Weight or resistance training is important as you age because muscle strength helps to hold back the years. Slowing down or preventing age-associated muscle loss will slow down the rate at which your body deposits fat. The ideal is three sessions a week of strength training doing exercises such as squats while holding weights and using weights to build strength in arm muscles.

See the professionals

Seek professional help from a gym or health club to work out a routine that is tailored to your specific age, ability and needs. Try to have at least one session with a trainer so that you learn to do exercises or use equipment safely. Talk to the trainer about your goals: improved strength or stamina or endurance or cardio-vascular fitness or overall health and fitness. Joining a club or an exercise class can be motivating because your progress can be monitored. You also have the advantage of a range of equipment at your disposal and professional help on hand to check that you are doing the exercises or using the equipment correctly. Most clubs have different challenges and fun activities so you do not lose your incentive or become bored and give up.

Join a class

Exercise classes are also a fun way to take exercise. The teacher or leader of the class does the thinking and you simply follow the workout, with the benefit of their expert advice to correct you when you do not perform a movement safely or effectively. Working as part of a class is very motivating and you will probably find that you work harder and keep going for longer than you would when working on your own.

A system such as Body Pump (details of classes available from Fitpro tel: 0990 133434) is ideal for those seeking a low-impact workout that combines aerobic activity with weights to tone and build strength and increase stamina. You can work at your own level with the weights and there are a variety of ways in which you can do the exercises to suit different abilities and levels of physical flexibility.

Body Combat is a martial arts fitness system that might appeal more to men and is also available from Fitpro.

Get fit at home

Consider buying home fitness equipment if you have the budget and if it is easier for you than travelling to a health club or local authority gym. Much of the professional fitness equipment that is available to health clubs is now sold as home fitness equipment from retailers such as Reebok (tel: 01865 886302 for mail order). The old-fashioned exercise bike now comes in various home-studio cycle models, from basic upright cycles to recumbent cycles with grip pulse and heart rate sensors. You don't even have to plug them in; many are self-powered (you pedal to power both the machine and its electronic display). Cross-trainers, with pedals on which you 'climb' a step or walk at the same time as pushing or pulling on arm poles, allow you to have an upper and lower body workout at the same time with virtually no impact, thus minimising any risk of injuries. There are also running decks or treadmills for home use.

The bottom line is this. If none of the above moves you, look at it this way. If you start doing something now and sustain it, at least you are not going to become any more decrepit than you are already. It's now or NEVER and at your age you need to walk to stand still . . .

Check Out Your Fitness Status

Question 1: What is your attitude to physical activity?

Circle the letter next to the statement which is closest to how you feel about physical activity:

a) I am not very physically active now and I'm too busy to become more active in the near future.
b) I am not very physically active, but I am thinking about increasing the amount of activity I take soon.
c) The amount of activity I take varies; sometimes I am physically active, other times not.
d) I am currently physically active on most days, but I have only begun this pattern within the last six months.
e) I am currently physically active on most days, and have been so for longer than six months
f) A year ago I was physically active on most days, but in the last few months I have been less active.

How active are you?
To answer the next two questions, consider last week (the seven days previous to yesterday). If last week was unusual, for example because you were on holiday, or you couldn't do what you normally do because of illness, think about the most recent typical week.

Question 2: How many times during that week did you do any of the following?

Vigorous physical activity (activity which made you breathe hard or sweat) for at least twenty minutes continuously, e.g. running, squash, vigorous swimming, stair climbing, aerobics, tennis, football, fast cycling, cycling over hilly ground, heavy lifting/carrying, digging.
Times per week (please circle):

0   1   2   3   4   5   6   7   7+

Question 3: How many times during that week did you do any of the following?

Moderate-level physical activity (which made you breathe a bit harder or made you feel warm) for at least thirty minutes (you can count two periods of fifteen minutes' continuous activity, as long as they were on the same day), e.g. brisk walking, easy cycling over flat ground, carrying medium-weight objects, heavy housework (for example, floor scrubbing), dancing, easy swimming, golf, gentle tennis, cricket.
Times per week (please circle):

0   1   2   3   4   5   6   7   7+

How did you score?

If your answer to Question 1 was statement (a) and you circled 2 or less for Question 2 and 4 or less for Question 3:
Then (as you have probably guessed) you are not active enough. Building up to thirty minutes of activity a day will improve your health. There are benefits to being active. You do not need to sweat to help your health. Activity needs to be of a moderate intensity. That means anything which makes you feel warm and breathe slightly more heavily than usual. Every little bit of activity counts. Any activity you can do can help you on the road to a healthier,

active life. Even small bouts of activity, spread throughout the day, will help your health in many ways. Think about becoming more active. Ask yourself if you would really like to be more active. Active people say that activity is Fun; it gives you more energy, helps you sleep, helps you relax and gets you out and about to meet friends. Taking more physical activity is a great way to control stress, improve concentration and feel better about yourself. Go on – think about it now. It will add years to your life and life to your years.

If your answer to Question 1 was statement (b) or statement (c) and you circled 2 or less for Question 2 and 4 or less for Question 3:
You are probably already thinking about becoming more active and you may even feel just about ready to do something about it. But did you realise that probably all you have to do is a little bit more activity, a little more often? The key to success is to choose activities that you enjoy and that are realistic for you. Why not have a go? Try to build up your activity levels. There are lots of ways to do it. Why not use the stairs instead of the lift, walk part or all of the way to work or to the shops? Go for a walk at lunchtime – invite a colleague to go with you for a chat on the way. Start slowly and gradually build up the amount you do. And don't worry: you do not have to be a sporty type. Any activity is better than none. Neither do you need great chunks of time. Have fun increasing your activity level in your daily life.

If your answer to Question 1 was statement (d) and you circled 3 or more for Question 2 and/or 5 or less for Question 3:
Congratulations. You are already on your way to a healthier active life. Now that you have started being active try to build up to doing thirty minutes of moderate activity on most days of the week. Progress slowly – any activity is better than none. Be prepared for setbacks. There will be times when it is difficult to be active, for example when you go on holiday or when you are particularly busy. Don't worry about it, although you could try to plan ahead. For example, think of how you could be more active on holiday. Could you build in more walks and use the car less? Or if you are

busy at work, could you walk some or all the way home? You could also try setting some goals now which are challenging but realistic and achievable. Keep a record of your activity so you can see your progress. Write down your goals, including the type of activity you want to do and for how long. Keep a check on how well you are achieving these. If they are too difficult, don't give up; modify your goals to make them slightly easier before you move on.

You are probably already benefiting from being active by having fun, socialising, feeling less stressed and more energetic. You will probably already be benefiting from better weight control.

If your answer to Question 1 was statement (e) and you circled 3 or more for Question 2 and / or 5 or less for Question 3:
Well done, you are already on the road to an active healthier life. Keep on moving as you are doing. Here are some tips for the times when it is harder to stay active. The main thing is not to worry; look on these times as temporary setbacks and aim to return to being active as soon as possible. You might like to have a Plan B for the times when you cannot pursue your regular exercise regime. For example, if you are on holiday or away from work, plan another activity that you can do instead. Set yourself goals and make them challenging yet achievable. Recognise your successes and congratulate yourself. Give yourself small rewards if these help to keep you motivated. Try to build activity into your social life; this is a good way to stay motivated. Build in reminders to be active around the house, or even the office. If there are no fitness posters around the building – for example, reminding people to use the stairs rather than the lift – suggest that some be introduced. Above all, Stay Active.

If your answer to Question 1 was statement (f) and you circled 2 or less for Question 2 and / or 4 or less for Question 3:
It's a pity that you are no longer as active as you were. But do not worry about it. All sorts of things can interrupt regular activity, such as illness, demands of home or job, the weather, the time of year – or even injury. Try to remember what you liked best about being active. Was it having fun, socialising, reducing stress, having

more energy and better weight control? If your circumstances have changed, you might want to find a new activity rather than readopt a previous activity. Remind yourself that being active is about doing a little more, a little more often. Start again slowly and gradually build up the amount you do until you are back at the level you were, or you have built up to thirty minutes of moderate activity on at least five days a week. Try to choose an activity that you will enjoy, or enjoy going back to. Good luck – and stick with it to stay younger.

CHAPTER FOUR

Don't Gain Weight, Lose Weight

Middle-age spread is not inevitable

For many people, gaining in years is synonymous with gaining in girth. But it need not be so. If you Eat to Beat Your Age and stay active, you will not find yourself arriving at middle age with a spare tyre. However, if you are already there and in possession of one, then Eating to Beat Your Age will help you lose it gradually, safely and permanently.

If you would like to lose weight straightaway, the Anti-Weight-gain Plan on the following pages provides a calorie-counted diet to give you the results you want a bit more quickly.

It is not a crash diet because weight lost that way is almost inevitably regained. It is a plan that will allow you to get a taste for healthy eating. And even if you do not want to lose weight, you can still use it as an Anti-Ageing Eating Plan – just increase the portion sizes (within reason) to suit your appetite or needs.

However, before I unveil the eating plan let's share a few more secrets about the vital links between your body weight and your prospects for a long and active life.

How you put on weight

You know by now that you put on weight if you eat more calories than you use up. The gradual weight gain experienced by most people as

---

they age is slow and steady; it happens gradually and insidiously over a prolonged period. Theoretically, about one pound (or 0.45kg) of fat is stored for each 3,500 kilocalories of excess energy intake.

When you eat food, you use up about 60 per cent of the calories to maintain basic body functions at the body's resting rate. Another 10 per cent is needed for digestion, absorption, transport and deposition of nutrients. The remaining 30 per cent is used for non-resting energy expenditure, primarily in the form of physical activity. It is this third component, non-resting energy expenditure, that you can probably vary the most by becoming more active (see Chapter 3; apologies for bringing the matter up again if you have already decided to become more active).

Tip   Fat is more likely than starchy foods or protein to be laid down as body fat, so getting the balance of your diet right by eating foods in the right proportion, i.e. more starchy foods, fruit and vegetables, and less fat (see Chapter 1), also helps prevent weight gain.

If You Eat Less, Will You Live Longer?

It's a popular idea that being slim and losing a lot of weight by dieting will help you live longer. Several studies (with humans and animals) have led some scientists to claim that the secret of a long and active life is to eat less. Cutting calories by a third to about 1,800 a day is claimed to result in a longer, healthier life. This assumes a calorie intake for the average sedentary adult as shown opposite.

In one American experiment based at the University of California in Los Angeles, a group of eight volunteers lived in a sealed dome called a Biosphere in the Arizona desert. During the period of the experiment, they worked six days a week on the land

| | Calorie intake | |
Age	Men	Women
19–50	2,550	1,940*
51–59	2,550	1,900
60–64	2,380	1,900
65–74	2,330	1,900
75+	2,100	1,810

*Note   Pregnant women need an additional 200 calories per day for the last three months of the pregnancy. An additional 450 extra calories a day are required for the first month of breastfeeding, rising to 570 extra calories a day if breast milk is the baby's only food until it is six months old.

---

to be self-sufficient and restricted their diet to 1,800 calories a day. After two years of this 'Good Life' (without respite to Margo and Jerry's for a quick G & T) all eight had lost weight and had 20 per cent lower blood pressure and lower blood cholesterol levels, plus a 30 per cent lower risk of diabetes. They claimed to experience increased mental clarity and vitality.

But living longer on less may not be as attractive a proposition as it seems (*if*, indeed, it was ever attractive to you). For a start it encourages unnecessary dieting, or excessive weight loss, with the associated health problems. However, the theory has gained credence among some scientists who support the hypothesis that metabolism is linked to longevity (see the Introduction). This decrees that you have a fixed amount of metabolic activity for your life. Metabolism is the process of burning food and oxygen to live. If you systematically eat less, you slow your metabolism and you live for longer, or so the argument goes. Evidence to support this includes the fact that smaller animals have faster metabolic rates and shorter lifespans. Cutting the calorie intake of monkeys results in the monkeys living longer.

Many animal studies support the thesis. Research on mice, rats and fruit flies shows that a 30 per cent cut in calories can lead to a

30 per cent longer life. A 30 per cent reduction in calories in a rhesus monkey's diet can lead to increased levels of HDL (good) cholesterol, which gives a lower risk of heart disease and lower blood pressure. Monkeys on a lower-calorie diet have also shown a slower decline in production of the naturally occurring human growth hormone, DHEA, which is used as a marker of ageing. But it has no proven benefits for humans.

Tip   By the way, taking DHEA as a youth drug is not a good idea. You may see it advertised on the Internet along with melatonin and HGH (human growth hormone) with claims that it can give you everlasting youth, do for you what Viagra does, keep you looking twenty into your seventies and so on. In the UK it is considered to be a medicine so it is not allowed to be sold over the counter as a supplement. The only way you can get it (legally) is if a doctor provides a private prescription – it's not available on the NHS.

The dangers of eating less to live longer

If you are tempted to try this (Margaret Thatcher was reported to practise it by always leaving the table still feeling a little hungry), be very careful. Do not mistake it as legitimisation of dangerous crash diets, or the mainly female practice of smoking to suppress appetite and therefore weight. And do not use it as an excuse to make self-imposed changes to your diet such as skipping meals, avoiding red meat, avoiding sugar, not eating bread, potatoes or other starchy foods.

Self-imposed dietary restrictions can result in:

- an acute dietary shortage of calcium, iron, magnesium, B vitamins and other nutrients, which has serious detrimental effects on physical and mental abilities
- tiredness that does not leave enough energy to be sufficiently

physically active to maintain even a moderate level of fitness
- reduced attention span, poor short-term memory and slow responses caused by anxiety and preoccupation with dieting and body shape
- uncontrolled eating episodes (binges). If you impose a regime of unnatural restrained eating, you will either overeat at subsequent meals or suffer excessive hunger which increases the desire for high-fat foods. High-fat foods are associated with weight problems more than starchy and sugary foods.
- 'night eating syndrome', characterised by skipping meals during the day and bingeing in the evening and at night

Dieting and restrained eating are ultimately ageing

Yo-yo dieting (or weight cycling) can also have an ageing effect on the body. In the long term, intermittent dieting (especially on crash or very low calorie diets of between 600 and 1,000 calories per day), followed by a return to poor eating habits, and usually habitual overeating, causes weight to yo-yo. This sort of on–off dieting is more dangerous to long-term health than being slightly overweight all the time.

Crash diets cause the metabolic rate to drop in a starvation response and weight then tends to be regained more quickly each time the diet is stopped as the body tries to replenish energy stores. The result is that habitual dieters end up heavier than non-dieters.

Warning: Not for mothers and a few others

There are periods in everybody's life when it would be dangerous to restrict food or to diet in any way. This applies particularly to the following groups:

- Pregnant women should not eat less: the nutrition it receives in the uterus affects a baby's health in adult life. Poor nutrition leads

---

> to low birth weight and problems in adulthood such as heart disease and diabetes.
>
> - Women who want to become pregnant should not eat less: fertility decreases with dieting and slightly plumper women are more fertile.
> - Breastfeeding mothers, teenagers, children, the sick, ballerinas and acrobats!
> - Mothers with young daughters: habitual restrained eaters and dieters pass on their bad habits and fads. Eat a normal balanced diet in the company of children and provide them with the same.

Survival of the Fattest?

In fact, the majority of scientific evidence, as I see it, shows that being at your optimal weight, or BMI, even a tad above, but not very overweight or obese, is probably the best for a healthy long life – so long as you are also physically active and on the right side of fit.

Being fashionably thin, with a body mass index or BMI (see page 149) of less than 18, for example, is not a vital ingredient in the elixir of life.

More than 78 per cent of underweight women (with a BMI of 18 or less) die before their eighty-fifth birthday, compared with 72 per cent of obese women (with a BMI of 34–36) and only 65 per cent of plump women (with a BMI of 26–28). In men the figures are similar: life expectancy is lowest in men with the lowest BMI and highest in the medium-to-plump category. More than half of very thin men (with a BMI of 18–19) die before their seventieth birthday, compared with 35 per cent with a BMI of 24–25 and 41 per cent who are obese. The optimal BMI for adults is 20–25.

A low BMI is 'a significant predictor of shortened survival', according to several studies. Of course, it could be argued that a high death rate among people with a low BMI may just be a reflection of the fact that their low BMI is a result of disease or malnutrition. Also that had they been healthy individuals who chose to eat less, then they would have lived longer. But studies that have set out to show the effect of dieting on health conclude, in the main, that whether dieting helps you to live longer depends on how healthy you were before you started dieting.

One study of 43,000 middle-aged (between forty and sixty-four) healthy American women who were not obese showed that they gained little benefit from dieting to their optimal weight. Only middle-aged women with obesity-related health problems showed a decrease in premature death rates if they lost weight.

Go for fat loss, not weight loss

The type of weight lost during dieting is extremely important. It has only recently been realised that among people who are not *very* obese, fat loss is anti-ageing, but general weight loss can increase mortality. This goes against the popular view that associates *any* weight loss with increased health and longevity.

It is fat loss, not weight loss per se, that encourages a longer, healthier life and reduces the risk of premature death. People who lose body fat tend to live longer than those who lose muscle and who are therefore more likely to die earlier.

Researchers studying the body fat changes of around 2,000 people in the Tecumseh Community Health Study and nearly more than 2,700 people in the Framingham Heart Study found that individuals who had lost body fat were less likely to die earlier than those who had lost overall body weight. Yet despite this it still remains true to say that considerable weight gain in later adult life, even over a short period, is not a benign process; it is harmful to health. Avoiding this slow weight gain from youth to middle age is an important anti-ageing tool. Unchecked weight gain is a severe health risk which could lead to obesity, heart disease, diabetes, cancer or other diseases of ageing which restrict the enjoyment of living.

Fitness not fatness predicts survival

So, what should you do? If you are a little overweight, rather than dieting, you will be better off increasing the amount of exercise that you take to get fitter and then any weight you need to lose will gradually disappear, as if by magic!

Middle-aged men, in particular those who are not obese but who are overweight, seem to benefit most from increased physical activity. Women may like to try a bit of behavioural modification and take a healthier attitude to their shape!

If you do have a weight-related problem, such as high blood pressure, insulin resistance or glucose intolerance, its effects can also be mitigated with increased physical activity and fitness, independent of weight loss. Before you embark on any attempt to lose weight you should be aware that lean people are not necessarily at less risk of disease – unless they are also fit. An American study from the Cooper Institute for Aerobics Research in Dallas shows that a low fitness level is a strong predictor of premature death. The study tracked 25,000 men and 7,000 women over eight years. It found that low fitness levels predicted ill health to the same extent as being a smoker.

Anti-Ageing Weight Control – the Best Way to Do it

A low-fat healthy diet packed with flavour to get the taste buds tingling and the senses reeling, and nutrients to slow the ageing process, is the only strategy that really works. In the long term the secret to preventing age-related weight gain is eating that matches your food needs to your lifestyle. Adjust the amount you eat so that energy in and energy out are in balance. This approach positively encourages you to enjoy a wide variety of different foods, each of which has its own health benefits. Getting the balance right has the added benefit of permanent weight loss, albeit at a slower rate than a crash diet, which gets results through temporary loss of water, stored energy or muscle – not fat.

Do not be put off by talk of balanced diets because healthy eating promotes what we all enjoy – tucking into a plate of delicious food. Combine good food with being more active, and the years may stand still . . . for a while.

How much you have to change your food habits to eat healthily and eat the right amount depends, of course, on what and how much you eat now. But you do not have to give up any particular food. Even if you are anxious to lose weight, you should not deny yourself food such as chocolate, sugar or any other food previously thought of as 'bad'. Just eat them in moderation or as treats.

Fatty foods are burned more slowly as you age

Controlling the amount of fat you eat is particularly important for weight control as you age. The ability to burn off fat from a large meal decreases with age. While people aged fifty and over seem able to burn off fat from smaller meals at the same rate as younger people, larger meals present a problem. This might be a further explanation of why people put on weight as they age (it certainly adds to the risk of heart attacks after large meals – see box on page 233).

A Tufts University study has shown that women in their twenties can burn off 246 fat calories from a 1,000 calorie meal, containing 350 calories of fat, compared with only 187 fat calories burned by women aged fifty and over. So the older women will have added 163 calories to their body fat stores, compared with 104 in the younger women.

However, after eating a smaller meal of between 250 and 500 calories, comprising 30 per cent fat, the older women burned off as much fat as the younger women. If the findings are confirmed, this is a persuasive argument for eating several small lower fat meals per day rather than one or two large ones to keep off body fat.

Easy ways to lose fat

- Eat tastier bread that does not require butter to make it edible.
- Eat bread and crackers without butter or margarine with soup, cheese or cold meat.
- Dispense with spread when toast is topped with moist foods like sardines, baked beans, scrambled eggs, hummus and other dips.
- Don't butter bread for sandwiches; add extra salad to the filling for moisture. Top jacket potatoes with low-fat yogurt or fromage frais flavoured with herbs, spices or garlic.
- Don't add butter to cooked vegetables before serving.
- Learn low-fat cooking techniques.
- Choose low-fat staple foods: milk, meat, yogurt and so on.
- Replace fatty snacks with fruit, dried fruit or starchy low-fat snacks.
- Eat more salads (all year round).

Does drinking wine make you fat?

When you drink wine with a meal, do you unconsciously adjust the amount you eat to compensate for the calories in the wine? Or is the net effect a greater calorie intake than if you did not have the wine with the meal? If it is the latter, then it is easy to see how weight gain can occur over time, especially as more and more people drink wine with food more frequently.

Well-conducted food studies have come to different conclusions when trying to answer this, and more research needs to be done to clarify the relationship between alcohol and food intake. Some things, however, are clear. In studies where people have been given an apéritif of wine or beer, they have eaten more at the subsequent meal than when the apéritif did not contain alcohol. Meals also last longer when alcoholic apéritifs are taken – the rate of eating is faster and the duration of eating is longer. Food energy intake is also higher during the following twenty-four hours. So apéritifs are very effective at stimulating and increasing the appetite and food intake which is not compensated for during the rest of the day.

Yet not everyone who habitually takes an apéritif or drinks wine with meals is overweight, which has led some researchers to suggest that not all calories from alcohol are absorbed by the body. However, studies show that the body burns off the calories from alcohol before it burns off other calories, and in particular fat. In fact, alcohol intake promotes body storage of fat. So in this respect alcohol is fattening and ageing.

Snack happy

If snacks are carefully chosen, they can increase your intake of vital nutrients and not just be an additional source of empty calories. Snacking and frequent eating are characteristic of people who are not overweight. While snacking could potentially lead to excess eating, it seems that snacking prevents over-consumption at meals. Main meals tend to be higher in fat than snacks which are most often carbo-hydrate-based; fat is more likely to be turned into body fat than starchy foods. Taking a greater proportion of your calorie intake in the form of starchy snacks can also have a beneficial effect on the ratio of starch to fat in your diet. Spreading out your calorie intake over the day in smaller meals and more frequent snacks might also make you more active (as we saw in Chapter 3). However, choose your snacks carefully. People who frequently snack on sweet and savoury biscuits, cakes, sugar and chocolate confectionery are not necessarily heavier or fatter than others, but they do have a lower intake of the important anti-ageing antioxidant, vitamin C.

Working out your body mass index

About 44 per cent of men and 35 per cent of women in the UK are overweight, which means they have a body mass index (BMI) of 25–30. Ten per cent of adults are obese with a BMI greater than 30. If the trend continues, 18 per cent of men and 24 per cent of women will be obese by the year 2005. The direct health care costs of obesity in the UK are estimated at more than £195 million a year! The annual market for slimming products is £2 billion.

Body mass index (BMI) is a good indication of whether you are the correct weight. To work out your BMI:

1. Measure your height in metres and multiply the figure by itself (see chart below for conversion of imperial to metric).
2. Measure your weight in kilograms.
3. Divide your weight by your height squared (i.e. the answer to Question 1).

Imperial height chart with approximate metric equivalents

4' 10"	1.45m
4' 11"	1.50m
5' 0"	1.52m
5' 1"	1.55m
5' 2"	1.57m
5' 3"	1.60m
5' 4"	1.62m
5' 5"	1.65m
5' 6"	1.68m
5' 7"	1.70m
5' 8"	1.72m
5' 9"	1.74m
5' 10"	1.78m
5' 11"	1.80m
6' 0"	1.82m
6' 1"	1.85m
6' 2"	1.88m
6' 3"	1.90m
6' 4"	1.92m
6' 5"	1.95m
6' 6"	1.98m
6' 7"	2.00m

Check your result against the table below. But before you do, inclusion of this alternative method of working out whether you are the correct weight comes with one more warning not to take it too seriously. Stocky people, and girls up to nineteen years in particular, may appear to be overweight when using this method. So do not be misled. Be honest with yourself: if you are of a stocky build, do not try to lose weight unnecessarily.

Category	BMI Range
Underweight	Less than 20
Ideal	20–25
Overweight; advisable to lose weight if you are under fifty	25–30
You should lose weight	30–40
Definitely too fat; lose weight now	Greater than 40

Even if your BMI falls within the ideal range and you feel you are the right weight, you still need to eat and exercise to beat your age, and to look good and feel even better. Eating to Beat Your Age provides the vitamins, minerals and other substances that allow you to enjoy optimum health and fitness for as long as possible. It also provides the vitamins and minerals needed for a highly tuned immune system that keeps you fighting fit.

Rather than chasing unrealistically low BMIs, it is better to adopt an attitude to food that prevents further weight gain when you are in your forties because people who stay the same weight in middle age live longest and are generally healthier so that they can fully enjoy their longevity. To share the benefits that they experience, aim to weigh the same at age sixty as you did at thirty because weight gain is associated with a shortened life expectancy up to age seventy-five!

Are you an apple or a pear?

As we have seen, health risks (particularly those of heart disease and diabetes) are higher when there is extra fat deposited around the abdomen. We all have an in-built genetic predisposition that determines what basic shape we are: whether the essential fat on our bodies is deposited around hips, breasts and upper arms (the case for most women) so that they are pear-shaped, or whether the excess fat deposited is abdominal (on tummies) so that most men and some women are apple-shaped.

If you are apple-shaped and you become overweight you are at greater risk of heart disease and diabetes than pear-shaped people. If in a moment of idle curiosity, or just for the fun of it, you would like to find out whether you are an apple or a pear, read on.

Assess your waist-to-hip ratio
Measure your waist and hips. Divide the waist measurement by the hip measurement to get your waist–hip ratio. For example, if your waist is 86cm (34in) and your hips 102cm (40in), your waist–hip ratio will be 86 divided by $102 = 0.84$. The ratio should be less than 0.95 in men and less than 0.87 in women.

- There is another rule of thumb as far as waist measurements are concerned. If a man's waist measures more than 94cm (37in), or a woman's 80cm (31in), they are categorised by some doctors as overweight. Waists do thicken with age, a phenomenon often referred to as middle-age spread. If you are younger and already have such a spare tyre – act now! It is this abdominal fat that increases the risk of heart disease and diabetes.

Your waist can interfere with your lungs

Did you know that your spare tyre could interfere with your lung function? An eight-year study at a London hospital revealed that men and women who put on weight and acquired middle-age spread between the ages of thirty-two and fifty-nine compromised their breathing. Body-fat stores around the waist seem to be responsible for their poorer lung function.

What all this amounts to is that the more overweight you are, the younger you will be when disease strikes. There is, for example, a direct relationship between weight and the age at which heart disease begins.

On the other side of the equation, or scale, if you go too far with weight loss, your lightness of being will have serious ageing consequences.

The way to longevity is the middle way. This will be very heartening news to most of you because simply staying within your BMI range gives you freedom from fashionable thinness and diets. It puts the emphasis on being more physically active and on living life to the full. See the next chapter . . .

The Anti-Weight-Gain Plan

This is a diet designed to Beat Your Age *and* your weight. Here's how it works:

It's very simple:

Women who want to lose weight   should choose one breakfast, one lunch, one evening meal and one snack per day.

Women who want to follow a healthy anti-ageing eating plan   should choose

Either breakfast – 2 servings, lunch – 2 servings, evening meal – 1 serving, plus 3 snacks a day;
Or one breakfast, one lunch, evening meal – 2 servings, plus 3 snacks a day.

Men who want to lose weight   should choose one breakfast, lunch – 2 servings, one evening meal – 1 ½ servings, plus 1 snack per day.

Men who want to follow a healthy anti-ageing eating plan should choose

Either breakfast – 2 servings, lunch – 2 servings, evening meal – 2 servings, plus 1 snack and 1 special snack a day;
Or choose one breakfast, lunch – 2 servings, evening meal – 2 servings, plus 1 snack and 2 special snacks a day.

Before you start

- Try not to rely on the same meal every day! The more varied your diet, the more varied your nutritional intake and the greater the ability of your food to make an anti-ageing contribution to the way you look and feel.
- Follow the plan for up to four weeks (twenty-eight days), then take a break.
- Take eight drinks (non-alcoholic) a day. Make as many of the drinks as you can water and diluted fruit juice.
- Keep tea and coffee to a minimum (try herb or fruit teas). All drinks are taken without sugar. Use skimmed milk, if required, in hot drinks.
- Slices of bread are medium-thick from a large loaf.
- No spread or salad dressings are to be eaten, unless stipulated.
- Fruit juice is unsweetened, e.g. orange, apple, grapefruit, pineapple, tomato. A glass is 125ml/4fl oz.
- If it suits your lifestyle, you can of course eat the meals listed as evening meals for lunch and vice versa.
- The lists of recommended snacks are on pp. 190–92.

Alcohol
While wine and beer and other drinks might have a place in your normal healthy eating plan, they are not built into the weight loss programme because nutritional quality of food is paramount when quantity is reduced.

How much weight will you lose?

Assuming your body uses just under 2,000 calories a day if you are a woman or around 2,500 if you are a man, then after a week on the *Eat to Beat Your Age* Anti-Weight-Gain Plan, which provides 1,800 calories per day for men and 1,200 calories per day for women, you will have lost more than 5,000 calories, the equivalent of more than 0.5kg or nearly 1 ½lb of fat.

Add to that the usual water loss that occurs during the first week of a diet and the amount could double to around 3kg or 6 ½lb weight loss.

After the first week you can expect to lose a further 0.5kg or around 1 ½lb of fat a week – and more if you increase the amount of physical activity you take.

In a month you could lose between 5 and 6kg or 11 lb to 1 stone. Again, it's worth emphasising that this is not crash dieting. **Weight lost at this moderate – but effective – speed is permanent, provided you continue on broadly the *Eat to Beat Your Age* lifestyle lines after the diet**.

Achieving this weight loss on 1,200 or 1,800 calories a day is the least painful way to lose weight, too.

Should you ever feel the need to return to the Anti-Weight-Gain Plan, it is safe to do so.

Breakfast Bar

Choose one breakfast each day.
All breakfasts also include:

* 1 glass of water, with twist of lemon if liked
* 1 glass (115–125ml = 1 wine glass) of fruit juice

Tea, coffee, or fruit/herb teas as liked; use skimmed milk where required.

1. 1 cereal or breakfast substitute bar, 1 apple.
2. Half a grapefruit, 4 ready-to-eat prunes, 1 small pot of

low-fat natural/vanilla yogurt, 1 slice of toast with a scraping of low-fat spread and 2 tsp preserve.

3. Half a papaya sprinkled with fresh lime juice, 100g/3½oz (8–10) strawberries, 1 slice of toast with a scraping of low-fat spread and 2 tsp preserve.

4. Fruit Smoothie drink – combine 150ml/¼ pint low-fat plain yogurt, 150ml/5fl oz orange juice, 1 small ripe banana. Liquidise together. Make just before serving.

5. 1 wholemeal hot-cross bun or similar spiced fruit bun, toasted, with a scraping of low-fat spread, 2 tbsp serving of fruit compote (made with fresh or dried fruit).

6. 1 grilled sausage, 75g/3oz baked beans, 1 grilled beafsteak tomato.

7. 2 slices wholemeal toast with a scraping of low-fat spread and Marmite.

8. 25g/1oz whole wheat or bran flakes or Shredded Wheat or whole wheat breakfast biscuit (e.g. Weetabix) with half a small banana or 4 prunes, and 125ml/4fl oz skimmed milk.

9. 1 wholemeal muffin with 10g/2 tsp polyunsaturated margarine/butter and 2 tsp preserve.

10. 1 low-fat natural yogurt poured over chopped fruit: (e.g. 1 small pear and 1 apple), 1 slice of toast with a scraping of low-fat spread and 2 tsp preserve.

11. Porridge made with 40g/1½oz porridge oats or oatmeal, 150ml/¼ pint skimmed milk, served with extra milk, if liked, and 1 tsp honey or equivalent to sweeten.

12. 115g/4oz dried fruit compote and 1 small pot vanilla/natural low-fat yogurt.

13. 1 reduced-fat croissant with 1 tsp preserve (no spread).

14. 1 poached egg on 1 slice wholemeal toast (no spread).

15. 1 wholemeal fruit scone with 1 tbsp Greek yogurt and 2 tsp jam.

16. 1 blueberry muffin (90 per cent fat-free variety).

17. 1 slice wholemeal toast with 1 grilled rasher lean bacon and 1 large sliced/grilled tomato.

18. 1 scrambled egg (no fat, a little milk if necessary) on 1 slice

wholemeal toast (no spread), 1 grilled beefsteak tomato or 10 cherry tomatoes.

19. 1 generous slice cantaloupe melon with 8–10 fresh strawberries or 100g/3½oz raspberries or blueberries or mixture of both, plus 1 slice toast with scraping of low-fat spread and 2 tsp preserve.
20. 1 Savoury Breakfast Croissant (see recipe) – no spread.
21. 1 Carrot and Raisin Muffin (see recipe).
22. Home-made Hazelnut Muesli (see recipe), 1 slice of toast, spread with 10g/2 tsp margarine and 2 tsp preserve.

Recipes

- Use organic ingredients wherever possible.
- Flour is plain, white and unbleached unless stated otherwise.
- Eggs are medium in size (if organic are unavailable, use free-range).
- Teaspoon and tablespoon measures are level for baking powder, cornflour and liquids. Elsewhere please indulge your personal preferences. For example, if you particularly like the flavour of ground cinnamon, ginger or mustard then make it a rounded teaspoonful (or two, according to the recipe). If you are trying to lose weight, use level spoon measures of high-calorie ingredients such as sugar, redcurrant jelly or sunflower seeds.

Breakfast Bar Recipes

Savoury Breakfast Croissant

(makes 16)

450g/lb white flour
115g/4oz each wholemeal flour and polenta (maize meal/flour)
1 sachet or 3 level tsp dried yeast
284ml/½ pint buttermilk (or milk soured with a few drops of lemon juice)

75ml/2½fl oz water
30ml/2 tbsp sunflower oil
150g/5oz matured cheddar, grated
75g/3oz pine kernels or sunflower seeds, lightly toasted

Mix the flours in a bowl and stir in the yeast. Heat the buttermilk until it is lukewarm and stir into the flours with the water, oil and cheese. Knead on a floured surface for 10 minutes. If the dough seems dry, add a little more water, warmed to the same temperature as the milk. Place the dough in a bowl and cover. Leave in a draught-free warm place for 40 minutes to double in size. Knead again for 2–3 minutes, kneading in the pine kernels or sunflower seeds. Cut the dough in half and roll out each half to a circle. Cut into eight segments (like the spokes of a wheel). Roll each segment from the broad outer edge towards the central point to make the croissants. Place on two greased baking trays. Cover and leave as before for 30 minutes until doubled in size. Brush with single cream or milk or lightly beaten egg and bake for 15 minutes in an oven preheated to 200°C/400°F/Gas Mark 6. When cold, freeze those that are not wanted at once, or store in an airtight container for 2 days.

Carrot and Raisin Muffins

(makes 10)

200g/7oz white flour
3 tsp baking powder
1 tsp cinnamon
55g/2oz ground almonds
55g/2oz muscovado sugar
100g/3½oz raisins
1 carrot, grated
2 eggs
45ml/3 tbsp sunflower oil
120ml/4fl oz skimmed milk

Sift the flour, baking powder, cinnamon, ground almonds and sugar into a bowl. Add the raisins and carrot, making sure they are coated with the dry ingredients to stop them sticking together. Stir in the lightly beaten eggs, oil and milk. Line a muffin pan with 10 paper muffin cases and spoon in the batter. Bake in a preheated oven at 190°C/375°F/Gas Mark 5 for 25 minutes or until well risen and an inserted skewer comes out clean. When cold, freeze those that are not wanted at once, or store in an airtight container for 2 days.

Hazelnut Muesli

(1 serving)

1 tbsp rolled oats
4 hazelnuts, chopped
1 tsp sunflower seeds
150ml/ ¼ pint apple juice
half an eating apple, grated

Mix the dry ingredients and place in a cereal bowl. Stir in the apple juice, cover and leave to soften and soak in the fridge, or a cool place, overnight. In the morning stir in the grated apple. Add more apple juice to taste.

Eat soup for lunch when slimming

Drinking a couple of glasses of water before a meal is an old slimming trick to help fill you up for fewer calories. Eating foods with a high water content reduces the calorie content of the meal and, in the case of a food like soup, also helps fill you up. Don't forget, though, that 'cream of' and 'creamed' soups may have a high fat and therefore high calorie content.

Lunch Bar

Choose one lunch each day
All lunches also include 1 piece of fruit, unless stated otherwise.

- Sandwiches are made from 2 slices of thick-cut wholemeal bread, but can be varied with other wholegrain breads on occasion, as preferred.

- Tea, coffee or fruit/herb teas as liked; use skimmed milk where required.

1. Tuna sandwiches – filled with 75g/3oz tuna canned in water (drained), quarter of a red/green pepper (seeded and chopped), 25g/1oz cooked sweetcorn kernels.
2. Half a carton of soup (e.g. carrot, pumpkin, tomato, bean), 1 wholemeal roll, 1 low-fat fruit yogurt.
3. 2 taco shells filled with mixed salad, 25g/1oz grated cheddar cheese, 55g/2oz canned beans.
4. 1 ready meal of your choice, not more than 350 calories, e.g. Lean Cuisine (Findus) and Weight Watchers frozen ranges or supermarket chilled/frozen convenience meals.
5. 75g/3oz reduced-fat hummus, 2 pieces crispbread, large assortment of crudités (raw vegetables) for dipping into the hummus.
6. Egg sandwiches – filled with 1 hard-boiled egg, mashed with 1 tsp low-calorie mayonnaise, seasoning and 25g/1oz chopped watercress, with green salad or raw carrots to serve.
7. Quarter of a ciabatta loaf, topped or filled with 40g/1½oz reduced-fat mozzarella, 1 sliced tomato and shredded basil leaves.
8. Sardines on toast – half a can of sardines in tomato sauce on 1 slice of toast, served with watercress and orange salad (no dressing).
9. Avocado salad – half an avocado, sliced, on a large bed of

mixed salad, topped with 3 drained anchovy fillets, 1 wholemeal roll.

10. 1 small slice wholemeal quiche with green salad (no dressing).

11. Ham salad – 55g/2oz sliced ham with a large mixed salad.

12. Crunchy pitta parcels – 1 wholemeal pitta bread, filled with a quarter of an apple, 1 stick celery, 55g/2oz grapes, half a carrot, all diced, and bound together with 1 tbsp reduced-calorie mayonnaise and 1 tbsp grated cheddar.

13. Waldorf baked potato – half a medium baked potato, topped with Waldorf salad – half an apple, ½ tsp lemon juice, 1 stick celery, 25g/1oz walnuts, shredded lettuce, all bound together with thick-set natural yogurt flavoured with fresh herbs.

14. Californian walnut salad – iceberg lettuce, spinach leaves, tossed in oil-free salad dressing, topped with 25g/1oz walnut pieces, 3 fresh dates, stoned and chopped, or 25g/1oz raisins.

15. Prawns on rye – 2 thin slices pumpernickel bread, topped with 100g/3½oz shelled cooked prawns, 1 sliced baby beetroot, diced cucumber and 1 spring onion.

16. 3 slices Parma ham (prosciutto), 1 large fresh fig, 1 generous slice cantaloupe melon, quarter of a ciabatta loaf.

17. Greek baked potato – 1 medium baked potato, topped with 40g/1½oz feta cheese and 1 tomato, both diced and mixed with 3 black olives, served with grated carrot and sliced cucumber.

18. Omelette – 2-egg omelette filled with 2 tbsp peas, 1 tbsp cooked spinach, 1 tbsp grated Parmesan, served with 3 new potatoes and 1 grilled beefsteak tomato.

19. Grilled trout – 1 trout fillet, grilled and served with 3 new potatoes and 2 portions of other vegetables of choice.

20. Grilled chicken – 1 small chicken breast, grilled and skin discarded, served with 3 new potatoes and 2 portions of other vegetables of choice.

21. Grilled mackerel – 1 mackerel fillet, grilled and served with 3 new potatoes and 2 portions of other vegetables of choice.

22. Italian Pasta Soup (see recipe).

23. Mozzarella and Tomato Coulis Salad (see recipe), with 2 crispbreads.

Lunch Bar Recipes

Italian Pasta Soup

(1 serving)

1 stick celery, diced
half an onion, diced
1 clove garlic, crushed
1 rasher lean back bacon, diced
200g/7oz can chopped tomatoes
150ml/¼ pint vegetable stock or water
55g/2oz pasta shells
1 small carrot, grated
fresh parsley, chopped
15g/½oz Parmesan, grated

Place the celery, onion, garlic and bacon in a pan, cover and sweat for about 3 minutes, stirring to prevent sticking. Add the tomatoes and stock and cook for 10 minutes. Add the pasta and cook until al dente (cooked but still firm). Remove from heat, stir in carrot and parsley. Sprinkle Parmesan at table.

Mozzarella and Tomato Coulis Salad

(1 serving)

55g/2oz reduced-fat mozzarella, thinly sliced
2 ripe flavourful tomatoes
fresh basil leaves
freshly ground black pepper
2 ripe tomatoes, skinned
1 tsp olive oil
1 tsp white wine vinegar

Arrange the cheese, tomatoes and torn basil leaves on a dish and season. Liquidise the skinned tomatoes, add the oil and vinegar and pour over the salad. Garnish with more basil.

Main Meal

Choose one of the following meals each day.

1. Gammon steak with Spiced Red Cabbage (see recipe)
    1 gammon steak (150g/5oz), grilled
    1 small portion boiled potatoes (115g/4oz)
    Pudding: Fruit Brûlée or Yellow Fruit Bake (see recipes)

2. Bumper Burger (see recipe)
    1 small burger bun
    1 mixed green-leaf salad, no dressing
    half a carton reduced-calorie coleslaw
    Pudding: 2 scoops fruit sorbet

3. Chicken Chop Suey (see recipe)
    Pudding: fresh fruit salad (in fruit juice, not heavy syrup)

4. Super Salmon Fish Cakes (see recipe)
    1 portion each of green beans, carrots and peas
    3 new potatoes
    Pudding: fresh fruit salad (in fruit juice, not heavy syrup)

5. Chicken Tikka (see recipe)
    1 portion Spicy Potatoes (see recipe)
    1 generous tbsp mango chutney
    Pudding: 2 scoops fruit sorbet

6. Pork Kofte Kebabs (see recipe)
    Medium portion boiled brown rice (175g/6oz)
    1 large mixed salad
    Pudding: fresh fruit salad (in fruit juice, not heavy syrup)

7. Caramelised Pork and Apples with Spinach Mash (see recipe)

8. Cheese and Spinach Soufflé (see recipe)
   1 large mixed salad
   Pudding: Fruit Brûlée or Yellow Fruit Bake (see recipes)

9. Simple Prawn Curry (see recipe)
   1 poppadom
   1 tbsp Indian relish/chutney
   1 portion Spicy Potatoes (see recipe)
   Pudding: fresh fruit salad (in fruit juice, not heavy syrup)

10. Potato Gnocchi in Tomato Sauce (see recipe)
    2 generous portions vegetables (other than potatoes)
    Pudding: 2 scoops fruit sorbet

11. Salmon Kedgeree (see recipe)
    Pudding: 1 piece of fruit

12. Minestrone (see recipe)
    1 slice French wholemeal stick (7.5cm/3in)

13. Meatballs with Red Pepper Sauce (see recipe)
    2 tbsp peas
    3 tbsp boiled rice

14. Chicken in Tomato Sauce (see recipe)
    1 medium portion (100g/3½oz) spinach
    1 red pepper, char-grilled
    3 tbsp boiled rice
    Pudding: Fruit Brûlée or Yellow Fruit Bake (see recipes)

15. Bouillabaisse (see recipe)
    1 medium slice French bread (7.5cm/3in)

16. Marinated Swedish Herring (see recipe)
    4 new potatoes, boiled and garnished with chopped dill
    2 small beetroot, boiled
    Pudding: Carrot and Raisin Muffin (see Breakfast Bar
    recipes), warmed, with 1 tbsp half-fat crème fraiche

17. Bagna Cauda (see recipe)
    Pudding: 1 piece of fruit

18. Thai Hot and Sour Soup (see recipe)
    Thai Prawn Salad (see recipe)
    2 prawn crackers

19. Salmon Steak with Pesto Crust (see recipe)
    3 medium portions vegetables (other than potatoes)

20. Eastern Fish Cakes (see recipe)
    2 portions green vegetables
    3 tbsp boiled rice
    Pudding: 1 amaretti biscuit with strawberries

21. Sweet and Sour Pork Stir-Fry (see recipe)
    4 tbsp boiled rice
    Pudding: 1 individual fruit yogurt and 1 Jaffa Cake

22. Seared Hot Tuna Niçoise 'Salad' (see recipe)

23. Pissaladière (see recipe)
    1 large mixed salad
    1 red pepper, char-grilled
    Pudding: 1 piece of fruit

24. Goan Fish Stew (see recipe)
    4 tbsp boiled rice
    1 generous portion green vegetables

25. Vegetable Risotto (see recipe)
    Pudding: Fruit Brûlée or Yellow Fruit Bake (see recipes)

26. Hash Brown Beanies and Spicy Tomato Sauce (see recipes)
    2 Hash Brown Beanies per person
    2 medium portions vegetables (other than potatoes)

27. Mediterranean Vegetable Pie (see recipe)
    150g/5oz portion boiled potatoes
    Pudding: Fruit Brûlée or Yellow Fruit Bake (see recipes)

28. Spinach Lasagne (see recipe)
    Pudding: Fruit Brûlée (see recipe)

29. Barbary Duck Breast Salad with Tabbouleh (see recipes)
    1 large pitta bread
    Pudding: Yellow Fruit Bake (see recipe)

Main Meal Recipes

Spiced Red Cabbage

(4 portions)

half a medium red cabbage
2 dessert apples, peeled and sliced
115g/4oz raisins
2 tbsp demerara sugar
4 tbsp red wine vinegar
3 tbsp redcurrant jelly
6 tbsp water
3 cloves
1 tsp ground cinnamon

Preheat the oven to 180°C/350°F/Gas Mark 4. Slice the cabbage, cutting away the stalk, and wash well. Put all the ingredients into a 25cm/10in ovenproof dish and pack down well. Cover with a lid and bake for 1 hour, stirring every 20 minutes or so until cabbage and apples are soft. Alternatively, cook in a saucepan with a well-fitting lid over a gentle heat, stirring occasionally to prevent sticking. Season to taste.

Bumper Burgers

(1 portion)

225g/8oz very lean minced meat (beef, lamb, chicken)
1 onion, diced
1 tomato, chopped
1 small carrot, grated
1 tsp ready-made mustard
freshly ground black pepper

Put all the ingredients in a bowl and mix well, or for a finer mixture blend in a food processor. Form into one large bumper burger. Grill for about 8 minutes each side.

Chicken Chop Suey

(3 portions)

150g/5oz noodles
45ml/3 tbsp vegetable oil
400g/14oz chicken, cut into thin strips
2 tsp cornflour
100ml/3½fl oz soy sauce
¼ tsp ground ginger
15ml/1tbsp wine vinegar
juice of 1 orange
150ml/¼ pint water
200g/7oz pak choi leaves, shredded
200g/7oz bean sprouts
4 spring onions, sliced
225g/8oz canned bamboo shoots or water chestnuts,
sliced thinly

Put the noodles on to boil or steam. Drain when cooked, cover and keep warm. Heat 2 tbsp of the oil in a wok or a large pan and fry the chicken for 7 minutes. Mix together the cornflour, soy sauce, ginger, vinegar, orange juice, water and the rest of the oil to make a smooth paste. Add the vegetables and the paste to the pan and continue cooking, stirring occasionally, for another 5 minutes. Mix in the noodles and serve at once.

Super Salmon Fish Cakes

(3 portions)

350g/12oz salmon fillet
250g/9oz cold boiled potatoes
1 tbsp fresh dill, chopped
1 tbsp reduced-fat mayonnaise
seasoning
55g/2oz fine breadcrumbs
1 tbsp oil for frying

Put the salmon in a saucepan with almost enough water to cover. Bring to simmering point and poach for 5 minutes. Drain and when cool enough to handle, flake the fish from the skin and bones. Mash the fish with the potato, dill, mayonnaise and seasoning and form the mixture into 3 fish cakes. Roll in the breadcrumbs and fry lightly in the oil for 4 minutes on each side. Serve at once.

Chicken Tikka

(3 portions)

2.5cm/1in piece fresh root ginger, peeled and grated
2 cloves garlic, crushed
15ml/1 tbsp lemon juice
1 red chilli, deseeded and chopped finely
115g/4oz natural Greek yogurt
½ tsp turmeric

1 tsp ground coriander
1 tsp ground cumin
450g/1lb skinless chicken breast, boned and cubed

Mix the ginger, garlic, lemon juice and chilli to a paste. Stir into the yogurt with the spices. Put the chicken in a bowl, cover with the paste and stir well. Leave covered in the fridge for several hours. Preheat the oven to 180°C/350°F/Gas Mark 4 and oil a baking tin. Spoon the chicken into the tin and bake for 20 minutes, turning once or twice to cook evenly. Alternatively, grill on skewers for 15 minutes, turning occasionally.

Spicy Potatoes

(3 portions)

450g/1lb potatoes, washed
15ml/1 tbsp vegetable oil
1 onion, diced
4 tomatoes, skinned and chopped
30ml/2 tbsp curry paste
2 tbsp fresh coriander leaves, chopped

Boil the potatoes whole in their skins for 10 minutes. Drain. Put the oil in a pan. Add the onion, tomatoes and curry paste. Cover and cook over a high heat for 10 minutes. Stir occasionally. Chop the potatoes and add to the pan. Cover and cook on a low heat for 10 minutes, being careful not to overcook. Remove from the heat and stir in the coriander leaves.

Pork Kofte Kebabs

(3 kebabs)

225g/8oz ground lean pork
1 onion, chopped
1 clove garlic, peeled and crushed

1 chilli, deseeded and chopped
2 tsp tomato purée
half a packet fresh coriander leaves, chopped
half a packet fresh parsley, chopped
24 cherry tomatoes
1 red pepper, deseeded and cut into bite-sized pieces

Put all the ingredients (except tomatoes and red pepper) in a food processor or mixing bowl and combine well. Form the meat paste into balls and arrange on 3 skewers alternately with the cherry tomatoes and red pepper. Cover the kebabs and refrigerate until needed. Grill or barbecue under a high heat for 10–15 minutes, turning frequently.

Tip   To soften red peppers before cooking, either halve and char-grill, peeling off the skin when blackened, or microwave in a covered dish for 4–5 minutes.

Caramelised Pork and Apples with Spinach Mash

(3 portions)

500g/1lb 2oz potatoes, peeled and chopped
225g/8oz fresh spinach leaves
22.5ml/1½ tbsp extra-virgin olive oil
10ml/2 tsp lemon juice
3 green dessert apples (e.g. Granny Smith, Golden Delicious
25g/1oz butter
55g/2oz demerara sugar
1 large leek, washed and cut into thin strips about 7.5cm/3in
450g/1lb pork tenderloin
2 tbsp plain white flour
seasoning

Boil the potatoes until tender. Wash the spinach thoroughly and put in a pan. Cover without adding water and cook for 3–4 minutes. Drain. While the potatoes and spinach are cooking, quarter and core the apples (no need to peel) and cut each quarter into 4 slices. Drain the potatoes, reserving 50ml/2fl oz of cooking water, and mash the potatoes with the reserved water, olive oil and lemon juice. Season to taste and stir the spinach lightly into the mash to give a thick marbling effect. Melt the butter and sugar in a wok. Add the apples and leeks and cook over a moderate heat for 5 minutes, stirring well until the apples are browned and slightly softened. Slice the tenderloin into about 12 medallions and toss in the seasoned flour. Add to the apples and leeks in the pan and cook for a further 7 minutes, turning once or twice. Add 50ml/2fl oz hot stock or water and stir well to thicken. Serve at once.

Cheese and Spinach Soufflé

(3 portions)

45ml/2 tbsp olive oil
40g/1 ½oz white flour
450ml/16fl oz skimmed milk
75g/3oz Gruyère, grated
225g/8oz frozen spinach, defrosted and drained
3 eggs, separated
freshly grated nutmeg
freshly ground black pepper

Oil a 16.5cm/6 ½in soufflé dish and dust with flour. Heat the oven to 200°C/400°F/Gas Mark 6. Stir the oil and flour in a saucepan over a moderate heat to make a smooth paste. Gradually whisk in the milk to make a smooth sauce. Stir in the cheese and spinach. Remove from the heat and cool slightly. Beat in the egg yolks and season to taste with nutmeg and pepper. In a clean bowl, whisk the egg whites until stiff but not dry. Fold the whites into the soufflé mixture. Pour into the prepared dish. Bake for 30–35 mins until well risen and an inserted skewer comes out clean.

Simple Prawn Curry

(3 portions)

2 onions, diced
2–3 cloves garlic, crushed
2 green chillies, deseeded and diced
22.5ml/1½ tbsp vegetable oil
500g/1lb 2oz large ripe tomatoes, skinned and chopped
1 tsp ground cumin
1 tsp ground coriander
350g/12oz cooked peeled prawns

Sauté the onion, garlic and chillies in the oil for a good 5 minutes. Add the tomatoes and spices and cook for a further 10 minutes at a moderate heat to break down the tomatoes. Stir in the prawns and cook for a further 5 minutes over a gentle heat. Serve at once.

Potato Gnocchi in Tomato Sauce

(3 portions)

For the gnocchi
675g/1½lb potatoes, peeled
115g/4oz plain flour
half an egg, lightly beaten
15ml/1 tbsp olive oil
2 tbsp Parmesan, freshly grated

For the tomato sauce
15ml/1 tbsp olive oil
1 medium onion, chopped
1 clove garlic, crushed
400g/14oz canned tomatoes, chopped
15ml/1tbsp tomato purée
1 tbsp fresh basil, chopped
1 tbsp fresh parsley, chopped
freshly ground black pepper

First, make the gnocchi. Boil the potatoes until cooked and season as you mash. Put the mash on a floured board. Make a well in the centre and quickly work in a small amount of the flour, egg and oil, using a fork. Gradually add the rest of the flour, egg and oil to make a firm dough.

Put the dough in an oiled freezer/sandwich bag or put on a plate and cover with cling film or freezer paper. Leave for 20 minutes in the fridge. Heat the oven to 190°C/375°F/Gas Mark 5 and lightly oil a 22cm/9in diameter ovenproof dish. Next, make the tomato sauce.

Heat the oil in a pan. Add the onion and garlic and cook until translucent. Stir in the remaining sauce ingredients, cover and simmer for 15 minutes. Roll the gnocchi dough into a long sausage. Boil a large pan of salted water. Cut 2.5cm/1in pieces of dough, roll them into egg shapes and pop into the water to poach for 5 minutes. They should float to the top when cooked. Remove with a slotted spoon and place in the ovenproof dish. Pour over the tomato sauce, sprinkle on the Parmesan and heat through in the preheated oven.

Salmon Kedgeree

(3 portions)

450g/1lb salmon, tail piece
15ml/1 tbsp vegetable oil
½ tsp ground cinnamon
5 green cardamom pods, bruised
150g/5oz basmati rice, washed
½ tsp turmeric powder
450–600ml/¾–1 pint water or fish stock
25g/1oz flaked almonds, toasted
2 eggs, hard-boiled
1 tbsp fresh coriander or flat-headed parsley, chopped,
plus leaves to garnish

Poach the salmon in enough water to almost cover for 10 minutes. Drain and cool. Remove the skin and bones and flake the fish.

Cover and place on one side. Heat the oil, add the cinnamon and cardamom, and fry for 2–3 minutes. Stir in the rice and cook until golden. Add the turmeric and the water or fish stock and stir well. Cover the pan and cook on a low heat for 15 minutes. Add the salmon and continue cooking until the liquid has been absorbed and the rice is cooked – about another 10 minutes. Remove from the heat and stir in the almonds and chopped coriander or parsley. Garnish with the sliced or quartered eggs and coriander leaves and serve hot or cold.

Minestrone

(2 portions)

30ml/2 tbsp olive oil
1 large onion, diced
2 cloves garlic, crushed
2 carrots, diced
2 sticks celery, chopped
115g/4oz French beans, sliced
2 tsp fresh thyme leaves
2 courgettes, sliced
450g/1lb tomatoes, chopped, or 400g/14oz can tomatoes
1.2 litres/2 pints chicken or vegetable stock
400g/14oz can cannellini beans
55g/2oz macaroni, or other pasta for soup
60ml/4 tbsp fresh parsley, chopped
salt and freshly ground black pepper

To serve:
1 tbsp Parmesan per person, freshly grated

Heat the oil in a large saucepan, add the onion and garlic, and cook until they begin to soften. Add the remaining ingredients up to and including the tomatoes. Stir well. When all the vegetables have been added, pour in the stock. Bring to the boil, cover and simmer for about 40 minutes until all the vegetables are tender. About 15 minutes before the end of cooking, drain and rinse the beans, then stir them in, together with the pasta, parsley and seasoning.

Meatballs with Red Pepper Sauce

(4 portions)

350g/12oz extra-lean minced lamb
1 large onion, chopped
2 cloves garlic, crushed
1 tbsp fresh coriander, chopped
55g/2oz pine kernels, lightly toasted
seasoning

For the sauce
1 red pepper, deseeded and chopped
1 onion, chopped
15ml/1 tbsp vegetable oil
3 ripe tomatoes, skinned and chopped
seasoning
7.5ml/½ tbsp vegetable oil, for frying

Place all the meatball ingredients, except the pine kernels, in a food processor and purée to a smooth mixture. Stir in the pine kernels. Form into balls in the palms of your hands and place on one side, or in the fridge, until needed. Next, make the sauce. Sweat the pepper and onion in the oil until softened. Add the tomatoes, cover and cook for about 15 minutes until soft. Transfer to a food processor or liquidiser and blend to a purée. Return to the pan, season and thin to the desired consistency with water. Lightly fry or grill the meatballs until golden-brown, turning to cook evenly. Remove from the pan and drain on absorbent paper. Place in a serving dish and pour over the red pepper sauce.

Chicken in Tomato Sauce

(3 portions)

1 onion, diced
2 sticks celery, diced
1 red pepper, deseeded and diced
30ml/2 tbsp olive oil
1 strip orange zest, blanched
400g/14oz can tomatoes
seasoning
3 skinless chicken breasts, boned
30ml/2 tbsp dry sherry e.g. Fino

Sauté the onion, celery and red pepper in half the oil for about 10 minutes until softened. Add the orange zest and tomatoes. Cover and cook for a further 20 minutes. Liquidise in a food processor. Season to taste.

Lightly brown the chicken in the rest of the oil. When sealed, add the sherry and when hot, carefully burn off the alcohol by holding a match to the contents of the pan. Pour the sauce over the chicken. Cover and cook for a further 20 minutes on a moderate to low heat.

Bouillabaisse

(3 portions)

The greater the variety of white and oily fish (not shellfish) the better. Traditionally the broth is eaten first, followed by the fish.

2 onions, chopped
2 cloves garlic, crushed
1 small bulb fennel, chopped
60ml/4 tbsp olive oil
450g/1lb tomatoes, skinned and chopped
1 bouquet garni (parsley stalks, bay leaf, sprig of thyme)
1 strip orange zest, blanched

600ml/ 1 pint fish or vegetable stock
pinch saffron strands, steeped in 2 tbsp boiling water
375g/ 12oz white fish (whiting, monkfish, John Dory, red mullet,
haddock, flounder)
375g/ 12oz oily fish (mackerel, eel, bass, sardines)

For the garnish
4 tbsp fresh parsley, chopped

Gently fry the onion, garlic and fennel in half the olive oil until soft
but not browned. Add the tomatoes, bouquet garni, orange zest
and stock, bring to the boil and continue to boil for 10 minutes.
Add the rest of the olive oil, the saffron and its soaking water, and
the fish (in the order in which they will take to cook) and bring to
boiling point. Boil for about 10 minutes until all the fish is cooked.
(Boiling is important because it amalgamates the olive oil into the
stock.) Adjust seasoning and ladle into serving dishes, ensuring
everyone gets a fair selection of fish. Sprinkle with the parsley.

Marinated Swedish Herring

(2 portions)

Note: This recipe requires 2 days' preparation.

6 herring fillets
25g/ 1oz sea salt
300ml/ ½ pint water
4 shallots, diced
1 carrot, diced

For the vinegar solution
1 tsp whole allspice
1 tsp black peppercorns
1 tsp white mustard seeds
1 bay leaf
300ml/ ½ pint white wine vinegar

75ml/5 tbsp water
2 tsp demerara sugar

Place the fish in a shallow dish. Sprinkle with the salt and add the water. Cover and leave overnight in the fridge. Next day, rinse and pat dry on kitchen paper and cut into 2.5cm/1in pieces. Layer the fish and the diced vegetables in a 1.25kg/1.2 litre (3lb/2 pint) Kilner jar. Blend together the ingredients for the vinegar solution and pour over the fish. Move a skewer round in the jar to distribute the seasoning evenly. Store in the fridge for 1 week before use. Keeps for 2 weeks.

Bagna Cauda

(3 portions)

An Italian sauce for serving with crudités (sliced vegetables which are dipped into the 'warm bath' of sauce).

150ml/¼ pint olive oil
25g/1oz unsalted butter
55g/2oz anchovies (1 can), drained and chopped
2 cloves garlic, crushed
55g/2oz ground walnuts
55g/2oz fine white breadcrumbs

Serve with crudités (e.g. celery, peppers, cucumber, radicchio, chicory, carrots, fennel)

Put the olive oil and butter in a saucepan over a low heat until the butter has melted. Stir well to combine. Add the anchovies, garlic and walnuts and continue to cook over a low heat for 5 minutes. Remove from the heat and add the breadcrumbs. Stir well and place in a dish over a source of heat to keep warm (traditional ceramic bagna cauda dishes have a compartment for a night light beneath them. Bagna cauda literally means warm bath). Wash and trim a selection of vegetables and arrange on a serving dish to offer with the bagna cauda.

Thai Prawn Salad

(2 portions)

55g/2oz creamed coconut, grated
2 tbsp hot water
150ml/¼ pint natural yogurt
juice of half a lime
pinch cayenne pepper (chilli powder)
3 spring onions, chopped
225g/8oz shelled prawns

For the garnish
1 heart of a large crispy lettuce, finely shredded
1 mango, peeled, stoned and sliced
1 tbsp fresh coriander, chopped

Mix the coconut and water in a bowl. When cool, add the yogurt, lime juice and cayenne (chilli). Stir the spring onions and prawns into the dressing. Arrange the lettuce on individual serving plates. Top with prawns in their dressing and arrange mango slices around the edge. Garnish with coriander.

Thai Hot and Sour Soup

(2 portions)

350g/12oz large raw prawns, shelled (reserve shells)

For the stock
1.2 litres/2 pints water
1 dried chilli
2 kaffir lime leaves
2.5cm/1in piece fresh root ginger, roughly chopped
1 stalk lemon grass, bruised
1 onion, chopped

For the soup
1 carrot, cut into julienne strips
juice of 1 lime
2 tbsp coriander leaves
10ml/2 tsp fish sauce

Place the prawn shells and the rest of the stock ingredients in a saucepan and bring to simmering point. Cook for 20 minutes. Strain and reserve the liquid. Place the prawns and carrot in the saucepan and return the strained stock to the pan. Bring to boiling point. Stir in the lime juice and coriander leaves and bring back to simmering point. Remove from the heat. Stir in the fish sauce. Ladle into serving dishes.

Salmon Steak with Pesto Crust

(3 portions)

3 × 150g/5oz salmon steaks
10ml/2 tsp olive oil
juice of half a lemon
seasoning

For the crust
2 tbsp ready-made pesto (or see recipe below)
55g/2oz very fine breadcrumbs, toasted

For the pesto
25g/1oz fresh basil leaves, stripped of their stalks
2 cloves garlic
25g/1oz pine nuts
55g/2oz Parmesan, grated
60ml/4 tbsp olive oil
sea salt and freshly ground black pepper

Brush the salmon steaks with the olive oil and cook under a hot grill for about 5 minutes. Remove the grill pan from the heat and turn the steaks. Leave on one side. If making the pesto, put the basil, garlic, pine nuts, Parmesan and half the olive oil in a food processor and purée until smooth. Drizzle in the rest of the oil. Season to taste. Stir the breadcrumbs into the pesto. Spread the pesto over the uncooked side of the fish steaks and replace the grill pan under the heat. Cook for about 5–7 minutes, until the crust is crisp and the fish cooked.

Eastern Fish Cakes

(3 portions)

370g/12oz mackerel fillets, skinned
225g/8oz coley fillets, skinned
1 clove garlic, crushed
1 onion, chopped
½ tsp ground cumin
½ tsp ground coriander
1 tbsp tomato purée
salt and pepper

Place all the ingredients in a blender or food processor and purée to a smooth paste. Form the mixture into 3 fish cakes. Lightly fry the fish cakes in a frying pan in 1 tbsp oil for 5 minutes on each side until golden. Remove from the pan and drain on absorbent kitchen paper.

Sweet and Sour Pork Stir-Fry

(3 portions)

30ml/2 tbsp vegetable oil
350g/12oz lean pork fillet, cut into thin strips
1 clove garlic, crushed or finely sliced
quarter of a green cabbage, shredded
1 small broccoli head
2 carrots, cut into sticks
1 red pepper, deseeded and sliced

For the sauce
2 tsp cornflour
45ml/3 tbsp dark soy sauce
150ml/¼ pint orange juice
1 tbsp tomato purée
2 tsp demerara sugar
15ml/1 tbsp wine vinegar

First, make the sauce. Slake the cornflour with the soy sauce and put into a saucepan with the remainder of the sauce ingredients. Whisk well as it comes to simmering point and thickens. Remove from the heat and set aside. Heat the oil in a large wok and stir-fry the pork strips for 2 minutes. Add the rest of the ingredients in order of hardness and continue cooking until the vegetables are cooked almost to the crispness you prefer. Pour over the sauce and heat through. Serve at once with rice.

Seared Hot Tuna Niçoise 'Salad'

(3 portions)

450g/1lb small waxy salad potatoes, scraped and halved
2 lettuce hearts, one crispy, one soft-leaved
3 × 125g/4½oz tuna steaks
4 eggs, hard-boiled and quartered
55g/2oz anchovy fillets, drained
175g/6oz French beans, cooked
4 plum tomatoes, skinned and quartered
75g/3oz black olives

For the vinaigrette
45ml/3 tbsp extra-virgin olive oil
1 clove garlic, crushed
45ml/4 tbsp red wine vinegar
1 heaped tsp Dijon mustard
2 tbsp fresh mixed herbs (parsley, chervil, thyme), chopped

Boil the potatoes until just cooked. Drain. Make the vinaigrette by placing all the ingredients in a clean screw-top jar and shaking vigorously. Pour half the dressing over the warm potatoes. When all the salad ingredients are ready, sear the tuna steaks on both sides in a hot pan brushed lightly with olive oil. Cooking time is dependent on whether you like your tuna steaks rare or well done. Assemble the salad by placing a layer of lettuce on the base of a salad dish. Place the tuna in the centre, topped with egg quarters and half the anchovy fillets. Arrange the potatoes, beans and tomatoes around the tuna. Scatter over the olives and remaining anchovy fillets. Pour over the remaining dressing.

Pissaladière

(4 portions)

175g/6oz ready-made shortcrust pastry

For the topping
625g/1lb 6oz onions, chopped
2 cloves garlic, crushed
60ml/4 tbsp olive oil
400g/14oz can chopped tomatoes
2 tsp fresh thyme leaves
75g/3oz black olives
2 × 55g/2oz cans anchovies, drained
sea salt and freshly ground black pepper

Heat the oven to 200°C/400°F/Gas Mark 6. Roll out the pastry and use it to line a lightly oiled shallow 20cm/8in flan tin. Line the pastry case with greaseproof paper and baking beans and bake blind for 15 minutes. Gently fry the onions and garlic in the olive oil for 7 minutes. Add the tomatoes and thyme, and simmer for about 15 minutes until a thick sauce has formed. Season. Spread the tomato mixture over the pastry base. Arrange the anchovies and olives over the top and heat through in the oven for up to 10 minutes; any longer will dry out the tart.

Goan Fish Stew

(3 portions)

55g/2oz dried tamarind, chopped
150ml/5fl oz boiling water
2 cloves garlic, crushed
1 tsp ground coriander
1 tsp ground cumin
2.5cm/1in piece fresh root ginger, peeled and grated
½ tsp freshly ground black pepper
½ tsp ground turmeric
pinch of salt
1 onion, chopped
1 tbsp vegetable oil
75g/3oz creamed coconut, grated
175g/6oz cod fillets, skinned and cut into large chunks
1 medium (225g/8oz) mackerel, filleted, skinned and
cut into strips

Put the tamarind in a small bowl and cover with the boiling water. Leave to soak for 30 minutes. Strain through a sieve, pressing through as much pulp as possible. Lightly fry the garlic, spices and onion in the oil for about 3 minutes until the onion has softened. Stir in the tamarind pulp and liquid and the coconut, and continue to cook for 3 minutes on a high heat, stirring to prevent sticking. Lower the heat and add the fish to the pan. Cook for about 7 minutes or until the fish is cooked, stirring occasionally.

Vegetable Risotto

(3 portions)

20g/¾oz dried mushrooms (e.g. porcini, morels,
ceps) or 115g/4oz fresh mushrooms
30ml/2 tbsp olive oil
2 cloves garlic crushed

1 onion, chopped
1 red pepper, diced
1 green pepper, sliced
3 sticks celery, chopped
225g/8oz risotto (Italian arborio) rice
pinch saffron strands
450ml/¾ pint vegetable bouillon or chicken stock

To serve:
2 tbsp Parmesan per person, freshly grated

Soak the dried mushrooms (if using) according to the instructions on the packet (usually 15 minutes in boiling water). Heat the oil in a large, heavy-based pan and sauté the garlic, onion, peppers and celery for 10 minutes, until softened. Stir in the rice and fresh mushrooms (if using) and cook for 5 minutes, stirring to prevent sticking. Add the saffron, the stock and the dried mushrooms (if using). Include the mushroom soaking water, but be careful not to add any grit from the bottom of the bowl in which they have soaked. Simmer for 20 minutes or until the rice is cooked.

Hash Brown Beanies

(makes 8, or 4 portions)

1 onion, diced
30ml/2 tbsp vegetable oil
40g/1½oz butter
225g/8oz sweet potatoes, cooked and cubed
450g/1lb potatoes, cooked and cubed
2 tbsp fresh parsley, chopped
3 tbsp flour
100ml/3½fl oz skimmed milk
seasoning
pinch ground paprika, cayenne or chilli, whichever you prefer
400g/14oz canned or cooked beans
(e.g. kidney, borlotti, black-eye)

Sauté the onion in half the oil and 15g/ ½oz butter for 10 minutes. Transfer to a mixing bowl and add the potatoes, parsley, flour, milk, seasoning and spice. Put the beans in a food processor and chop roughly. Transfer to a mixing bowl, and combine with the potato mixture together well. Lightly oil an 8-cup muffin pan or use crumpet rings or metal scone/biscuit cutters of 7.5cm/3in diameter. Divide the remaining oil and butter between 2 frying pans. Put 4 rings in each pan and pack the mixture into the rings. Cook for 10 minutes on each side over a medium heat. If using the muffin pan bake in a preheated oven (200°C/400°F/Gas Mark 6) for 20 minutes.

Spicy Tomato Sauce

(3 portions)

1 onion, diced
2 cloves garlic, crushed
2 red chillies, deseeded and finely diced
1 tbsp fresh thyme leaves
30ml/2 tbsp olive oil
400g/14oz can tomatoes
30ml/2 tbsp tomato purée

Sauté the onion, garlic, chillies and thyme in the oil for 10 minutes. Add the tomatoes and the tomato purée and simmer over a low heat for 30 minutes. Liquidise or sieve the sauce to desired consistency, adding stock to thin it if required. Reheat if necessary.

Mediterranean Vegetable Pie

(3 portions)

1 aubergine, diced
75g/3oz green beans, diced
half a red pepper, diced
125g/4½oz pack half-fat mozzarella, sliced

115g/4oz can pinto beans
half a 225g/8oz pack filo pastry
25g/1oz unsalted butter, melted

Dice the vegetables and steam until slightly softened. Transfer to a mixing bowl and combine with the cheese and beans. Brush a pie dish (850ml/1½ pint) with some of the butter. Line the dish with a triple layer of filo pastry, brushing between the layers with enough butter to hold the sheets in place but not covering each sheet. Let the excess hang over the edge of the dish. Put the vegetable mixture into the pie dish. Fold the filo pastry back over the filling. Use the remaining filo to make a triple-layer lid. Brush the top with the remaining butter and bake for 35 minutes.

Spinach Lasagne

(3 portions)

1 red pepper, halved and deseeded
1 yellow pepper, halved and deseeded
4 plum tomatoes, skinned and sliced
300ml/½ pint passata
450g/1lb spinach, cooked and drained
450g/1lb low-fat fromage frais
½ tsp ground nutmeg
200g/7oz sheets fresh lasagne

Heat the oven to 190°C/375°F/Gas Mark 5. Flatten the pepper halves and char under a hot grill until black and blistered. Set aside and when cool enough to handle remove the skin and slice the flesh into strips. Mix in a bowl with the tomatoes and passata, and season (add a dash of Tabasco, if liked). In another bowl mix the spinach, fromage frais and nutmeg, and season. Boil the lasagne in plenty of water for 5 minutes (or as long as instructed on the pack – it may even be ready-to-use) without pre-cooking. Drain. Make up the lasagne by layering alternately half the tomato filling, lasagne, half the fromage frais filling and lasagne.

Repeat, but make the fromage frais the last layer. Cover with foil and bake for 25 minutes – remove foil for the last 5–10 minutes if you like the top browned.

Barbary Duck Breast Salad

(3 portions)

3 Barbary duck breast fillets

For the marinade
45ml/3 tbsp shoyu or soy sauce
2 green chillies, deseeded and grated
2.5cm/1in piece fresh root ginger, peeled and grated
juice of 1 orange
1 clove garlic, grated
mixed green salad leaves to serve

Put the duck fillets in a shallow dish. Mix the marinade ingredients together and spoon over. Cover and marinate in the refrigerator for 12 hours or overnight, turning occasionally. Heat the grill (or barbecue) to high and grill the duck for 4–5 minutes on each side. Remove the skin and serve, either whole or cut in strips, on a bed of green salad.

Tabbouleh

(4 portions)

115g/4oz bulgur wheat
half a cucumber, chopped finely
1 green pepper, deseeded and finely chopped
4 spring onions, finely chopped
6 tbsp fresh mint, chopped
juice of 1 lemon
salt and pepper

Put the bulgur in a saucepan and cover with water. Bring to the boil, cover and simmer for 15 minutes or until the wheat is tender and the water has been absorbed. Mix the remaining ingredients with the cooked bulgur. Serve at room temperature.

Yellow Fruit Bake

(6 portions)

2 pears, cored and sliced
4 small bananas, peeled and halved
3 peaches, stoned and sliced
2 star fruit, sliced
40g/1½oz brown sugar
40g/1½oz butter

Heat the oven (if using) to 180°C/350°F/Gas Mark 4. Put the fruit in a shallow dish and add the sugar and butter. Put into a medium oven (or under a hot grill or in foil over hot coals on the barbecue) and cook for 10–15 minutes, turning occasionally and basting with the sugar and butter and juices as the fruit cooks.

Fruit Brûlée

(1 portion)

115g/4oz unsweetened cooked fruit of choice (see below)
75g/3oz Greek-style natural yogurt
1 tbsp demerara sugar·

Place the fruit in a ramekin and top with the yogurt. Sprinkle with the demerara sugar and put under a hot grill until the sugar is bubbling. (Try it with apples, rhubarb with cinnamon, gooseberries with elderflowers, blackcurrants or pears.)

Snack list

Choose one of the following as your snack(s). The number of snacks allowed per day on the Anti-Weight-Gain Plan is given on pages 153–4. The number depends on whether you are trying to lose weight or whether you are using the plan as a healthy anti-ageing plan.

1 glass fruit juice
1 apple
4–5 fresh apricots
20 cherries
2 medium clementines (or other easy peelers, e.g. mandarins, satsumas)
3 fresh dates
1 dried date
2 fresh figs
1 dried fig
1 small bunch (about 20) seedless grapes (100g/3½oz)
2 small kiwi fruit
1 peach or nectarine
1 pear
2 large plums
1 rice cake
1 fig roll
1 jaffa cake
2 breadsticks (grissini)
3 matzos
1 poppadom
1 mini pain au raisin
1 mini ring doughnut

Double snack list

If your allowance is for more than 1 snack per day, you could have an item from this list, which is the equivalent of 2 standard snacks. See pages 153–4 for the number of snacks allowed on your plan.

1 large banana
1 raw lychee
1 handful (40g/1 ½oz) raisins or sultanas
1 low-fat fruit yogurt
1 small chocolate éclair
1 coconut macaroon
1 Cadbury's chocolate miniroll
1 Boots Shapers cereal/fruit bar
1 low-fat fruit fool or mousse
2 cheese-spread triangles
25g/1oz chocolate raisins
1 small teacake
1 raisin/maple syrup/Scotch pancake
1 slice malt loaf
1 slice wholemeal toast with 1 tsp low-fat spread
1 McVitie's Go-Ahead cake bar
25g/1oz Twiglets
25g/1oz plain or caramel/sugar-coated popcorn

Special snack list

Choose one of the following as your snack(s). The number of snacks allowed per day on the Anti-Weight-Gain Plan is given on pages 153–4. The number depends on whether you are trying to lose weight or whether you are using the plan as a healthy anti-ageing plan.

1 wholemeal hot-cross bun, spiced fruited bun or currant bun
1 wholemeal fruit scone and either 10g/2 tsp low-fat spread or 10g/2 tsp preserve
200ml/7fl oz chocolate milk or hot chocolate
1 Bath bun
1 individual packet of low-fat, unsalted crisps and 1 apple
1 granary roll spread thinly with black olive pâté or tapenade
25g/1oz nuts (1 small bag)
1 bagel

half a bagel, spread with 30g/2 tbsp low-fat soft white cheese
and 25g/1oz smoked salmon

3–4 dried dates

1 samosa

75g/3oz dried ready-to-eat pears, apricots or peaches

1 cup of soup and 1 bread roll

3–4 fish fingers

1 small jacket potato with 25g/1oz cottage cheese

2 slices wholemeal toast with 10g/2 tsp low-fat spread

1 scrambled egg on 1 slice of unspread toast

CHAPTER FIVE

Mind Over Matter

The speed at which you age, and the age to which you live, is also controlled by the way you think and the attitudes you hold. In this chapter you will find a wealth of ideas, surprises and techniques to keep you younger for longer.

The way you live is probably determined by your job, whether that is work in the conventional nine-to-five sense or work based around the family or in the home. When you meet people, they will probably ask you what you do and it will not have escaped your notice that the popular perception of success is defined by how far you have climbed your career ladder and what that means in material terms.

Climbing that ladder can be ageing, and problems with premature ageing arise when such success is achieved at the expense of mental and physical well-being. Eating a nutritionally poor diet, neglecting exercise, seeing little of family and friends and possibly drinking heavily and smoking, can easily become part of a 'successful lifestyle'. In these respects 'success' is neither sustainable nor conducive to slower, healthier ageing – no matter how glamorous a hectic lifestyle appears to others.

Even if you do not fit this stereotype there are many aspects of your life that could lead to premature ageing. We have already looked at diet, exercise and weight control. The strategies that follow will also be a great help.

One of the most important lessons to learn from this chapter is about your attitude of mind. The way you deal with the everyday stresses in your life can take years off the way you look and feel.

There is a lot of truth in the adage that you are as young as you feel – and the way you feel affects the way you look and the way you behave. So use these techniques and tips to alter your mindset, if necessary, and to become younger and feel fitter.

Reduce the Impact of Age on Your Mind

Ageing can decrease your body's ability to withstand stress, as your regulatory mechanisms can start to decline from the age of thirty. These changes mean that the older you are, the less your body is able to regulate pulse rate, blood pressure, oxygen consumption, blood glucose and so on when you are under stress. As the reserve ability to maintain balance in the body declines, the time you take to recover from injuries increases, and there is a greater likelihood that the stress of the injury will lead to complications or to acute or chronic illness. Anti-ageing nutrition will enable your body systems to function more efficiently in these circumstances, and good management of stress will help you reduce the damage and boost your immune system.

Managing Stress Effectively

Effective stress management does not mean total avoidance of stress. That is unrealistic, impossible and probably undesirable – unless you want to live life as an inanimate object rather than as a vital human being. Some stress can be beneficial. For example, the kind of stress that you experience before saying a few words in public or when starting a new job or going for an interview will sharpen your wits and help you deal with the situation. Stress can also be life-saving because it triggers the 'fight or flight' reaction, which will help you dash for safety from a fire or an attacker. Problems arise when the stress is unremitting.

What happens when you are under stress

- The muscles tense in preparation for physical activity. The hypothalamus in the brain alerts the pituitary gland (also in the brain) which releases hormones to bring the adrenal glands into action to produce adrenalin and noradrenalin to maintain the 'fight or flight' reaction.

- The liver releases some of its stored glycogen to boost blood sugar levels so that the muscles have enough energy to take action.
- The heart increases its pumping rate to get blood sugar to the muscles very quickly.
- Blood pressure rises.
- The rate of breathing increases so that the lungs can take in extra oxygen.
- Other areas of the body such as the digestive system, salivary glands and kidneys constrict or shut down to allow the blood to be diverted to the priority areas: muscles, heart, lungs and brain. This process will make you go pale as the blood leaves the body surface, and your mouth will become dry.
- The immune system stops dealing with infection to let the body cope with the emergency, and the skin starts to sweat to cool you down in anticipation of the overheating that will result when you fight or flee.

It is a brilliant system for priming the body for physical action. After the physical action has happened and the stress is no longer there, the body swiftly reverses the process and no harm is done. However, when stressful situations in everyday life repeatedly bring this mechanism into play and the cause of the stress does not go away and cannot be physically or psychologically resolved, then you are suffering from 'stress'. If you do not fight or flee, the wind-down process cannot happen.

What happens when you stay wound up

You can end up with:

- high blood pressure
- a shut-down digestive system that adapts by giving you permanent indigestion, diarrhoea or even ulcers

- chronic muscle tension
- headaches
- a dampened-down immune system, leading to frequent colds and infections

To top it all, you can develop allergies.

It almost goes without saying that stress can lead to exhaustion – and the whole process of unremitting stress is extremely ageing. In an attempt to deal with stress, many people turn to common props such as alcohol and drugs (medicinal and recreational) which have their own inevitable ageing effects.

Constant stress means that you live on adrenalin, which uses up all your mental and physical energy, leaving you tired and less effective at what you do. Being stressed can disrupt your best efforts to follow a healthy diet or lifestyle and in time this will add to the ageing effect and will lead to ill health.

Learning appropriate techniques to recognise the signs of stress and to take action to manage it are essential anti-ageing tools. Some very basic strategies are given below, but if you are not confident that you can deal with it yourself, or if you need specific behaviour or therapy techniques, seek help from your GP or other appropriate health provider to find the causes of your stress and develop ways to manage it.

The following quizzes will help you make a rough assessment of what level of stress, if any, you are under.

Basic Stress Quiz

This quiz will give you a general idea of how stressed you are, if you do not already know! Just gauging your situation may be enough. If you want to examine your stress level in more detail, take the In-Depth Stress Quiz too, and read the advice that follows it.

If you have experienced any of the following in the last year, score 1 point for each:

- longer working hours
- worry about finances
- starting a new job/course
- chronic sleep problems
- lack of regular exercise
- poor eating habits
- conflicts between family and work commitments
- partner's new job or other conflicts and problems as listed above

The following score 2 points each:

- new marriage
- divorce or break-up of long-term relationship
- family disagreement
- moving home
- assuming care of elderly relative

The following score 3 points each:

- legal problems
- illness or injury
- problems with drugs or alcohol
- death of family member or close friend
- serious illness of family member or close friend
- birth of a child

Enter total points here _____

What is your score?

0–8	low stress
9–19	medium stress: start stress management techniques
20–36	highly stressed: seek help

In-Depth Stress Quiz

1.   Image

Are you:

a)	unhappy with the way you look?	Yes	No
b)	worried that you are not fashionable enough?	Yes	No
c)	Constantly having 'bad hair' days and spotting new wrinkles?	Yes	No
d)	plagued by fears that you look old-fashioned?	Yes	No

2.   Work

Are you:

a)	confident that you are achieving what you want to?	Yes	No
b)	about to move or lose jobs?	Yes	No
c)	behind with your work?	Yes	No
d)	unhappy at work or under too much/too little pressure?	Yes	No

3.   Props

Do you:

a)	rely on cigarettes/drink/other to get you through the day?	Yes	No
b)	get comments about the large amount of alcohol you drink?	Yes	No
c)	eat a poor diet, or not have much interest in food?	Yes	No
d)	drink as many as six or more coffees or colas a day?	Yes	No

4. Health

Do you:

a)	get a lot of headaches?	Yes	No
b)	suffer from nervous digestive complaints?	Yes	No
c)	hardly ever get a regular 6–8 hours' sleep at night?	Yes	No
d)	avoid exercise and other physical activity?	Yes	No

5. Emotions

Are you:

a)	prone to going 'berserk' when things go wrong for you?	Yes	No
b)	easily irritated, even by small things?	Yes	No
c)	anxious or worrying about something most of the time?	Yes	No
d)	feeling under pressure from work, home, family or elsewhere?	Yes	No

Your score

Score 0 for each No you ticked.
For each Yes, score the following:

1.	a) 2	b) 1	c) 2	d) 2
2.	a) 3	b) 6	c) 3	d) 4
3.	a) 5	b) 6	c) 3	d) 4
4.	a) 4	b) 4	c) 3	d) 4
5.	a) 5	b) 2	c) 4	d) 3

Total score _____

What your score means

Your score is an indication of how well you cope with stress, i.e. whether you overreact. There are two ways of dealing with stress: internally and externally. Making 'internal' improvements means changing your attitudes and habitual responses; 'external' changes involve alterations to your environment, such as going to bed earlier or replacing some of your coffee, cola or alcohol drinks with alternatives.

Score 0–10   Some people might say that you have reached the age of wisdom. You probably do have a mature attitude to life and health and are coping well with ageing. Try to maintain your positive outlook and independence of thought. You are in a good position to continue to work hard and achieve a lot, but make sure that you are also enjoying yourself to the full.

Score 11–20   With a little bit of effort you could become happier and more relaxed. Try to identify which are the avoidable stresses in your life and try to eliminate them. Try to better understand your emotions and those of family and friends. Take steps to improve your diet and increase physical activity. Find a relaxation technique (meditation, yoga, stretch and tone classes, swimming) that you can practise regularly and you will soon find that you feel more relaxed and confident about yourself, your appearance and your future.

Score 21–40   You need to take practical steps now to alter your personal habits so that you eat better, sleep better and exercise more. Working all of these changes into your routine will greatly improve your vitality and stamina and reduce anxiety. If you feel reluctant to change, consider that it is a lot easier to change your old habits than it is to change the world (even if the world could do with radical modifications, in your view). It's time to face the fact that life is about compromise. So, take stock, write down realistic medium-term goals and learn to express your feelings and needs openly and without hostility.

Score 41–70 Reducing stress in your life, and your reactions to situations that are stressful for you, is going to involve quite a bit of work, gaining greater insight into your own character and personality. Learning to accept responsibility for your problems and behaviour is important, as well as modifying your quick, often heated, responses. This will mean a combination of reorganising your lifestyle and making a big effort to change and reduce your reliance on social props. At the top end of the scale (55+) you are probably going to need counselling and behavioural advice to sort out long-held feelings of resentment and difficulty in personal relationships. Good luck.

Eat to beat stress

Stress increases your body's need for **vitamin C**, either because of increased consumption or decreased uptake. It is not known exactly how much extra vitamin C, or other vitamins and minerals, your body needs to cope during stressful periods without leaving you depleted. But it highlights the need to eat lots of nutrient-dense foods – and in general avoid an excessive intake of alcohol, caffeine and sugar which deplete the body of nutrients.

The **B vitamins** are needed for your nervous system to function and cope with the effects of stress. The mineral **magnesium** appears to be depleted when there are high levels of stress hormones in the bloodstream. As magnesium activates the B vitamins and is involved in turning food into energy, it is easy to see why requirements might increase during periods of stress.

For good food sources of these nutrients, see pages 110–13.

Stress and your weight

If stress is interfering with your eating habits, then you need to deal with your emotions before you can deal with your diet. Moods can trigger our urges to overeat for comfort and to cheer ourselves up. The habit of rewarding yourself with food can be exacerbated by stress. Stress can also have the opposite effect and cause loss of appetite.

The stress of dieting can threaten your health and well-being. Yo-yoing weight in particular is ultimately ageing because of the strains it puts on the body. A cycle of gaining and losing weight can also lead to ugly skin folds. The ideal is to remain the same weight through adult life. People who stay the same weight in middle age as in their youth (provided they were not obese then!) generally live longer and enjoy a healthier life.

The way you think can increase your stress levels

Thinking in absolute terms is ageing. Absolute thinkers tend to be perfectionists and control freaks who are unable to compromise.

Are you the sort who becomes angry when crossed or at inappropriate times (disregarding the fact that there is never really an appropriate time to be angry)? Do you get mad in traffic jams or when trains are late or in other situations that are beyond individual control? This is wasted effort because there is nothing you can do about these things and being stressed only makes it worse.

Frequent anger leads to poor mental health, and to poor relationships in the family and at work. The inability of absolute thinkers to cope creates more stress for themselves, their partners and their children. Such long-term stress is harmful to health and very ageing. Studies show that absolute thinkers are more likely to consult their GPs with problems such as insomnia, headaches and tiredness.

Thinking in non-absolute terms is, as you have guessed by now, anti-ageing. Non-absolute thinkers tend to be flexible and able to negotiate, see shades of grey and tolerate differences. They stay younger for longer.

Basic strategy for relaxing

Set time aside for yourself   Block it off in your diary if necessary. Do not view it as a waste of time, even if it does seem like a luxury. Taking time for yourself, on a regular basis, will add to your productivity and efficiency because it will enable you to relax. Use 'your' time to do something you enjoy – reading, going to the cinema, visiting an art gallery, gardening, listening to music, getting some fresh air, cycling, taking more exercise, doing an evening class. It is important to have absorbing hobbies or interests as you age and have more time to yourself. You will return home or to work refreshed and with a better attitude of mind. And when you are not concentrating hard on your work, but doing something else, you might find that you think more creatively and that answers to problems just pop into your head when you least expect them. (See also sleep, page 215).

Mind over Grey Matter

Eating to Beat Your Age is good for you and you had better believe that . . . This is not a threat, merely an extension of a phenomenon shown in an American Cancer Risk Behavior Study: that those people who *believe* a healthy diet is important really do eat more fruit and vegetables. It also works another way: those people who perceive their health to be good eat 30 per cent more fruit and vegetables than those who think their health is poor. The better you feel about yourself, the healthier the food you eat, which is good because you need to eat nutrient-dense food to keep your brain (and therefore your mind) functioning well as you age.

Foods rich in antioxidants are particularly important for quenching free-radical damage to brain cells and maintaining normal brain function. In a study of 1,800 middle-aged men and women, those with the poorest cognitive function (thinking, reasoning skills, etc.) had the lowest blood levels of antioxidants vitamin E and beta-carotene. Vitamin E was most strongly associated with better brain performance. Other factors such as age, education and variables were taken into consideration.

Don't lose grey matter because you might go grey

Memory tests on older people have also shown the highest scores among those with the highest intakes of fruits and vegetables.

These individuals also had the highest blood levels of vitamin C and beta-carotene. Other measures of judgement, perception and reasoning showed highest scores among those tested who had the highest levels of vitamins C and E.

These three antioxidant vitamins (or perhaps another as yet unknown substance found in the foods containing them) are thought to be responsible for the greater brain power. It is likely that the antioxidants prevent damage to brain cells known as neurons. They probably do this by preventing free radicals from breaking down cell structure so that brain cells and nerve cells cannot function properly.

- Lowering your levels of stress will also improve your memory as you age. High levels of stress hormones appear to be partly responsible for a decline in brain cell function in old age. If stress hormone levels can be controlled, improved· memory could follow.

Eat to beat brain power loss

The following foods and nutrients can have a positive effect on your brain power:

- Vegetables and fruit, especially yellow, orange and green; nuts and seeds; vegetable oils or spreads fortified with vitamin E.
- B vitamins are also needed for efficient brain work. People aged fifty and over who do best at cognitive tasks (e.g., repeating numbers in reverse order, drawing geometric shapes) are those with the highest levels of vitamins B_6, B_{12} and folates. Older people (over sixty) can become deficient in vitamin B_{12}, as we have seen, because their reduced gastric juices do not allow for the nutrient's absorption.
- Folates are found in pulses, kidney beans, etc; green leafy vegetables; orange juice.
- Vitamin B_6 is found in vegetables and fruit; animal proteins; seaweed.

- Vitamin B12 is found in meat, fish, poultry, cheese; some fortified vegetarian foods; fortified breakfast cereals.

Eat to beat memory loss

While we are on the subject of mind and brain power, what about nutrients for your memory? Folic acid, iron, riboflavin and vitamin B12 help to improve memory and mental alertness. As do the omega-3 fats in oily fish and nuts, and the zinc in oysters and pumpkin seeds. Not only could you look younger if you eat these foods, but you won't keep forgetting things!

Other good sources of memory-enhancing B vitamins and choline (not a true vitamin but a member of the B vitamin complex and linked to lecithin, a natural emulsifier that keeps fats in suspension and is found in the brain) are breakfast cereals, bread, eggs and liver.

It has been known for a long time that omega-3 essential fatty acids (EFAs) are vital for foetal brain, nerve and eye development, and for baby and infant development. Now evidence is coming to light that they may help prevent us declining into a second childhood. Initial studies suggest that lack of omega-3 fatty acids (or an imbalance between omega-6 and omega-3) may play a role in the physical brain changes that characterise Alzheimer's disease and its associated loss of memory and intellectual performance.

One of many studies shows that baby rats fed a diet in which the fatty acid content was saturated had a lower ability to learn and remember than those fed a diet where the fat content was either monounsaturated or polyunsaturated. Immune processes are also thought to be involved in Alzheimer's disease, and omega-3 fatty acids may have an anti-inflammatory role (as have fish oils in alleviating some of the symptoms of rheumatoid arthritis) in preventing this illness.

Maternal amnesia

Do not eat liver to enhance your memory if you are pregnant. Liver contains dangerously high levels of vitamin A which may cause birth defects. Frankly, there is nothing you can do to save your failing memory after childbirth (maternal amnesia will run its course . . .)

Lower your blood pressure to increase your brain power

It's true that your brain shrinks in volume as you age, but this is not necessarily a sign that you are losing your memory or becoming feeble-minded; it usually just means that it takes you longer to process information. And this can be made worse by high blood pressure. As we have seen, in a typical unhealthy British diet, blood pressure rises with age (see Chapter 1).

People in their mid-fifties and older with high blood pressure show a more marked slow-down in mental abilities and their brains shrink more quickly. If you have high blood pressure which is not treated or reduced during middle age, you are likely to be among those with the greatest loss of cognitive (thinking, reasoning) ability by the time you are seventy. This is probably due to a build-up of brain fluid, a sign of small undetected strokes.

- Treatment with vitamin C can lower high blood pressure. In a small American trial patients given supplements of vitamin C – one 2g dose followed by 500mg per day for a month – showed an average reduction of systolic pressure from 155 to 142, and of diastolic pressure from 110 to 100.

How do you know if your blood pressure is high?

Blood pressure readings give two figures. The highest number is the systolic pressure and the lowest number is the diastolic pressure (see box below). Your pulse is the pressure wave in the arteries with each heartbeat.

In the UK medical intervention for high blood pressure is usually only given when blood pressure reaches 160/100, if you are otherwise healthy. In the US treatment is given much earlier, as high blood pressure is considered to be upwards of 140/90. In the UK you would only get treatment at 140–159/90–99 if you had other related health problems.

Systolic and diastolic

Systolic pressure is caused by the contraction of the heart muscle and the recoil of the aorta (the main artery leaving the heart) as the blood surges through it.

Diastolic pressure is recorded during relaxation of the ventricles between beats; it reflects the resistance of the small arteries in the body and the load against which the heart must work.

In terms of its effect on brain power, systolic pressure has the greatest relevance. Men who have had a systolic pressure above 140 for fifteen years experience a 50 per cent greater cognitive (mental) decline than men with normal blood pressure. Men in their sixties and seventies who have had a systolic pressure of 140 for twenty-five years experience 100 per cent more cognitive decline.

The good news is that high blood pressure is not inevitable with ageing. Weight loss, regular physical activity, moderate to low alcohol intake, low sodium intake and eating more vegetables and fruit all help reduce elevated blood pressure.

Music intelligence in the third age

Back in the 1990s it was reported that you could enhance your IQ by more than two points if you listened to Mozart while doing maths. Specifically, there was a temporary improvement in IQ (particularly in the ability to think ahead and see symmetries and patterns) among students who listened to a Mozart piano sonata. Inevitably headlines followed that you could improve your maths if you listened to Mozart while you did it.

Since then other studies have failed to confirm the earlier findings or they have produced a lesser effect than the original work. Even though music intelligence is not yet thoroughly proven, you could still give it a try whether you are a candidate of the University of the Second Age or the Third Age – and see if you can become smarter with age using music.

Keep the mental cogs turning

It is a common myth that all elderly people become senile. Although changes do occur in the nervous system, senility is *not* inevitable with age. While some slight slowing of thought and memory seems to be a normal part of ageing, there is evidence that if you engage in mental activity you will keep your cognitive abilities (thinking, reasoning and so on) sharp, just as physical activity keeps your body strong.

As you age there will be physical changes in the nervous system. Brain weight may decrease significantly from its maximum in young adulthood. The number of nerve cells decrease, and each cell has fewer branches (dendrites). Some nerve cells lose their coating (a process called demyelinisation). These changes slow the speed of message transmission. After a nerve carries a message, there is a short time when it must rest and cannot carry another message; ageing increases this period.

Some people will experience many physical changes in their nerves and brain tissue as they age; others will experience few. Some will have atrophy (brain shrinkage) and plaques (deposits); some will have plaques and tangles; some will have other changes. Although certain physical changes are typical of specific brain disorders, their amount and type are not necessarily related to changes in brain function.

Changes in capacity for memory, thought and reasoning,

while common in the very old, cannot be directly traced to atrophy or other physical brain changes. As the nerves degenerate, the senses of touch, vision, hearing and so on may be affected. Reflexes may be reduced or lost. Reflex changes increase problems with mobility and safety. Conversely, some reflexes that were present at birth and then lost through maturity (infantile reflexes such as the sucking and grasp reflexes) may reappear with advanced age. Something to look forward to . . .

Sudden decline is a serious sign

Delirium, dementia and severe memory loss are not a normal, expected part of ageing, and are probably caused by degenerative brain disorders.

Sudden decline in mental ability is not natural with old age and it can signal the onset of Alzheimer's disease, which is one such degenerative disorder.

By testing older adults repeatedly for up to fifteen years, researchers have shown that stability over time is central to distinguishing normal ageing from dementia. Although participants who were in the older age group when they first took the psychometric tests did not perform as well as those in the younger, in both groups people who remained stable over time did not go on to develop Alzheimer's.

Those who did develop Alzheimer's disease experienced an abrupt decline in ability. Any sudden change in performance is critical.

Maintaining stability requires a constant source of nutrients and emphasises the need for a nutrient-dense diet with age. It also emphasises that you must continue to use your mental facilities to keep them functioning well.

Eat to beat mental decline

Decreases in brainwave function have been seen in healthy persons older than sixty if their diet is short of the B vitamins thiamine and riboflavin and of the mineral iron.

Low thiamine status seems to be a particular problem. And the deficiency does not have to be great for there to be an effect: neuropsychological impairment can occur with mild deficits.

Other nutrients also promise some protection against depression and dementia. Diets containing high amounts of monounsaturated fatty acids can protect against cognitive decline in old age. As part of the Italian Study on Ageing, diet was assessed in nearly 300 people between the ages of sixty-six and eighty-four who were living at home. On average, about 17 per cent of the participants' energy intake came from monounsaturated fatty acids, a reflection of their olive-oil-rich diet. An evaluation showed a better mental state among those with the highest intake of monounsaturated fatty acids. The effect was most pronounced in people with a poor education. There was no association between other nutritional variables and memory.

This shows that monounsaturated fatty acids could be protective because they may help maintain the structural integrity of neuronal membranes, as does gamma-linoleic acid (GLA). Supplements of GLA have been taken for many years by people with multiple sclerosis and other neurological health problems related to demyelinisation to try to prevent rapid decline.

Another much smaller study showed that patients with dementia who were daily given 9.6g of omega-3 fatty acids had longer periods of remission than those not receiving the supplement. The authors of the study suggest that omega-3 fatty acids may stabilise mood. Patient interest in and acceptance of omega-3 fatty acids was high, because they were perceived as natural, with few, if any, side-effects. These are small findings, but more research is needed into the role of optimum nutrition in maintaining the functional integrity of the ageing brain. For more about omega-3 fatty acids, see oily fish, Chapter 2.

Improve your mood with food . . .

Much of this book gives practical ways to use the nutrients in foods to keep you younger and fitter than you might otherwise be. Habitually eating foods rich in nutrients will, over time, reap the greatest reward. But what you eat and drink can also have an immediate effect on your mood, energy levels and general zest for living life to the full. Some of these effects are related to our attitudes to food, for example the 'naughty but nice' attitude to chocolate (which is misplaced); others are specific physiological actions: for example, the stimulating effect of caffeine in coffee and the relaxant effect of alcohol.

- A glass of wine will have an effect on your mood.
- A cup of coffee will make you more alert.
- Chocolate can relieve tension, while also bringing on (unnecessary) feelings of guilt.
- Omega-3 fatty acids, found in oily fish and other foods, are being investigated for their beneficial effect on depression.
- Carbohydrate-rich snacks and meals are commonly eaten for comfort and there is scientific backing for this. Starchy and sugary foods increase uptake of the amino acid tryptophan by the brain, and tryptophan is needed to make serotonin which is a natural sedative. So eating more carbohydrate foods if you feel stressed is a natural nutritional self-medication.

. . . and activity

- Physical activity relieves symptoms of depression and anxiety, and improves mood.
- Regular physical activity reduces the risk of developing depression.
- Physical activity appears to improve the health-related quality of life by enhancing psychological well-being and physical function.

Reduce the Impact of Age on Your Body

You will have gathered by now that it is not obligatory to decline as you age. You are not *obliged* to have middle-age spread, lose your teeth and fall into a state of unfitness and decrepitude just because you are ageing.

Take heart

Your level of fitness is measured by the efficiency of your heart and lungs (see Chapter 3). Cardiac tissue, for example, undergoes only small metabolic changes due to ageing itself and cardio-respiratory (heart and lung) fitness can be maintained into advanced years. Without wishing to offend any reader, it is probably fair to say that much heart disease and lack of fitness, especially from as young as the thirties onwards, is brought about by a lifestyle of acute lack of physical activity, poor eating habits, severe weight problems, heavy smoking and a high alcohol intake. Such is the importance of the relationship between ageing, lifestyle and disease.

Digest this

Digestive complaints are frequent in the elderly, yet the gastro-intestinal tract does not automatically deteriorate over the years. Although there is a decline in gastric acid secretion, particularly in women from the age of thirty onwards, it should have no great effect in healthy people. The elderly may be notorious users of laxatives, and constipation is a common complaint, but little change with ageing has been found for intestinal transit times in healthy active adults: they can be the same whether you are twenty-five or seventy-five. In older adults who are constipated, slower transit times and decrease in faecal water content are most likely to be associated with factors other than age, such as lack of physical activity, not drinking enough water, altered diet and taking medications. All of which can be changed or improved.

Vitamin supplement sales literature might have you believe that the human gut automatically loses the ability to absorb vitamins and minerals as you age, but there are no significant differences in the absorption of most vitamins and minerals between healthy young and healthy old subjects, except, perhaps, possible problems in age with iron absorption. (However, too much iron can produce free radicals which are harmful, so this may be no bad thing, as long as you do not become anaemic.)

- An increased frequency of gallstones with age is thought to be due to an age-related rise in the ratio of cholesterol to phospholipids secreted in the bile. And that can be influenced by diet and exercise.

Conserve water

However, one area that does tend to go a bit wonky with age is the 'waterworks'. The renal blood-flow of an eighty-year-old is half that of a young adult. Even so, the ageing kidney remains remarkably capable of maintaining its fluid and electrolyte status at the age of 100, so long as it is disease-free.

Women beware   One serious problem that does occur with age, and is more pronounced in women, is a water-conservation defect which predisposes the elderly to dehydration. So it becomes even more important to remember to drink lots of water.

Men beware

Many men can be troubled, after the age of forty, with benign prostatic hypertrophy (BPH). It affects almost 90 per cent of men aged eighty or more. Hypertrophy of the prostate can eventually result in obstruction of the urethra and obstruction of the flow of urine from the bladder. Symptoms of urinary obstruction can begin as early as the age of fifty. The cause of BPH may be related to changes in the circulating hormones which occur with ageing. It is known that the ratio of oestrogen to testosterone increases in men as they get older.

Remember this

A certain loss of brain power with age is expected by most people, but again many studies have shown that even the elderly perform very well in tests of sustained attention. Long-term memory, especially the ability to retain large amounts of information over long periods of time, may decline from your forties, with the loss being greatest in those from lower educational and socio-economic backgrounds. This suggests that the effect is linked to nutritional and other environmental factors and not to ageing – so it can be slowed or prevented in part through diet and lifestyle.

Avoid diabetes

High blood sugar levels are more frequent with age but are not necessarily an ageing phenomenon; they are quite likely to be due to insufficient exercise, obesity, dietary changes and resistance to the effect of insulin on peripheral tissues. Again, exercise and diet can improve these.

Sound bite

Advances in the prevention of dental caries and periodontal disease, and the wider availability of dental care, mean that loss of teeth need not be a normal part of ageing.

Keep smiling

Good mouth hygiene is essential if you want to keep your teeth firmly rooted and not dancing about like virginal jacks (as Ben Jonson so vividly portrays loosened teeth that are the result of gum disease). So floss between your teeth every day, and brush your teeth effectively at least twice a day. Gum disease can also impair immunity and is associated with heart disease. The more gum and tooth decay you have the more likely you are to suffer a stroke or heart attack. The theory is that bacteria which promote dental problems also trigger a reaction in the immune system that causes arteries to swell, increasing the risk of heart disease and strokes.

Tip   Ensure your brushing and flossing technique is good by making an appointment with the dental hygienist at your dentist's surgery because bad brushing habits can add to the problems of receding gums.

Tasty as ever

Production of saliva and the ability to taste and enjoy food also does not decline as much with age as is popularly thought, even though the number of taste buds does. Recent studies suggest that there is only a modest change in taste recognition or enjoyment.

Sleep Well to Slow Ageing

While it is incontrovertible that lack of sleep can be both a cause and a result of stress, of direct relevance to this book is the fact that lack of sleep accelerates ageing.

What constitutes a good night's sleep is open to debate. There are those who believe the brain needs one hour's sleep for every two hours its owner is awake and alert. Without that amount, it is said that you will become slow and disorganised and suffer daytime sleepiness.

Continuous uninterrupted sleep in regular patterns is the best kind. This means that adults need eight hours (or more) to wake as fresh as a daisy and free from dark circles under the eyes. There are those who think we need only six hours (or less) for our beauty sleep to knit up those wrinkles. The ultimate test of how much sleep you need is how you feel and look during the day. If you are going round in a fog of sleepiness, then you need more sleep, but there is no point lying around in bed if you do not need the extra sleep. It will be far more invigorating to get up early and do some meditation, yoga, stretching exercises or go for a walk.

Lack of sleep could make you old before your time

Persistent sleep debt is making us age faster, warn scientists. Chronic or persistent sleep debt is how researchers describe the reduction in sleep from 12 hours a night at the turn of the last century to 7.5 hours a night in this new (third) millennium. In a recent study eleven fit young men received 8 hours' sleep for three nights followed by 4 hours for six nights and 12 hours for seven nights. They all ate the same diet.

During the days following the 4-hour nights, they took 40 per cent longer than normal to regulate their blood sugar levels after high-carbohydrate meals and their ability to secrete insulin fell by 30 per cent. These changes are most probably associated with the development of age-related diabetes and with weight problems.

Sleep deprivation also altered their hormone levels, notably increasing their risk of high blood pressure and the amount of stress hormones in their blood in the afternoon and evening. Raised cortisol levels at this time of day are typical of old people and are thought to be related to memory impairment. All the abnormalities disappeared when the volunteers slept for 12 hours a night.

It is a common myth that you need less sleep as you age. You continue to need the same amount of sleep that you have always needed as an adult, whether that is eight hours a night or twelve. The idea that older people need less sleep has probably arisen because older people are unable to sustain long periods of sleep. They suffer sleep disturbance which means they cannot sleep through the night. Instead they sleep in shorter periods, hence the tendency to doze off during the day.

Overcoming sleep problems – a quick guide

1. Get plenty of fresh air and exercise during the day, but do not exercise for at least one hour before bed.

2. Avoid drinks that contain caffeine during the evening. Some people find that they need to avoid them from lunchtime onwards. These drinks include coffee, tea, cola, chocolate and some other soft and fizzy drinks.

3. Eat early. Avoiding large and/or rich meals during the evening or late at night will help you sleep better. If you are hungry in the evening, have some breakfast cereal or a banana or a milky drink before bed.

4. Medicines can keep you awake. Check the ingredients with the pharmacist or your GP to see whether any drugs you are on contain caffeine (or other substances) that might cause sleep problems. Your doctor may be able to alter the dosage or timing or swap to another medicine.

5. Avoid alcohol before bed. Although alcohol may make you drowsy and a nightcap may get you off to sleep quickly, it can cause you to wake during the night and/or very early in the morning.

6. Establish a pattern. Going to bed at roughly the same time each night will help establish a regular sleep pattern. If you have a very late night, do not stay in bed too long the next morning to compensate and do not have a long daytime sleep, as this will have a knock-on effect on your sleep patterns.

7. Try not to worry. Anxiety can keep you awake at night so that you turn things over and over in your mind. Write them down and tell yourself you will deal with them in the morning when you are refreshed.

8. Stay cool. Keep the bedroom airy and cool; use extra bedclothes and covers to keep you warm rather than keeping the heating on as this is dehydrating and leads to fitful sleep.

9. Buy a hot-water bottle . . . Tests show that you will not fall asleep until the blood vessels in your hands and feet widen to

allow in more blood to heat the extremities. The body's natural (circadian) rhythms should make this happen at night, but if they don't – or if you miss the window of warm opportunity – use a hot-water bottle or wear socks and gloves in bed!

10. Eat more ginger! Ginger is a herbal remedy for circulatory problems and has been shown to improve circulation to the extremities, warming hands and feet. It also inhibits synthesis of the type of prostaglandins that can cause arthritic inflammation – so it should help ease aches and pains that might keep you awake.

Sleep to boost your immune system and prevent cancer

Sleep deprivation undermines the immune system. In one study, people who usually went to bed at 11 p.m. were kept up to 3 a.m. and were given only four hours' sleep instead of their seven to eight hours. They showed depleted defences against viruses and tumours and a dramatic reduction in their levels of interleukin 2, an important chemical for getting rid of cancer cells.

People who go to bed late miss out on slow-wave (non-dream) sleep and move swiftly into deep dream-sleep. During slow-wave sleep the immune system is replenished. Disruptions have the same effect if during slow-wave sleep you are, for example, woken by a baby or a noise. Getting more sleep the next night more or less recovers the levels of body defences, except of interleukin 2, the cancer preventer.

- In studies on students, twenty minutes' extra sleep a day was found to bring them back up to normal immune response level within a few days of a period of sleep deprivation.

Tip   Try to avoid exposure to viruses such as the common cold if you have lost sleep because you will be more susceptible to infection.

Sleep well to learn well

If you are learning a new skill or taking in knowledge during the day, you need rapid eye movement (REM) sleep in order to retain what you have learned. During REM sleep the new skill or knowledge is thought to be reactivated and consolidated. So if you are learning something new, it is probably important to get a good night's sleep afterwards.

Look Younger (How Much Younger is up to You)

The realisation that you are ageing and not immortal, as you believed (consciously or subconsciously) in your youth, can cause considerable psychological stress in itself, particularly if it takes you unawares. It can be a terrible shock to many people when they see the first signs of ageing: the first wrinkle or furrow on the face, the first grey hair, the realisation that attractive sun-kissed freckles have been replaced with liver spots; or in men, hair loss leading to baldness.

Reactions differ. It is an unusual person who welcomes these signs, but a realistic person will accept that these changes are merely a reflection of the way s/he has lived life to date. There may be minor irritation at the passing of time, but there will not be the overreaction of the fantasist who thinks that age cannot touch her (or him). However extreme or nonchalant our reaction to the signs of ageing, most of us do not like it and there are various steps we can take.

By the way, the first item on the list (Step 1) is obligatory for all *Eat to Beat Your Age* readers. You can pick and choose from the rest . . .

Step 1 (not an option at all): Stop whingeing about it After all, what do you expect? Just accept that things can only get worse . . . and from then on they will always seem better than they could be. You will be more optimistic and look less gloomy and therefore younger!

Step 2: Eat to Beat Your Age   Skin cells need plenty of vitamins and minerals so give them an edible facelift. Omega-3 essential fatty acids (EFAs) keep skin cells moist and strong by strengthening the cell membrane or wall. They encourage the production of strong collagen and elastin fibres in the dermis (the deepest layer), which help keep the skin supple and looking younger for longer. Deficiency in EFAs can result in dry skin. Skin needs feeding from the inside because it is being constantly shed in a cycle of between twenty-one and thirty days. Collagen and elastin also need protein, but this is not something to be concerned about. If you eat enough calories, your diet will almost certainly provide you with enough protein. In fact most Western diets provide more than we need.

Step 3: Take vitamin pills to save your skin   There is definitely a case for the judicious use of dietary supplements. Supplements of beta-carotene and vitamin C and E have been shown to help prevent and treat photo-ageing (sunlight-induced ageing) of the skin (in the case of vitamin E, both as pills and in skin creams). These antioxidant vitamins limit DNA damage and consequential cancerous changes. In addition, the antioxidant minerals copper and zinc (see good food sources of antioxidant nutrients, pages 56–8), iron (protein foods), calcium (dairy foods) and the B vitamins (starchy foods and meat) are needed for healthy skin, eyes, teeth and hair and nails. (See page 103 for optimum antioxidant supplementation.)

Step 4: Go to the hairdressers   and have a fringe cut – a light feathery one will hide a lined forehead or a frown. Better still, take your hairdresser's advice and have your hair modernised. A very good cut in a modern, not extreme, style will take years off you. Of course, you need to wear clothes that complement the haircut – so a classic look may be the least extravagant option.

Step 5: Learn make-up tricks   Reshape your face with make-up. This can be particularly helpful because as you age, prominent facial features become even more prominent. For example, big noses look larger, small eyes appear smaller, and pouting (non-silicone variety) lips become thinner. The best way to succeed is to learn the tricks from a professional. Book an appointment with a make-up artist or beautician to teach you how to apply make-up for the best, and most natural, effect. Some make-up counters in department stores offer this service, but make sure you like the products first. If you want to practise yourself, here's how:

- To make a wide nose smaller, apply shader to both sides of the nose from bridge to nostrils, blend in with a moisturiser and put highlighter down the centre from the bridge to the tip.
- To shorten a long nose, apply shader on the tip of the nose and blend in. Wear hair off the face.
- To make eyes larger, have your eyebrows shaped by a professional, and learn how to use an eyebrow pencil to accentuate the natural arch of the brow just above the pupil, and to extend the brow to the outer corner of the eyes.
- Fill out lips by drawing in the shape you want with a natural-coloured lip pencil, then filling in with lip colour. Use a special lip base to prevent lip colour leaking into the feathery lines around the mouth that become accentuated with age.

Step 6: Use appropriate cosmetics   Some ranges of cosmetics have been specially made for the more mature face. For example, the Estée Lauder range Resilience Lift features in its advertisements the fifty-four-year-old American Karen Graham who agreed to come out of retirement as a model to promote cosmetics for women aged over forty. After all, it is a bit of an insult to be sold anti-wrinkle creams by advertisements that obviously feature women under thirty, twenty or even mere teenagers! A good cosmetic cream for the forty-plus should contain ingredients to feed your collagen, elastin and keratin, plus antioxidants and an SPF (sun protection factor) of about 15 (plus whatever other miracle skin products may have been discovered since this book was written . . .) These anti-ageing cosmetics are expensive, but some do have a degree of clinical proof that they have a visible effect, albeit limited, on surface lines (although none gets rid of wrinkles completely).

Step 7: Consider less drastic forms of cosmetic surgery This includes collagen replacement therapy, in which artificial fat is injected into lines and wrinkles to smooth out the creases; a non-surgical facelift, in which a minute current is passed through rollers on the face to tighten muscles; a skin peel/laser treatment, to remove old skin to allow new smooth skin to grow. Or Botox injections, in which a purified version of the food-poisoning bacterium *clostridium botulinum* – brand-name Botox – is injected into your forehead to freeze your facial muscles and remove the frown lines. The muscle-paralysing injection can last up to five months. It will simply stop the production of the furrows that are caused when we unconsciously frown up to 1,000 times a day. (It is also used underarm to prevent sweating!)

Step 8: Consider serious cosmetic surgery Talk to your GP about consulting a reputable aesthetic plastic surgeon for a facelift. Decide with the surgeon (and your nearest and dearest, if they are in on the secret) which course of action would be most useful: eye-bag removal? Lifting of jowls? Removal of saggy neck skin? If you don't mind the tugging, pulling, scalpels, bruising, bandages and post-operative wretchedness, then you may be rewarded by your friends and acquaintances telling you how well or how wonderful you look after you have recovered. Take arnica and vitamin E tablets to aid recovery.

Step 9: Put on weight to fill out your wrinkles This is the eminent advice of Dame Barbara Cartland who maintains that thin women look haggard and gaunt, especially after forty. She has a point . . .

Give Your Face a Lift – Wear Comfortable Shoes

Badly fitting shoes can make you look ten years older! A pained facial expression and a certain amount of deeply etched wrinkles can, according to some chiropodists, be a reflection of a lifetime spent hobbling around in ill-fitting shoes. When you think about it, it makes sense: happy feet means fewer wrinkles. Choosing the best shoes (like diet and exercise habits) should start early in life. Because the twenty-six bones in your feet do not fully set until you are eighteen years old, great importance is put on training fitters of children's shoes to measure and fit their shoes correctly. But once we are adults, we can cram our feet into any unsuitable footwear with the enthusiasm and determination of an Ugly Sister faced with Prince Charming's equerry and a glass slipper two sizes too small.

Even if your feet have been cared for in childhood, damage can still be done to adult feet by wearing the wrong shoes. The ideal shoe to reduce facial wrinkles (and damage to the feet) will have heels no higher than 4cm/1.5in. This, of course, refers to everyday wear; the occasional evening spent tottering on stilettos is fine so long as you do not end up breaking your ankle. The back of the ideal shoe will prevent the heel from sliding up and down while walking. The sole should be flat with a gentle slope upwards under the toes. The upper part that covers the top of the foot should be leather or another natural material that allows the feet to breathe. There should also be a fastening to hold the foot in the shoe – slip-on shoes have to be either too small for the foot or must be held in place by gripping and curling the toes. Shoes should also be able to bend as the foot bends so that the foot is able to move naturally – slip-ons tend to be stiffer to help keep them from slipping off.

To check whether your shoes fit correctly (if you have nothing better to do, or want to keep small children amused for a while by giving them a practical project), stand barefoot on a thin piece of card and mark the position of your longest toe and your heel. Draw round your foot (or feet) and cut out the resulting shapes. Fit this inside the shoe; there should be a 7–14mm gap

(0.25–0.5in) between the end of the card and the heel of the shoe. The width of the shoe should be the same as the widest part of your foot while standing. Your shoes should also be wide enough to allow you to wiggle your toes.

If you suffer from swollen feet, put your shoes on when you get up, before your feet have had a chance to swell.

- It is a myth that you need to 'break in' new shoes; they should fit comfortably from the time they are bought. If they don't, then they don't fit, so don't buy them!

Never soak your feet; it's bad for them

To keep you and your feet sweet, wash your feet every day in warm soapy water, but do not soak them as this creates the right environment for fungal conditions such as athlete's foot. Rinse and dry them well, especially between the toes. Rub a moisturiser into dry skin. If you have soggy wet skin on your feet, particularly between the toes, dab with surgical spirit on cotton wool. Get a chiropodist to cut away any corns or hard skin. Keep your toenails short and cut them straight across. Do not wear tight socks, stockings or tights – allow your toes to wriggle. Exercise your feet throughout the day, especially if sitting at a desk. Keep your feet moving to keep the circulation pumping and to maintain your feet at a comfortable temperature.

Look Younger, Have a Head Massage

Since we are looking after ourselves from head to toe, and we have just dealt with the feet, what about an Indian head massage? It is a traditional technique that is catching on here, with good reason. You may have experienced a short version with a few minutes of massage while having your hair washed at the hairdresser's. The longer version of about ten to fifteen minutes involves lightly massaging oil into the scalp.

Its main function in Indian society is to maintain the hair's glossy appearance and to stimulate the circulation, and thus the nourishment, to the hair follicles which keeps the hair thicker and luxuriant for longer. It is also believed that it helps prevent greying. Because the technique can relieve tension headaches and eye strain, and may be extended to the neck and shoulders, it can help other stress-related muscle tensions. The result is that you can look fresher, younger and more relaxed after a head massage.

Those who might benefit include people with poor posture or who spend long hours in front of a computer screen or in any other similar position. Other benefits of head or gentle face massage may be improved drainage of blocked sinuses.

Smoking

You know what I am going to say:

'Stop!'

Giving up smoking is a complicated process for most people. To give up successfully you have to really want to. For some people, finding out the main reason why they smoke helps them give up, but if the motivation to smoke is complex, then stopping will also be harder. Learning to dislike the habit enough is a great incentive.

The immediate benefits of giving up

These include:

- no longer smelling horrible
- having more money to spend
- greater resistance to coughs, colds and other illnesses
- a higher level of fitness to allow you to enjoy life more

The longer-term benefits

More years of active life   If you started smoking young, continue to middle age and then give up, it is estimated that you can almost reverse your risk of dying from complications related to smoking. If you stop before middle age, you avoid almost all the risks.

Fewer wrinkles The free radicals generated by smoking cause skin damage and result in smokers having more, and deeper, wrinkles than non-smokers.

How to live ten years longer

An analysis of two US trials that included 385,400 people* concluded that low blood cholesterol, low blood pressure and not smoking increases life expectancy by almost ten years. Public health policy should therefore concentrate on preventing high blood cholesterol and high blood pressure and discouraging people from smoking, say the researchers at the Northwestern University Medical School, Chicago. Hear! Hear!

* The Multiple Risk Factor Intervention Trial and the Chicago Heart Association Detection Project in Industry trial.

Giving up smoking does not mean that you will gain weight

Fear of gaining weight is a major disincentive among women who might otherwise try to give up smoking. But not everyone puts on weight when they stop smoking. When appetite that was previously suppressed by smoking recovers, it is normal to put on a few pounds. However, this weight can be lost in a matter of months once you are comfortable enough to accommodate adjustments to your food intake and take more physical activity. The main thing is to stay positive. Remember, your body no longer burns up extra calories trying to detoxify itself from the poisonous by-products of smoking. If your appetite increases, you will probably not have to eat less, just differently.

Exercise helps smokers give up

Being more active when you stop smoking will also help prevent weight gain. Some research shows that combining high-intensity aerobic exercise with other measures helps women quit smoking successfully. In one controlled trial, the women who exercised were more likely not to take up smoking again one year after giving up than were the controls, who received counselling but took no exercise.

Ginseng – a 'Smart' Aid for the Third Age?

Ginseng is popular with athletes because it helps the body increase its resistance to physical and emotional stress and fatigue. Ginseng is generally stimulating and can increase alertness and concentration as well as stamina and strength. There are several different types of ginseng: Korean (*Panax ginseng*), American (*Panax quinquefolius*) and Siberian (*Eleutherococcus senticosus*). Siberian ginseng is said to be the most therapeutic. Ginseng works best if taken for short periods. Six weeks of taking the supplements followed by a two-month break and then a period of taking them for another six weeks is one way. For a more sustained effect, two weeks on and two weeks off may be preferred. Do not take ginseng near to bedtime as it can cause insomnia. Do not use it if you have high blood pressure, during pregnancy or while breast-feeding.

Studies of Siberian ginseng show that it is an adaptogen, which means that it supports the body under stress. It can promote healthy function of the adrenal gland and improve the use of oxygen in exercising the muscles. Endurance and mental acuity have been shown to be enhanced in Russian studies, from where claims also come that Siberian ginseng supports the immune system and the liver.

The Sun Has Got his Hat on – Have You?

You would have to have come from another planet if you were of an age to be interested in this book and you had not heard that exposure to the sun causes skin cancer. Even the weather forecasters use little icons of sunscreen bottles, sunhats and sunglasses to remind us to protect ourselves from the sun's rays.

There is no doubt that exposure to sunlight, particularly leading to sunburn and especially in the very young, can lead to skin cancer, eye cataracts and accelerated skin ageing.

For inveterate sun lovers

In all this quite proper concern and education, it is easy to overlook the basic human love of the sun and the instinctive desire – even urgent drive among some people – to get out in its rays during the summer. Many people love spending time in the sun. And until recent knowledge of the link between sun and skin cancer, there was advice to do just that.

Nature-cure clinics in the early part of the 1900s advised patients to take air baths. This quaint old-fashioned way of describing sunbathing was more about enjoying the fresh air, and it was done with considerably more clothes on than in modern sunbathing, hence the concomitant increase in skin cancer. Air baths were not taken to the sunbathing extremes of the typical modern tourist, who leaves an indoor job in the northern hemisphere on a Friday evening and is fully exposed to the sun's rays in the hottest part of the day on a beach in the Mediterranean or Caribbean the next morning. Clearly that is asking for trouble, but in moderation and taking appropriate precautions such as plenty of sunscreen applied regularly, sunglasses, sunhat and shade during the hottest part of the day, the sun can make you feel and, paradoxically in the short term, even look a lot younger.

The effect of the sun has been measured and evaluated and shown to help reduce the frequency of depression. A moderate amount of sun can help skin conditions such as psoriasis. The action of sunlight on the skin in making vitamin D enhances bone health, and may even reduce the risk of heart disease – but it's true there are other less risky ways of achieving these results.

How big a risk are you prepared to take?

Accepting that sunbathing, like everything else in life, is not without risk, some people might feel that its potential benefits for them outweigh the ageing factor. Weighing the pros and cons might determine the depth of suntan that you are prepared to risk.

Obviously fair-haired people are most vulnerable and they are at greatest risk of skin cancer from repeated exposure to the sun. Like those of any other form of radiation, the effects of the sun are cumulative, so the more you go for it, the more potentially damaging they are.

Regardless of whether or not it is possible to achieve one safely, a suntan will have an ageing effect on the skin. Wrinkles and age spots are like the rings and knots on a tree; they advertise your age. And if you do not wish to do this in those terms, the best course of action is to avoid the sun and to become a zealot in your use of sunscreen products. It may also cost you a lot less in the long run. Having acquired the tan and the wrinkles that will inevitably follow, you may then feel in need of expensive special cosmetics or of cosmetic surgery to try to reduce or reverse the damage.

Anti-ageing sun and skin tips

We may stock up on our sun creams and lotions for overseas holidays but we should also use them every day for protection against repeated exposure to the sun at home.

- Use a moisturiser with a sun protection factor (SPF) of 15 daily from March to the end of October.
- Choose a foundation with an SPF of at least 15 and also a moisturiser with a sun protection factor in it.
- Exposure is more related to time of day than intensity of sunshine, so stay in the shade between 11 a.m. and 3 p.m.

- To avoid ageing, avoid getting a tan. Sunscreen does not make getting a tan safe – a tanned skin is a damaged skin! It reduces the risk of burning, which in turn reduces the risk of skin cancer. But whether the long-term use of sunscreens can prevent skin cancer is not yet known.
- Apply sunscreen twenty minutes before exposure and reapply frequently – don't forget nose, ears and back of neck. If you wait until the skin reddens and tingles, that is too late.
- For children (that's when anti-ageing measures should start) use sunblock with an SPF of 30.
- You need sunscreens to protect you from UVB rays, the ones that cause sunburn. Sunscreen products show how much protection they offer by giving their SPF (sun protection factor) followed by a number. The higher the SPF number, the longer you can spend in the sun. Ten years ago most sunscreen products had SPFs of less than 10; today most product ranges also include SPFs of 15 to 20 – some up to 50.
- To be effective sunscreens need to be applied thickly. Among manufacturers there is an internationally agreed application rate of two milligrams per square centimetre of skin. Studies show that people typically apply between 0.5 to $1.3mg/cm^2$. As a result most people only get 20 to 50 per cent of the protection they expect, which is why some people who use sunscreens still get sunburnt.
- A star rating on sunscreen products indicates protection against UVA rays, the ones that cause ageing. Everyone needs at least ★★★ but ★★★★ is better.
- Most people should use an SPF of 15 or more unless they have naturally brown or black skin.
- Wear sunglasses for protection against harmful rays that can result in eye cataracts. Look for the British Kitemark BS2724: 1987.
- Cover up with a hat and loose-fitting cotton clothing.
- Drink plenty of cool non-alcoholic drinks to prevent dehydration.

Eat to beat suntan damage

Sunbathers given daily supplements of vitamins C and E during an American dermatology trial were better protected than sunbathers who received a placebo (dummy tablet). Those who took the vitamin pills received 2g of vitamin C and 1,000 IU of d-alpha-tocopherol (or natural vitamin E).

In another, Australian trial, 1,600 people were given one of the following: a daily application of an SPF 15+ sunscreen to the head, neck, arms and hands, and beta-carotene supplementation (30mg per day); a sunscreen plus placebo tablets; beta-carotene alone; or a placebo alone. Participants were followed up for four and a half years. The trial showed that squamous-cell carcinoma, but not basal-cell carcinoma (the two less serious of the three types of skin cancer, malignant melanoma being the most dangerous), seems to be prevented if sunscreen is used routinely in the long term. Beta-carotene was shown to be neither beneficial nor harmful.

Do Vegetarians Age Better?

A major seventeen-year study of 11,000 vegetarians and health-conscious people in the UK tried to discover any connection between a vegetarian diet and causes of death. In particular, the researchers looked at daily consumption of wholemeal bread, bran cereals, nuts or dried fruit and fresh fruit and salad.

During the seventeen-year follow-up, the group studied had a death rate of about half that of the general population before the age of eighty. After smoking was adjusted for, daily consumption of fresh fruit and/or daily salad was associated with a 24 per cent reduction in mortality from heart disease, a 32 per cent reduction in death from stroke and a 21 per cent reduction in all causes of death compared with less frequent consumption.

The UK study was initially set up to test the hypothesis that daily consumption of wholemeal bread (as an indicator of a high-fibre diet) and a vegetarian diet are associated with a reduction in deaths from heart disease caused by narrowing of the arteries by cholesterol deposits; but fruit turned out to be more significant. This is in line with other studies from around the world that have looked at the health effects of frequent versus infrequent consumption of fruit or fruit juice and green salad. These other studies concluded that a high intake of vitamin C and of beta-carotene in the form of fruit is the protective factor against heart disease.

The low death rate among fruit eaters is comparable to findings in similar trials: one of German vegetarians and health-conscious people; the Oxford Vegetarian Study; and a study of Californian Seventh-Day Adventists. Vegetarians show low death rates for diseases of the circulatory and respiratory systems. Their low rates of death from cancer of the bronchus and lung, compared with the general population, is probably mainly accounted for by the low proportion of smokers among vegetarians and the health-conscious. Other factors such as levels of physical activity may also have been protective.

Will Beany Babies (vegetarians) live longer?

Both vegetarian and non-vegetarian diets can be equally healthy (or unhealthy). However, vegetarians, I am sure, would like me to point out studies that suggest their diet can be the healthiest. For example, one study compared over twelve years the death rates of 6,000 non-meat eaters with those of 5,000 meat eaters, and discovered that vegetarians were nearly 40 per cent less likely to die of cancer and 30 per cent less likely to die of heart disease than meat eaters.

These findings do not mean that meat is harmful, but because Beany Babies have a higher intake of pulses, nuts, vegetables, fruit and cereals, they are likely to be eating more protective nutrients and have a lower saturated-fat intake. Pan-European studies also associate high intakes of vegetables and fruit with lower incidence of heart disease, cataract and some cancers. The results may also be influenced by the fact that overall, vegetarians tend to have a healthier lifestyle; the studies show that many vegetarians exercise regularly and are non-smokers.

Don't let the funeral in Four Weddings be yours . . .

If you saw the eponymous film, the following will not come as a surprise to you. Deaths from heart attack are far more likely after a high-fat meal such as is traditionally enjoyed at Christmas, birthdays, Thanksgiving – and even weddings . . .

Overweight middle-aged men with excess fat in the abdomen area, and with low levels of HDL (the beneficial type of cholesterol), are most likely to have a heart attack after a high-fat meal. For at least six hours after such a meal, the effect of the fat on the arteries makes them unable to fully expand or to handle any rush of blood flow that may be needed during physical exertion or emotional stress. That is why people who already have clogged arteries often suffer heart attacks soon after high-fat meals.

Tips

- Taking antioxidant vitamins before such a meal – 800 IU of vitamin E or 1g of vitamin C – has in trials allowed arteries to expand to accommodate surges in blood flow for up to six hours after eating.
- Taking 3–4g of omega-3 fish oils per day for a month has lowered circulating levels of triglycerides; more so during fasting and modestly after meals.

Eat to Boost Your Immune System

Good nutrition is now generally accepted as vital for healthy immune responses to fight off everything from the common cold to cancer. And since the immune system's efficiency declines as we age, this is yet another compelling reason to focus on food for long-term health. All the body's first-line defences against infection rely on a good supply of nutrients. To give examples of these defences, we are protected by our skin; by the mucous membranes in our gut and lungs; by the action of less easily understood general body defenders, such as phagocytic cells, which swallow up invaders, and by natural body chemicals such as interferon.

In addition we have a second line of defence: antigens, which are a specific defence against previously encountered infections. For example, once you have had measles/chickenpox/mumps – or the vaccine against mumps and measles – the antibodies produced by your body for that specific disease should prevent you from getting it again. Of course, in abnormally sensitive (atopic) people, immune responses can result in allergies, which are inappropriate reactions to other external antigens such as food or pollen.

Feed up your natural defences

In very malnourished people, immune response processes (such as phagocytosis – the engulfing and destroying of invading bacteria) are poor, leaving them open to infection. Deficiencies of the minerals iron and zinc and of vitamin A compromise their immune system. It is likely that only a small drop below the level of our daily requirement of these or other vitamins and minerals can alter or impair our immune response. This is not to say that supplements or megadosages are advisable because excessive intakes can also cause harm. Zinc is a case in point; while it is a popular remedy for the common cold (and is also involved in wound healing), too much can be harmful and reduce immune defences.

As we age there is a fall in the number of active cells within the immune system. Lack of variety in the diet, eating only a limited range of foods or a low quantity of poor-quality foods can all suppress the immune system. Eating well can help combat the effect of ageing on the immune system. Trials with elderly patients given supplements of vitamin E have shown that the immune system can in effect be switched back on. Vitamin E does this by turning off a major inhibitor of the immune system, a type of prostaglandin that increases with age. The elderly who received the supplements also suffered fewer infectious diseases and required less antibiotic treatment than their contemporaries.

Foods and nutrients for a healthy immune system

- Carotenoids – as antioxidants and for their role as scavenger cells that kill invaders: **eat more** yellow, orange and red fruit and vegetables.
- Vitamin B6 promotes production of white cells which fight infections: **eat more** nuts, spinach, potatoes.
- Folates to increase white blood cell activity: **eat more** beans, pulses, etc., lettuce, peas.
- Vitamin C for its antioxidant powers and to raise levels of a substance called immunoglobulin, an antibody which protects against infection by bacteria and viruses: **eat more** vegetables and fruits, especially citrus.
- Vitamin E to stimulate immune responses: **eat more** wheatgerm, vegetable oil, whole grains.
- Selenium, another antioxidant that also attacks invading bacteria: **eat more** tuna, eggs, wholemeal bread.
- Zinc promotes wound healing and is a defence against the common cold: **eat more** seafood, eggs, wholemeal bread.

Sunshine immune boost

A certain amount of the ultraviolet (UV) radiation in sunlight is good for health and helps the body produce vitamin D, but too much UV exposure can suppress the immune system and lower the body's resistance to infection and cancer. Research shows that the immune function of people on low-carotenoid diets is suppressed more when exposed to the sun than people with higher blood levels of beta-carotene.

Never say you'll have your Martini stirred again

Speculating on why secret agent James Bond seems so healthy in his long-lived popularity, Canadian researchers tested the antioxidant properties of Bond's favourite drink, 'shaken, not stirred' Martinis, reports the *British Medical Journal.*

'As Mr Bond is not afflicted by cataracts or cardiovascular disease, an investigation was conducted to determine whether the mode of preparing Martinis has an influence on their antioxidant capacity,' stated the researchers.

They found that shaken Martinis had a far greater antioxidant activity than stirred Martinis and that both were more effective than gin or vermouth alone. Which led them to conclude '007's profound state of health may be due, at least in part, to compliant bartenders . . .'

Is HRT the Anti-Ageing Tool for You?

About one in five women aged between fifty and sixty-four takes hormone replacement therapy (HRT). And anyone who has ever read anything about the subject will be aware of the high-profile women who attribute at least some of their youthful good looks and energy to HRT. This is probably not surprising as they must in part be persuaded of its potential benefits in order to take it, and no one has ever tested them with a placebo to see otherwise . . .

But is HRT the fountain of youth at which all women should be drinking, once they reach the menopause? It is tempting, particularly as it offers the prospect of enhancing the quality of one-third of a woman's life.

Why would you want to take HRT?

Some of the benefits of HRT can be life-transforming:

- increasing life expectancy by more than three years
- helping to maintain skin elasticity
- helping to maintain bone density to prevent osteoporosis
- slowing periodontal disease, the inflammation that affects the tissues that support the teeth, thus preventing tooth loss
- enabling an active sex life
- producing feelings of improved well-being
- possibly helping to prevent Alzheimer's disease because of its antioxidant activity (oestrogen seems to be as powerful as vitamin E in its effect on nerve cells and may cross the blood–brain barrier more easily than vitamin antioxidants)

So it is not surprising that many women want HRT, yet many more women who could benefit from it do not take it.

Menopause symptoms

The therapy was developed to alleviate the symptoms of the menopause, which happens around the age of fifty, although some women can experience symptoms from the age of forty. During the menopause, which occurs over two or three years, there is a reduction and cessation of oestrogen production, the ovaries stop producing eggs and periods also stop. The symptoms of oestrogen reduction include hot flushes, night sweats, sleep disturbance, palpitations, irritability and/or depression, vaginal dryness, recurrent urinary infections and bone mineral loss, which can lead to osteoporosis and more fractures. The loss of oestrogen also increases the risk of heart disease, and speeds up cognitive (mental) decline.

How can HRT help?

HRT, as tablets, skin patches or implants under the skin, was developed to alleviate these symptoms. Recent trials have even found snorting HRT to be effective, and unlike snorting cocaine it seems not to damage the nose, ears or throat! And soon there will be vaginal rings and gels.

However, HRT does not work for everyone, particularly if the wrong form of treatment is chosen – and there is a price to pay.

Giving oestrogen stimulates the cells of the endometrium, the lining of the uterus (or womb), which can lead to cancer. Women on HRT have six times the risk of endometrial cancer after five years' use. To combat this, progestogen is also given. This is a drug version of the natural female sex hormone progesterone. Progestogen counters oestrogen's stimulation of the endometrium to reduce the risk of cancer; it induces monthly shedding of the uterine lining so that periodic bleeding occurs. However, progestogen may have other side-effects, too, such as weight gain, fluid accumulation and headaches. For women who have had a hysterectomy, oestrogen alone can be given.

Oestrogen has been shown to reduce the demineralisation of bones and the subsequent risk of fractures, but when a woman stops taking HRT bone loss accelerates, so there is little, if any, lasting benefit to the bones. It is not yet known how long it is safe to take HRT.

A 50 per cent reduction in heart attacks and strokes is also claimed for women on HRT but this is debatable, as the type of women who take HRT tend to be healthier than their counterparts before they start.

Do the pluses outweigh the minuses?

Whether the benefits of reduced risk of heart disease outweigh the increased risk of developing breast cancer (albeit probably only the uncommon, highly treatable forms) for those taking HRT is another factor in the equation of pros and cons. The current statistics are that around 130 women per 100,000 die of breast cancer between the ages of sixty-five and sixty-nine compared with 590 per 100,000 who will die from heart disease or stroke. The figures rise to around 150 per 100,000 dying from breast cancer between the ages of seventy and seventy-four and, 1,075 per 100,000 dying from heart disease and stroke.

Unfortunately there is no definitive answer because the results of the first ten years of a long-term study comparing the health of women taking HRT with those who do not will not be available until 2008 and the subsequent ten-year follow-up will not be through until 2018.

Pros and cons of HRT

Benefits – relieves menopausal symptoms, lowers risk of heart disease, lowers risk of osteoporosis.

Possible benefits – preserves cognitive abilities, reduces the risk of Alzheimer's disease, helps maintain youthful looks, reduces the risk of colorectal cancer.

Hazards – higher risk of breast cancer, higher risk of endometrial cancer.

Possible hazards – higher risk of ovarian cancer, higher risk of thromboembolism (blood clots in veins), unknown long-term side-effects.

Eat to beat menopausal symptoms

Instead of accepting what the menopause throws at you, or trying to just grow old gracefully (or disgracefully, whichever you prefer), you could try some other anti-ageing strategies, such as improving your diet to increase your nutritional buffer against the onslaught of menopausal symptoms:

- Increase your antioxidant intake to take advantage of their anti-inflammatory benefits to combat hot flushes. This applies particularly to vitamin E, shown in one trial to help reduce hot flushes. Vitamin E is found in olive oil, avocado, tuna and fortified spreads. To increase intake of other antioxidants, eat more fruit and vegetables and complex carbohydrate foods.
- Swap from meat sources of protein to fish, oily fish in particular, and more soya-based foods such as tofu, soya milk and meat alternatives made from soya protein. An Oriental

239

diet could have positive advantages because the Japanese, for example, have no word for 'hot flush', the menopause being such a symptom-free event in the life of Japanese women eating the traditional national diet. The main difference between a traditional Eastern diet and a modern Western diet is the large proportion of vegetables, beans and particularly soya products, and the low fat content, with much of the fat coming from fish. There is also the inclusion of mineral-rich seaweed products (but see tip below). But first you need some sushi cookery lessons! The main ingredient of the Japanese diet to which the harmonisation of hormonal changes has been attributed is the phyto-oestrogens in soya (see soya, Chapter 2).

Tip   Seaweed as sold in supermarkets as a vegetable side dish to a Japanese or Chinese meal is in fact cabbage fried to be crispy. Go to a health food shop or ethnic store for true seaweed products.

Phyto-oestrogens as tablets

Trials with phyto-oestrogen supplements have shown that they can reduce hot flushes. Although only a few small trials have been done so far, isoflavone supplements have been shown to have the potential to reduce the risk of heart attacks and strokes, but whether they are as effective as HRT remains to be seen.

In addition, the long-term effects of taking these 'natural' supplements is not yet known. And some experts warn that they might also trigger hormone-dependent cancers in susceptible women.

Osteoporosis drugs may share HRT benefits

An American trial has shown that the selective oestrogen receptor modulator (SERM) drug raloxifene, currently licensed to treat osteoporosis in post-menopausal women, significantly reduces the risk of breast cancer. In a three-year trial, more than 7,500 women below the age of eighty-one were chosen at random to take either raloxifene or a placebo and were followed for three and a half years. There was a 76 per cent lower risk of breast cancer among the women taking raloxifene than among those taking the placebo. Thirteen cases of breast cancer were diagnosed among the 5,129 post-menopausal women taking raloxifene, compared with twenty-seven cases in the 2,576 controls.

The drug shares similarities with phyto-oestrogens (see soya, page 89). It is one of a new generation of selected action oestrogens that are believed to mimic the effects of oestrogen in reducing bone loss and cholesterol, while inhibiting oestrogen's ability to increase the risk of some forms of breast cancer. Although raloxifene does not seem to cause an increase in uterine cancer, it was associated with increased incidence of deep-vein thrombosis and pulmonary emboli. A larger, long-term study of 22,000 women comparing the cancer-preventing effects of raloxifene and tamoxifen (the anti-breast-cancer drug) started in 1999.

Brain power, oestrogen and HRT

Oestrogens may also improve cognitive function (thinking, reasoning, etc.) in post-menopausal women. Oestrogen treatment altered brain activation patterns in women who were given verbal memory tasks. Activation responses are associated with everyday memory function, for example remembering telephone numbers. However, new studies have failed to deliver the early promise that oestrogen could halt cognitive decline or slow the progression of Alzheimer's. More studies are needed.

HRT: what should you do?

The decision to take HRT or not is one that can only be made after discussing the issues and your personal health history with your GP. As you have seen, there are plenty of other things you can do, through diet and exercise and lifestyle, to reduce the symptoms.

HRT Recipes

Why not bake yourself a cake rich in phyto-oestrogens? HRT 'cake' has become popular and cereal bars rich in phyto-oestrogens are promoted as a preventative against breast cancer. Here are my recipes for Beat Your Age phyto-oestrogen-rich cakes and bakes. Safe for all ages!

HRT Sweet Ginger Flapjacks

(makes 8)

55g/2oz demerara sugar
115g/4oz margarine
2 tbsp syrup from a jar of stem ginger
150g/5oz oats
75g/3oz soya flour
2 pieces stem ginger, chopped
55g/2oz pumpkin seeds
25g/1oz linseed

Butter or grease a 17.5cm/7in square tin and heat the oven to 180°C/350°F/Gas Mark 4. Put the sugar, margarine and syrup in a pan or a microwave-proof jug and heat until melted together. Stir well. Stir into the dry ingredients and spoon into the tin. Bake for 20 minutes. Remove from the oven and cut through at once into fingers or squares. Leave in the tin until cold, then recut before removing and storing in an airtight tin.

HRT Blueberry Muffins

(makes 8)

55g/2oz soya flour
55g/2oz wholemeal flour
1 tsp baking powder
55g/2oz date purée (see below)

1 large egg
25g/1oz linseed
25g/1oz sesame seed
125ml/4fl oz soya milk
25g/1oz melted butter
115g/4oz blueberries

Heat the oven to 190°C/375°F/Gas Mark 5 and put 8 large paper muffin cases on a baking tray or grease a muffin baking pan. Put the flours and baking powder in a mixing bowl. Add the date purée (below), egg and seeds. Beat to a smooth consistency, adding the soya milk and melted butter as you work until the mixture drops easily from a spoon. Stir in the blueberries and spoon into the muffin cases. Bake for 15–20 minutes.

Date purée

To make date purée, simmer dried dates in enough water to prevent them from sticking to the bottom of the pan and burning. When soft, beat to a purée with a wooden spoon.

HRT Oat Biscuits

(makes 18)

25g/1oz linseed
25g/1oz sesame seeds
55g/2oz butter or margarine, melted
55g/2oz demerara sugar
60g/2½oz soya flour
grated rind of 1 lemon
75g/3oz wholemeal flour
75g/3oz oats

Heat the oven to 190°C/375°F/Gas Mark 5 and grease 2 baking trays. Put the seeds, margarine, sugar and soya flour in a food

processor and blend to a sticky paste. Add the lemon rind. Mix in
the wholemeal flour and oats and gently knead to a manageable
ball of dough. Roll out on a lightly floured surface, to 0.5cm or just
over a quarter of an inch thick and cut out biscuits with a
7.5cm/3in cutter. Bake for 15 minutes until golden. Remove from
the oven and leave on a wire rack to cool and become crisp.

HRT Carrot Passion Cake

(serves 8–10)

55g/2oz butter
25g/1oz sugar
115g/4oz date purée
2 eggs
150g/5oz grated carrot
75g/3oz wholemeal flour
75g/3oz soya flour
2 tsp baking powder
1 tsp ground cinnamon
25g/1oz linseed
25g/1oz sunflower seeds
125ml/4fl oz soya milk
2 pieces stem ginger, finely chopped

Frosting
55g/2oz butter, softened
55g/2oz icing sugar, sifted
grated rind of 1 orange
few drops of orange flower water (optional)

Line the base of a 22cm/8in cake tin with silicone paper and heat
the oven to 180°C/350°F/Gas Mark 4. Cream the butter, sugar
and date purée together. Add the eggs, carrots, flours, baking
powder, cinnamon and seeds and beat together, adding the soya
milk to soften the mixture as you work. Fold in the ginger. Spoon
into the prepared tin and smooth the top level. Bake for 35–40

minutes. When completely cold, cover with frosting. To make frosting, beat all the ingredients together until soft.

Something else to chew on

Chewing gum may be socially unacceptable in some circles (and some countries), and disgusting when thoughtlessly discarded, but it has proven benefits in helping you keep your teeth, and in whitening teeth that may have become stained over the years by tea, coffee and red wine.

Chewing gum promotes saliva flow which helps clear food particles from the mouth. Saliva creates the right pH balance in the mouth to combat enamel erosion from acidic fizzy drinks, and it also provides minerals which help to repair acid attacks by bacteria which feed on the sugars from food and drink that stick to the teeth.

Chewing gums that are sweetened with sorbitol and xylitol also seem to have a protective effect against dental caries. In some countries their presence is flashed on the pack because the protective effect is well known. In the UK it is, apparently, not of enough interest to consumers, but you can find xylitol in Wrigleys Extra Gum, Oral-B Dental Health Gum (and in Orbit Gum for children). Ice White Gum contains sodium bicarbonate (baking soda) which has a whitening effect on the teeth – tests have shown that it can reduce 35 per cent of coffee and wine stains.

Put on a Happy Face

If I was to ask you now, 'What is the one ingredient missing (so far) for slowing ageing?' I think many of you might answer – laughter.

Laughter is probably one of the best anti-ageing medicines. But as humour is a personal thing, and as I do not know you personally, it is difficult to inject humour into a book such as this. You might find the television programme *Father Ted* amusing, I might fail to see anything funny in it; you might be a *Monty Python* fan, or you might be offended by *The Vicar of Dibley*, which others find hilarious. Humour is very personal. But it is essential for a long – and happy – life.

There is not a lot of medical research available to prove the point to you, but scientists have located where humour appreciation resides in the brain: it is a role of the right frontal lobe! This was discovered by testing patients who had focal damage in various areas of the brain. People with damage to this area had the most disrupted ability to appreciate humour. They found it hard to get jokes and they did not understand the humour in cartoons. Sadly they cannot have a humour transplant to solve the problem. Humour is not something you can put back once it has gone missing.

Although much of the evidence that laughter helps people get better is anecdotal from nurses and patients who say that it helps, there is little British research to support specific humour or laughter 'interventions' as beneficial in the short or long term. In the US and in France humour or laughter therapy is used in some hospitals.

France, for example, has Le Rire Médecin, a team of artists who work with medical care workers and perform regularly for children in hospital. There is an ethical code for the artists who aim to help children and their families cope with hospitalisation. The artist bases his or her work on respect for the dignity, the personality and the privacy of the child and his or her family. And they observe medical codes of conduct on confidentiality. Working as a team, they try to make humour and fantasy become part of hospital life.

What they do is based on the knowledge that if you can laugh, you may be helping yourself physiologically. Laughter prompts physiological changes that may be beneficial to the immune, endocrine and other systems of the body.

But whether various types of laughter or a sense of humour have different advantages is not known. For example, does laughing at a TV programme or the clowns' antics at the circus have the same effect as having a giggle with friends? And if you laugh at others' misfortunes, does that have the same biochemical effect as when your laughter is motivated by other emotions? Is it the laugh or the underlying feeling that is important? Researchers are now trying to answer these questions.

So far it seems that mirthful laughter decreases or lessens the effects of stress-related hormones. It also affects the immune system, increasing both the activity of cells that kill invading bacteria and viruses and the production of immunoglobulins. Mirthful laughter also increases the production and activity of interferon-gamma which prevents invading viruses from replicating, both immediately and into the next day.

These beneficial effects have been seen in people watching funny films or programmes but does being funny yourself or being able to laugh in stressful situations, at mishaps, or over other pitfalls of daily living, have a different effect?

In short, the answer is yes. Being able to produce your own humour in response to everyday events can also prompt the production of endorphins (natural opiates) and lessen the production of stress hormones.

And you do not have to be born funny. Learning to look on the bright side is something that can successfully be taught through behaviour therapy. Changing your outlook in this way has been likened to athletic training. You can learn to exercise a sense of humour in the same way that you can train your body to become fitter for life.

So go on, let's see a big smile.
Thank you, keep smiling.

Reduce the Impact of Age on Your Spirit

Is faith a good medicine to hold back the years?

As interest in alternative and complementary medicine has grown, the notion of linking medical to spiritual or religious care has become widely popular, especially in the USA. For many people, religious and spiritual activities provide comfort in the face of illness. Around thirty US medical schools now include in their curricula courses on religion, spirituality and health. This begs the question: 'Can religion and spiritual activities enhance health and slow ageing?' While nobody has satisfactorily answered this (either proving or disproving it), it might be worth exploring further to see if it could have an anti-ageing effect for you.

In a recent poll of 1,000 US adults, 79 per cent of the respondents believed that spiritual faith can help people recover from disease, and 63 per cent believed that physicians should talk to patients about spiritual faith. If this is the case, it would be interesting to ask the same respondents if they believe that faith can also help prevent or slow the onset of diseases associated with ageing? After all, prayer has been part of medical therapy in church congregations since time immemorial.

It has been said by others that the medicine of the future is going to be prayer and Prozac, with doctors asking what they can do to support patients' faith or religious commitment. Some patients may think that religious or spiritual matters are (like financial and marital matters) private and personal, even though all these aspects of life impinge upon our health and how well we recover from illness or avoid it – and, of course, whether we look younger or ten years older than our actual age.

Answering your prayers

Prayers may comfort, but do they work? One American trial, subject to stringent medical controls, suggests it can. A team of Christians from different denominations were recruited to pray for half the patients admitted to a coronary care unit. The patients were unaware of the prayers (and their consent to be prayed for was not sought!) Those who were prayed for got better more quickly than those who were not prayed for.

This is not really new. Studies in the past have measured the outcomes of disease against the frequency of church attendance or prayer. While some research has shown that religious attendance improves outcomes, other researchers have found that neither church attendance nor religious involvement is associated with lower mortality. Similarly, the degree of faith and private reflection has not been shown to increase mortality rates either way.

Other studies have shown that a greater degree of religiousness (assessed as service as a Roman Catholic priest, as a nun, Mormon priest, or Trappist or Benedictine monk) is associated with lower death rate and disease. But then these people are not inclined to smoke, drink, be promiscuous, eat meat or suffer stress (in the general application of the term).

The benefits of membership of a religious order, and the sense of support and belonging to a religious congregation, must confer benefits. While monks who take a vow of silence can hardly be described as sociable, the social side of being a member of a congregation or a prayer group must have health benefits, calculable or not.

Of course, religious or spiritual involvement may not necessarily be helpful. Religions have in the past promoted the idea that the vicissitudes of very old age and disease are due to moral failure, and that 'better' people are more deserving of health and longevity than less-good people. So linking spirituality or religion with health has the potential for burdening people who age more quickly or fall sick sooner with age-related diseases with the undeserved guilt of moral failure.

In truth earthly concerns about ageing are probably not high on the agendas of religious people because for them everlasting life after death is more important.

Even if religious activity does confer beneficial health outcomes, it is doubtful that it could be widely advocated like anti-ageing guidelines for giving up smoking or losing weight.

'Get a life' and live longer

This rather commonplace suggestion is quite apt if you apply it to healthy ageing. It seems that if you have a good social life, or you are socially active and/or productive or useful, then you will live longer. This also applies to people who are less healthy and less physically active. Regardless of physical fitness, if you are socially active you will live longer and see improvements in your health.

One American study followed more than 2,500 men and women aged between sixty-five and eighty. After thirteen years they concluded that social and productive activities are as effective as fitness activities in lowering the risk of death and that valuable social activities may help to increase the quality and length of life.

Get a grip on your life and think positive

Together with changes to the way you think and live your life, you have the potential for a longer, healthier and happier life right here in your hands. So be optimistic about your future. Optimists have a longer life than pessimists. If you want proof for what might seem a mere common-sense observation then here it is: researchers at the Mayo Clinic in Minnesota have found that people with a positive outlook live on average 19 per cent longer than those who are miserable.

It may be that optimists' immune systems are stronger because of their attitude of embracing life, or it may be that they seek medical help and act to get better rather than taking a fatalistic approach to their health and giving up when things go wrong.

Or it may be simply that they are happy to live in Minnesota where all the women are strong and all the men are good-looking . . .

CHAPTER SIX

Eat to Beat Your Age: Thirty-Day Anti-Ageing Action Plan

Do not feel overwhelmed by this action plan. It is designed to give you a series of starting points to put some anti-ageing strategies in place in your life. **You are not meant to do everything!** Some things will appeal more than others so have a go and find out what suits you best.

The aim is for you to have both a long-term healthy eating pattern and a regular physical activity routine in place by the end of the thirty days. You should also have a better understanding of your own mental attitudes and how much you need to change to ensure a happier, healthier future.

Day 1

From today:

- the food you eat
- the amount of physical activity you take
- the number of hours you sleep
- the way you perform and handle frustrations at work and at home
- the relationships you have with your family and friends

will all change for the better. They will work together to keep you younger than your chronological age.

Let's flesh out those statements one by one so that you can see in more detail how they might slow down the ageing process.

The food you eat   is going to help keep you young if you do two simple things:

- eat it in the right proportions (see Chapter 1)
- regularly eat lots of anti-ageing foods (see the list in Chapter 2)

The amount of physical activity you take   will keep you younger for longer if you increase it to:

- improve your fitness so that you have more energy
- control your weight so that you feel and look fitter and face a future with fewer health problems
- tone and shape you so that you look (and feel) ten years younger

The number of hours you sleep   will provide anti-ageing benefits if you adjust this so that you are no longer deprived of enough sleep. Towards this end, try to achieve a better balance between the potentially conflicting demands of work, fitness and family activities. Trying to fit too much in can reduce the number of hours' sleep you get. If you get enough sleep you will find that:

- your memory improves
- you will learn new things more quickly (instead of more slowly as you age)
- your body will repair and renew itself more efficiently, keeping you younger for longer

The way you perform at work   and handle the frustrations of working life can also be improved to bring anti-ageing rewards. It may mean opening a dialogue with your employer to overcome frustrations. This can be done either as an individual or through existing channels, depending on your circumstances. Explain what is demoralising about your job. Seek ways of broadening your horizons within work so that there is room for personal development. Consider adjusting your hours to relieve the stress of conflict with domestic or family commitments. If your working parameters can be altered, there could be benefits for your employer because you will:

- work more efficiently
- be more alert and responsive
- be less likely to take time off work through stress-related health problems
- have more time to concentrate on your own needs and your other interests (or do more work, if that's what you want!)

The relationships you have with your family and friends will improve if you can communicate better with them. Try to talk about your needs and their needs. Understand how they see things, how they feel. If you can explain yourself clearly, this will result in more meaningful conversations and should result in changes of behaviour that will bring:

- a greater level of satisfaction with your personal life
- deeper immunity to the vagaries of the outside world

Day 2

Think about those topics raised yesterday. Go for a thirty-minute brisk walk and mull them over. When you come back from your walk, you can do something practical: go through your store cupboard or fridge or freezer. Write a list of the foods that you habitually eat in a week. Include those you buy to consume at home and the foods you eat away from home. You will be expecting me to say that it's time to throw away the Pot Noodles and pies, banish the biscuits and condemn the chocolate to the bin. Wrong (waste not, want not), but it is time to buy more of other foods next time you go shopping so that there is less room in your cupboard, and more importantly in your diet, for foods that are full of fat, sugar, fiendish additives and fillers that rob you of nutrients. It's time to buy more fresh fruits and vegetables, more starchy foods such as bread, cereal, pasta and rice. Check out Chapter 1 and look at the pyramid model below to see what I mean about proportions. No foods are bad foods, as long as you eat them in the right proportions.

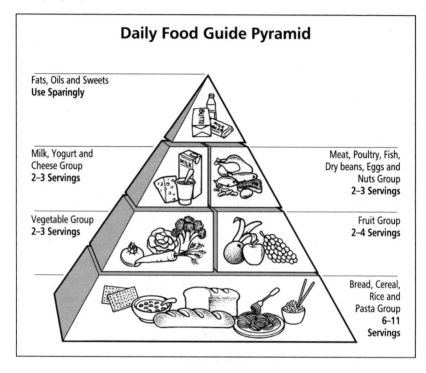

Day 3

Go for another thirty-minute walk, or two fifteen-minute walks if you are pressed for time.

Organise a fitness assessment. If you have not had one before, this can be done either at a private health club or gym or at a public gym run by the local authority. The assessor should:

- check your blood pressure
- measure your body fat. Using various methods, the

percentage of your body tissue that is fat, lean tissue and water can be measured. The assessor will tell you what is average or ideal for your age
- measure your level of cardio-respiratory fitness

Having found out where you are at (so to speak), the assessor or fitness instructor can work out a suitable activity programme tailored to your particular needs.

Think about what you will tell the instructor about your fitness goals. You want to turn back the clock, so you want to become more active to stay younger than your chronological age. How can becoming more active keep you younger? It can:

- improve your cardio-respiratory (heart and lung) fitness to give you more energy and improve your level of general fitness, keeping you younger for longer
- help prevent health problems such as heart disease, diabetes, weight gain etc. For a full explanation of all the benefits, see Chapter 3
- tone and strengthen your muscles to give you a better shape and improve your posture, to make you appear younger
- improve your circulation to benefit your complexion, hair, nails, eyes and general appearance

Discuss the ways in which you can become more active. Decide with the assessor what would suit you best – classes, gym work, swimming, jogging, team games. Work out a varied programme and agree a date (in a month's time) when you can review your progress.

Day 4

Build in another half an hour's activity today. For more ideas see Chapter 3.

Check how your diet is matching up to the food pyramid model. Use the chart (see over) to get an idea of the foods that you eat over a week. The number of pyramids for each food group is the number of servings you should be eating each day. Colour or shade in a pyramid (triangle) at the top for each serving of food eaten from the main food groups, then write what it was in the appropriate meal slot for that day. For example, if you have a bowl of cereal for breakfast, write 'cereal' in the breakfast compartment and fill in one grain pyramid. At the end of the week (Day 11), compare what you have eaten with the ideal. If

	SUNDAY	MONDAY	TUESDAY
Milk	△△	△△	△△
Meat	△△	△△	△△
Vegetable	△△△	△△△	△△△
Fruit	△△	△△	△△
Grain	△△△	△△△	△△△
	△△△	△△△	△△△
Breakfast			
Snack			
Lunch			
Snack			
Dinner			

you have several blank pyramids, you should try to include more foods from these food groups over the next few days. Conversely, if you run out of pyramids, you may be eating too much of a particular food.

- For what constitutes a serving of food from each food group, see Chapter 1.

WEDNESDAY	THURSDAY	FRIDAY	SATURDAY
△△ △△ △△△ △△ △△△ △△△	△△ △△ △△△ △△ △△△ △△△	△△ △△ △△△ △△ △△△ △△△	△△ △△ △△△ △△ △△△ △△△

Day 5

Begin the three-day detox mini anti-ageing diet. (If you do not want to follow this low-calorie eating plan, follow three days from the Anti-Weight-Gain Plan in Chapter 4).

On rising, a glass of water, with a squeeze of lemon.

Breakfast 1 glass (115ml/4fl oz) fruit juice (either freshly squeezed orange or grapefruit or red grape or tomato), 1 thick slice wholemeal toast, a scraping of low-fat spread, 1 medium banana. Green tea, herb or fruit tea.

- Although green tea is rich in phenols, it does contain caffeine, so avoid it if you prefer on this detox plan. On the other hand, green tea can also raise the metabolic rate, so it could help with weight loss, which might be one of your goals.

Lunch 1 bowl vegetable (not creamed) soup, 1 wholemeal or other multi-grain roll (no spread), 1 piece fruit.
Snacks (morning and afternoon): 1 cereal bar.

Evening meal 1 medium baked potato, dressed with natural low-fat yogurt mixed with chopped fresh chives and 1 crushed clove garlic, 1 small grilled trout or mackerel or herring. Salad of grated raw carrot, grated raw beetroot, cherry tomatoes, and watercress.

Drink at least 1 litre of water during the day, other drinks as required, such as fruit juice (see breakfast) or Fruit Smoothies (see page 156) or skimmed milk or soya milk or drinking yogurt.

Tip   Gunpowder tea is a green tea, but is slightly less pronounced in flavour than many green teas.

Day 6

(Day 2 of the three-day detox mini anti-ageing diet.)

On rising, a glass of water with a squeeze of lemon.

Breakfast 1 glass (115ml/4fl oz) fruit juice (as Day 5), 1 bowl of wholegrain breakfast cereal or muesli, with 1 small banana or 1 other fruit of choice, e.g. pear, apple, peach, prunes, 2–3 dried apricots, and 125ml/ ¼ pint skimmed milk or soya milk. Green tea, herb or fruit tea.

Lunch wholemeal sandwiches filled with poached salmon, avocado and watercress or lettuce (no spread).
   1 low-fat fruit yogurt.

Evening meal grilled chicken and red pepper salad – grill a chicken breast (discard the skin when cooked as this is where most of the fat is) and a red pepper. (Halve and deseed the pepper; grill skin-side up until blackened; then peel off the skin and slice.) Toss the grilled chicken and pepper with sliced tomatoes in an olive oil vinaigrette and serve with large mixed seasonal salad as colourful as you can make.
   Dried fruit compote and 1 natural yogurt.

Drink at least 1 litre of water during the day, other drinks as required, such as fruit juice (see breakfast) or Fruit Smoothies (see page 156) or skimmed milk or soya milk or drinking yogurt.
   Go for a thirty-minute brisk walk or find another activity.

Day 7

(Day 3 of the three-day detox mini anti-ageing diet.)

On rising, a glass of water with a squeeze of lemon.

Breakfast 1 glass (115ml/4fl oz) fruit juice (see Day 5), 1 whole-meal muffin topped with 1 poached egg. Green tea, herb or fruit tea.

Lunch   tuna salad, made with cold cooked brown rice, tuna (canned in water), sweetcorn canned without added sugar or salt, cubed cucumber, chopped fresh parsley, with 2–3 wholemeal crispbreads if required.

1 piece fresh fruit or 1 low-fat yogurt.

Evening meal   wholemeal pasta (75g/3oz dry-weight) with tomato and vegetable sauce. Either buy a tub of fresh chilled tomato sauce for pasta or make your own. Grill or microwave 2 back rashers of bacon to drain them of fat. Chop when cooked. Boil the pasta while you prepare the vegetable sauce. Sweat a diced stick of celery and small onion in a non-stick pan. Add 2–3 ripe roughly chopped tomatoes, or a small can of tomatoes, and continue cooking for 10–15 minutes. Stir in freshly grated carrots and chopped fresh parsley. Sprinkle over the chopped bacon. Serve with freshly grated Parmesan cheese.

Mango and melon fruit salad.

Drink   at least 1 litre of water during the day, other drinks as required, such as fruit juice (see breakfast) or Fruit Smoothies (see page 156) or skimmed milk or soya milk or drinking yogurt.

Go for a thirty-minute brisk walk or find another activity.

Day 8

Time to start your regular fitness activities. You need two or three sessions a week, combined with more activity in your everyday life. Walk more, climb stairs more, move about more, sit down less.

If you have to sit down for long periods at work or on journeys, get up and stretch frequently, build exercises into your sedentary time; circle ankles, pump feet, 'walk' your buttocks where you are sitting, flex your triceps (at the back of your arms) and your biceps (everyone knows where they are), rotate your shoulders regularly to alleviate stress, stretch one side of your neck by lowering your ear to your shoulder and at the same time push the opposite arm gently away from you to stretch out any tension in your neck. Contract and hold in your stomach muscles ten times for ten seconds every hour or so. Do the same with your pelvic floor muscles. There are other exercises, flexes and stretches you can do – check them out. Or you can just generally jiggle and wriggle about – fidgets burn more calories and keep their muscles moving.

Building fresh air into your new active lifestyle . . . is, well, invigorating! When did you last go for an invigorating walk or hike in the fresh air? Walking out in the open (away from exhaust fumes and pollution) is good for the mind and the body; it encourages creativity and keeps you fit. Do it today, or if not today, do not put it off for too long – mark it in your diary, if necessary, to make it a regular habit.

Skin care reminder If you are not already following the advice in Chapter 5, do so now:

• Use a moisturiser with a sun protection factor (SPF) of 15 daily during spring and summer. Sunlight produces ultra-violet radiation throughout the year. We tend to think that if it is cloudy or raining, there is not much ultraviolet light, but this is not the case.
• Exposure is more related to time of day than intensity of sunshine, so stay in the shade between 11 a.m. and 3 p.m.

Day 9

Have a Real Conversation with someone you know and someone you do not know. By this I do not mean observing etiquette by passing the time of day with comments about the weather but without revealing much of yourself or trying to find out about the other person's emotions and opinions. In a real conversation, we aim to find out how the other person feels and try to understand their views and attitudes. Having a real interest in others and endeavouring to break down misunderstandings and cynicism is the hallmark of people who keep a lively interest in the issues of the time, fuelling their longevity through mental agility and adventure.

- Check that you are including in your diet all the foods you need to eat regularly. Here are some: fruit and vegetables – five servings a day; bread, pasta, potatoes, rice and other cereals; yogurt; oily fish.

Day 10

Love thy neighbour (this is not always possible). But the point of mentioning neighbours is that it raises issues that can express your happiness level. If you covet your neighbour's (in the wider sense) wife/car/wealth/cat/whatever, it will add to a sense of dissatisfaction with your own life. If you think the grass is always greener in next door's garden or that the opposite side of the street is sunnier than your side, then you will not be happy. This is not a plea for complacent acceptance of your lot, but a suggestion that you turn any habitually negative thoughts around and make them positive. If you cannot be happy for the good fortunes of others, at least don't be envious.

- Tomorrow is another day (this is true even though it is a cliché) and the seemingly endless fresh starts, and daily renewal, of life present a tremendous opportunity for optimism and trying to get it right (again).

Day 11

Go wine tasting. Moderate drinkers have a lower death rate from all causes than abstainers, those who take only the very occasional drink and heavy drinkers. For moderate women drinkers aged over forty-five there is also a reduced risk of heart disease and stroke. Moderate drinking is two to four units a day, but not every day. If you want to know more about how alcohol might protect you, read the relevant sections in Chapters 1 and 2.

As you already know the most beneficial drink is red wine. Some white wines will also probably turn out to be beneficial, once all the scientific analysis is complete. To know more about wine, you need to taste more, and a wine tasting course is a serious suggestion. It will help you find out which wines you like and not waste your money on wines you find disappointing. You can also find out more about wines by popping into your local off-licence and supermarket wine department on tasting days.

The red wines that are potentially the most beneficial against heart disease, cancer and many inflammatory diseases such as osteoarthritis, are those produced in sunny climates. These wines contain the highest levels of phenols, substances which act as UV protectants (sunscreens) to the fruit, and so greater concentrations are found in the skins of grapes grown in sunnier climates. Look out for wine from Chile, Argentina, South Africa and Australia.

- How did you get on with your Pyramid Planner? Today is the day you should have finished filling it in for a week. Keep up the good work on improving the proportions of the foods on your plate.

Day 12

A choice of activities today. You could have an anti-ageing (HRT) baking day, if this is appropriate for you. The recipes for cakes full of anti-ageing phyto-oestrogens can be found in Chapter 5.

Alternatively, you could do an exercise in assessing your body image. The way in which you perceive yourself will have an effect on your level of self-confidence and your level of motivation. It will also have a knock-on effect on your health and ultimately the rate at which you age. You may think the questions below are obvious, but they touch on some important issues.

Do you:

- dislike seeing yourself in mirrors?
- avoid exercise because of your appearance?
- feel embarrassed to be seen in a swimsuit or shorts?
- compare yourself with others to see if they are a better shape than you?

- feel that other people think you are ugly or unattractive?
- joke about yourself to mask your sensitivity?
- spend a lot of time thinking about your appearance?

If you answered yes to all these questions you are very dissatisfied with your body. You are probably being too hard on yourself and you need to learn to ease off. You may need support from friends, but if you are overly concerned you may need to seek help from a health professional.

Your self-image will have some element of truth in it and a negative one probably indicates that you need to take active steps to lose weight (or gain weight), improve your posture or your dress sense. You might benefit from behavioural techniques to learn to accept yourself or to find motivation to change. Picture how you would like to be. Be honest with yourself in recognising whether that is possible and then take action through diet, exercise and improved mental attitude.

- Have you had a brisk walk or taken some activity today?

Day 13

Have you had breakfast today? Do you regularly eat breakfast? If you do not, you are missing out. On what? On lots of things: energy, improved performance at work or college, better weight control, better mood. There has been masses of research on the benefits of breakfast and all of it shows that you should make time for the first meal of the day.

- Put an extra special effort into your fitness training today (use up all that energy from breakfast).

Day 14

Yoga is so anti-ageing that I cannot think why I have not recommended it to you before. There are many different kinds of yoga, some dedicated more to meditation and some with greater emphasis on exercise. A combination of both will best meet your anti-ageing needs as this encourages a healthy mind in a healthy, supple and serene body. There are probably as many styles of yoga as there are teachers, yogis and gurus. In this country most teachers use Hatha yoga, which is chiefly concerned with exercises to improve posture and breathing. Sivananda yoga is more spiritual with chanting, meditation and fewer postures and Iyengar yoga emphasises the precision of its postures.

A good yoga teacher should teach you the correct way to do the postures (asanas) and exercises. They need to be done slowly and smoothly, held for a certain amount of time and then released in a controlled way. Gradually they become easier and more natural to you.

You should be taught how to concentrate on your breathing techniques. Yoga breathing is regular, slow and deep and is designed to alleviate stress and achieve tranquillity. Usually teachers will have a sequence of postures that are done (like a fitness routine) in a specific order, but it is not all that important to perform the postures in a particular order: just do them effectively. Incidentally, yoga will need to be supplemented by some cardio-vascular exercise, unless you do Astanga yoga which can be done '*à la* Madonna' so that it is aerobic (and sweaty). For teachers contact British Wheel of Yoga, 01529 306851.

Day 15

Become Mistress of your own Wardrobe (and this applies to chaps, too). Throw away the years by throwing away your (old) clothes. You know the rules – if you haven't worn it for a year, throw it away, give it away or sell it – do not put it back in the wardrobe. It is far better to have two or three outfits per season and wear them out than fill your wardrobe with the usual mismatch of ad hoc purchases, which is what most people do. You will look younger and more modern, feel younger and more modern, and be younger and more modern. So stop prevaricating and do it.

- The alternative to sorting out your wardrobe is to have a DIY sprouting day (i.e., learning how to sprout mung beans in a jam jar, see Chapter 2). Now which would you rather do? It's up to you.

Day 16

Juicing day. If you have not got into juicing, now is the time to learn. Freshly pressed fruit and vegetable juices are a revelation. They can easily become part of your new anti-ageing routine. You can produce endless variations of flavour and colour. If you think it is not worth investing in the equipment, consider that in a healthy well-balanced diet you may be drinking around three or more glasses of juice a day, so you would certainly make good use of a juicer. In fact, some of your kitchen equipment may already include juicing facilities, but perhaps you have not felt the need to use them until now. If you decide to buy a juicer, invest in a book about juicing which will give you all the recipes, techniques and information you need. You can adjust the vegetables and fruits you use to give you a boost of any particular anti-ageing nutrients you feel in need of. For example, you could juice to provide nutrients for eyes, hair, nails and skin, or to improve your lung function and protect yourself against degenerative diseases. Once you are set up, you could even have a detox juicing day, in which you 'eat' just juices (*not recommended for slimming or in the long-term, but great for occasional use*).

Day 17

While we are in the mood, what about a raw food day? Raw food has much to commend it. If ingredients are fresh, they will contain more vitamins and minerals when raw than when cooked. And the kinds of foods you eat on a raw food day – fruit, vegetables, nuts, seeds and yogurt – are nutrient-dense, which means they contain a lot of vitamins, minerals and other phyto (plant) nutrients per calorie. They give you more nutrition for the same number, or fewer, calories than processed, high-fat and sugary foods.

Day 18

This is the day to realise your dreams . . . Dreams help the brain sort out information stored away during waking hours. Often the brain will have taken in things that you only half noticed because you were busy doing something else. During dreams, current information and more distant memories come to the surface and are woven into visions, dramas and stories that prompt you to address unfulfilled desires. And not surprisingly middle age can be a fruitful time for such dreams and an apt time to ponder the meaning of them. It may sound rather far-fetched, but your dream could be trying to help you find your true self. The person arriving at the mid point of life may well be very different from the person who set out in childhood or adolescence. Indeed, middle age can be a time for people to reinvent themselves using all their experience of life so far. Consolidating who you are will make a sound foundation for the rest of your life, which is likely to be as long as the life you have already lived, particularly if you put in place all the health-enhancing strategies in this book.

So, how do you recapture or use your dreams? Keep a pad of paper and a pencil beside the bed and write down any scraps of dreams that remain in your mind on waking. By piecing together your dreams, or the contents of various dreams, over a couple of weeks or a month, a picture may begin to emerge of the direction you want your life to take from here on. Some people find it helpful to attempt to reenter their dreams and continue them using their active imagination. It is unlikely that anyone else can interpret your dreams as well as you, but if you describe them to others they may give you an interesting commentary or make illuminating observations about what the meaning of the dream might have been had they dreamt it.

There is no need to become morbid about ageing during this short interlude of introspection. It will not last for the rest of your life as it does for many women in traditional cultures where women cast off their colourful clothes and personality of youth, motherhood and middle age in order to wear black in perpetuity. Making time for contemplation and taking time to plan how you want to be in the future is a positive and optimistic exercise. And even if you do not find it helpful as a tool of self-discovery, at least you will have improved your memory by undertaking the exercise, which is in itself an anti-ageing activity.

Day 19

Imagine you have been invited as guest on *Desert Island Discs* (for the uninitiated, this is a radio programme on which the guest is hypothetically cast away on a desert island with only his or her favourite music for company). How important is music in your life? If it's not very important, give it more space. Music is a marvellous expression (by proxy perhaps) of your emotions and it can satisfy emotional needs. You can transcend the mundane with music (as with meditation) and it can release creative thought. It may even boost your brain power (see Chapter 5). Listen to your favourite music and try out more frequently other types of music too.

Day 20

Tense and relax. Tension control is an important concept and a vital technique. If you control tension in your life at the moment by smoking or drinking a lot or by overeating, you need to find other ways of coping because these methods are damaging to health and are ageing. Paradoxically, relaxing is an effective method of tension control. And tense and relax techniques can be applied virtually anywhere at any time.

The idea is to tense and relax each muscle group in turn from top to toe. You can do this sitting in an airport lounge, or at your desk or on the underground. (Or you can lie down in a quiet candle-lit room). Tense each muscle group for fifteen seconds and then relax it. Work through eyes, jaw, neck, shoulders, arms, abdomen, buttocks, legs, toes. The same kind of tension release can be achieved through meditation (both are preferable to medication, so put away the Prozac . . .)

• Look out of the window at the mystic mountains on the horizon (or even at the end of the street). Widen your field of vision. Not in order to take on the troubles of the universe, but to appreciate that there are many other ways around the world of doing things, seeing things, being things. You could also head off towards the horizon on a brisk walk or run. Have you taken your exercise today?

Day 21

Start of a two-day brain-boosting eating plan.

Breakfast 1 glass (115ml/4fl oz) fruit juice (either freshly squeezed orange or grapefruit or red grape or tomato), 1 serving of a fortified breakfast cereal with 1 medium banana, skimmed milk, 1 thick slice wholemeal toast and a scraping of low-fat spread. Black coffee or tea (or herb or fruit tea).

Lunch 1 wholemeal egg sandwich, green salad.
    1 low-fat yogurt.

Evening vegetarian bean-based curry or other pulse dish with plenty of green vegetables.
    Fruit Brûlée (recipe on page 189).

Drink at least 1 litre of water during the day, other drinks as required, such as fruit juice (see breakfast) or Fruit Smoothies (see page 156) or skimmed milk or soya milk or drinking yogurt.
    Go for a thirty-minute brisk walk or find another activity.

Day 22

Day 2 of brain-boosting eating plan.

Breakfast 1 glass (115ml/4fl oz) fruit juice (either freshly squeezed orange or grapefruit or red grape or tomato), 1 serving of muesli rich in nuts and dried fruit, with skimmed milk.

Lunch   peanut butter sandwiches.
1 banana.

Evening   stir-fry with chicken or oily fish and plenty of red, orange and green vegetables.
Fruit crumble with natural yogurt.

Drink   at least 1 litre of water during the day, other drinks as required such as fruit juice (see breakfast) or Fruit Smoothies (see page 156) or skimmed milk or soya milk or drinking yogurt.
Go for a thirty-minute brisk walk or find another activity.

Day 23

Five-minute brush-up. Body brushing stimulates the lymphatic system (the tiny network of vessels which clear waste from the cells) and also the circulation. It also removes dry skin. And it only takes five minutes.

Use a natural bristle brush (such as a long-handled back-scrubbing brush for use in the bath) or a loofah or a dry washcloth. Make small circular strokes, moving up your legs in the direction of your heart area. Once the chest has been reached, move to the top of the neck and brush down towards the heart. Follow with a shower.

Day 24

Sit up and take notice. If you are not doing 200 sit-ups daily, or equivalent abdominal exercises, then you will have to miss a turn and go back to Day 1 (only joking – fifty is sufficient). Nothing gives your age away more quickly than a saggy tummy (that's not true, of course, but it might motivate you). And tummies do not look after themselves. While I empathise with the Botticelli view of the ideal woman – that she be pear-shaped with a distinct belly – I also see the value of strong abdominal muscles, because they help support your back and improve your posture. Whether you do them each morning before dressing, or each evening before bed, you are not doing them in order to emulate emaciated models (they can only achieve that kind of flat stomach by starvation or colonic irrigation).

How to exercise abdominals safely

Lie on your back with your knees bent, hip-width apart and parallel. Keep your buttocks on the ground and keep your pelvis in neutral (not tipping up or down).

Raise your arms above your head, bend your elbows and let your fingertips touch behind your head. Breathe in.

As you breathe out, draw your navel in towards your spine and raise your shoulders off the ground so that your head comes up to view your knees. (Imagine you have a tennis ball between chin and chest so that your head stays in position and your chin does not fall to your chest.)

Breathe in as you gently lower your shoulders to the starting position. You should feel your abdominal muscles working during the lifting and lowering. Do not arch your back during the exercise. Repeat.

- If your neck begins to ache, cradle the weight of your head in your hands.
- As you improve, pause at the top of the lift and hold for a count of three.
- As your muscles become stronger, do the exercise so that your shoulders do not return completely to the floor between lifts.
- Once you are competent, a variation is the lateral abdominal sit-up in which you lift the right elbow towards the left knee that is raised to meet it, and vice versa. Do the same number of sit-ups towards each side.

Day 25

Face values. Time for a treat. Although skin care is not really a treat, it is an absolute essential, particularly with today's lifestyle of central heating, air conditioning, thinning ozone, harsh chlorinated water and all the other daily assaults upon the skin's natural moisture barrier that is trying desperately hard to keep your face looking radiant and glowing with health (to degenerate for a moment into cliché). You've got the picture? The point is: are you cleansing and moisturising your face effectively as you head for or through your forties? No time to lose – dedicate the rest of this anti-ageing action plan to investigating the best moisturisers and cleansers for you. Collect samples from every cosmetic counter at every chemist, department store, health food store and beauty shop that you can. Ask your friends and acquaintances for recommendations but bear in mind, however, that your friends may not share the same skin type as you; ask judiciously and not indiscriminately.

To feed your face from within, eat more avocados (for B vitamins and oils), more nuts and seeds, and use olive oil (it contains vitamin E) rather than saturated fats for cooking and in salad dressings. Other vegetable oils to consider are: grapeseed, rapeseed, sesame and walnut oils.

Day 26

Boost your immune system by regularly eating more:

- yellow, orange and red fruit and vegetables for their antioxidant carotenoids, whose role is to scavenge invading viruses and bacteria
- nuts, spinach and potatoes for vitamin B_6 to promote production of white blood cells which fight infections
- beans, pulses, etc., lettuce and peas for folates to increase white blood cell activity
- vegetables and fruits, especially citrus, for vitamin C to protect against infection
- wheatgerm, vegetable oils and whole grains for vitamin E to

stimulate immune responses
- tuna, eggs and wholemeal bread for selenium, another antioxidant that also attacks invading bacteria
- seafood, eggs and wholemeal bread for zinc, which promotes wound healing and is a defence against the common cold

Day 27

Have you paid off your sleep debt? The amount of sleep you have lost over the years may have accumulated to chronic proportions by the time you reach your forties. And persistent sleep debt may increase the severity of any age-related disorders you might be having problems with. We sleep 20 per cent less than our ancestors did. Our modern lifestyles mean that we work longer hours and extend our leisure activities well into the night. Why else would we have 24-hour petrol stations, 24-hour supermarkets, 24-hour cinemas and 24-hour gyms? We seem to be living in an anti-sleep culture that denies we have an internal body clock that tells us it is time to sleep when the sun goes down.

If you ignore your internal body clock and continuously override it (in the way that dieters restrain and override their natural appetite) you will find that your tiredness levels are yo-yoing just as an habitual dieter's weight yo-yos. If you suffer from this kind of chronic fatigue, you are likely to become a casualty of a road traffic accident, unproductive at work, irritable with those around you and a lot dimmer. Some experts calculate that you lose the equivalent of one IQ point the next day for every hour of sleep lost the previous night. You will certainly look and feel a lot older than you need look and feel because you need at least eight hours' sleep a night to knit up wrinkles and renew body cells.

Day 28

And now it's your Pharma Sutra guide to staying young and sexy. Many foods possess pharmacological properties that will keep you younger for longer (Chapter 2 is full of them). Some of those foods, and others, are also credited with aphrodisiac qualities. Among them are oysters, chocolate, asparagus, truffles, green-lipped mussels and lettuce – the diamonds of the pantry. I have no empirical evidence that they are good for your love-life, but I know they taste wonderful and can be enjoyed in many romantic settings. And if you indulge your paramour in these luxuries s/he will feel greatly valued. So tuck in and turn on.

Just one more thing before you do – eating these aphrodisiacs (if that is what they are) is much kinder to animals than using the supposedly sex-empowering 'foods of love' such as ground rhino horn, tiger parts, the meat of rare Amazonian river turtles and other sacrifices to Eros and Cupid that have resulted in species being hunted to the brink of, if not total, extinction.

While we are in Save the World mode, have you 'gone organic' yet? If not, visit the websites of two leading educational organic organisations: the Soil Association (www.soilassociation.org.uk) and Henry Doubleday Research Association (www.hdra.org.uk). For their telephone numbers see page 13, and while you are there, give Greenpeace a ring, too.

That's a good day's work; now enjoy your pharma sutra night.

Day 29

When you book a holiday, make it an anti-ageing one. It can be activity-based or culture-based or spiritually based, but make sure it is packed with food for your mind, body and spirit.

Day 30

And now – pack your bags for the rest of your life. Only take on board what you need to keep you younger for longer. Throw overboard all those old habits and vestments that you do not need. Be brutal. Be minimalistic. Remember on your journey that all journeys are dehydrating: drink plenty of liquid (that means lots of water) each day.

Bon voyage . . . and live to beat your age from now on.

Index